A VISION OF YEMEN

A VISION OF YEMEN

The Travels of a European Orientalist and His Native Guide

A Translation of Hayyim Habshush's Travelogue

ALAN VERSKIN

Stanford University Press
Stanford, California

Stanford University Press
Stanford, California

Printed in the United States of America on acid-free, archival-quality paper

Library of Congress Cataloging-in-Publication Data
Names: Ḥabshush, Ḥayyim, 1839–1899, author. | Verskin, Alan, translator, writer of introduction.
Title: A vision of Yemen : the travels of a European Orientalist and his native guide : a translation of Hayyim Habshush's travelogue / Alan Verskin.
Other titles: Ru'yā al-Yaman. English.
Description: Stanford, California : Stanford University Press, 2018. | English translation of: Ru'yā al-Yaman. | Includes bibliographical references and index.
Identifiers: LCCN 2018016759| ISBN 9781503607033 (cloth : alk. paper) | ISBN 9781503607736 (pbk. : alk. paper) | ISBN 9781503607743 (e-book)
Subjects: LCSH: Ḥabshush, Ḥayyim, 1839–1899—Travel—Yemen (Republic) | Halévy, J. (Joseph), 1827–1917—Travel—Yemen (Republic) | Jews—Travel—Yemen. | Jews—Yemen—Social life and customs. | Jewish-Arab relations. | Yemen (Republic)—Description and travel. | Yemen (Republic)—Social life and customs. | Yemen (Republic)—Ethnic relations. | LCGFT: Travel writing.
Classification: LCC DS247.Y42 H313 2018 | DDC 953.3/04—dc23
LC record available at https://lccn.loc.gov/2018016759

Cover design by Rob Ehle
Typeset by Bruce Lundquist in 10.25/15 Baskerville

For Maya, Hannah, and Daniel

הוֹדִיעֵנִי דֶּרֶךְ-זוּ אֵלֵךְ כִּי-אֵלֶיךָ נָשָׂאתִי נַפְשִׁי

Show me the way wherein I should walk,

for unto you I have entrusted my soul.

Psalms 143:8

CONTENTS

Acknowledgments xi

PART I: INTRODUCTION

Ḥayyim Ḥabshūsh and the European Explorers 3

The People and Politics of Yemen 39

A Note on the Text and Translation 57

PART II: *A VISION OF YEMEN* BY ḤAYYIM ḤABSHŪSH

Author's Note 63

1 Arrival in Yemen 65

2 Excavations in Ghaymān 70

3 Jews, Muslims, and Foreigners in Ṣanʿāʾ 80

4 Strangers among the Tribes 87

5 Clients and Patrons 96

6 Death and Ruins 128

7 Jews Bearing Arms 155

8 An Ordeal in the Desert 158

9 The Honor Code of the Najrānī Jews 168

10 Persecution 177

11 The Bedouin 190

12 The City of Mārib and Return to Ṣanʿāʾ 199

Glossary 213

Notes 215

Index 249

ACKNOWLEDGMENTS

I discovered Ḥayyim Ḥabshūsh's *A Vision of Yemen* more than a decade ago in Princeton University's student center. It was in an unassuming walk-in closet, grandiosely titled "The Princeton University Genizah Laboratory," which housed a few computers and filing cabinets and some books left by the late Professor Shlomo Dov Goitein. It was there that many social historians first got to know the people they would study and the people with whom they would study. As I idly browsed the books, I noticed this one. Goitein was primarily a medievalist, as I was. What had he seen in this modern travelogue? I picked it up and found that I couldn't put it down. I began to translate bits of it to show to Sadiq al-Azm, the professor and Syrian public intellectual with whom I was studying the history of orientalism. Translating it became my passion project. Over time, I told more and more people about it, and those people, appreciating what it meant to me, went out of their way to help me realize my own vision of *A Vision of Yemen*.

At Princeton, Mark Cohen and Avraham Udovitch discussed modern and medieval Judeo-Arabic with me. Andras Hamori initiated me into the world of Arabic poetry and graciously studied Ḥabshūsh's rhymed prose with me. David Bellos started me thinking about the theory and practice of translation. I further benefited from the expertise of Bat-Zion Eraqi Klorman, George Hatke, Bernard Haykel, and Norman Stillman. I owe a special debt of gratitude to Brinkley Messick, of Columbia University, for his unwavering enthusiasm for the project and for sharing his deep knowledge of Yemen with me.

This book has benefited immensely from my collaboration with the talented and collegial team at Stanford University Press. I thank Kate Wahl for recognizing the value of Ḥabshūsh's voice, and for encouraging me to put in more of my own. Mimi Braverman's copyediting has been both thoughtful and remarkably thorough. Carolyn Brown skillfully managed the entire production process, and Leah Pennywark has shepherded me from start to finish. I am sincerely grateful to all of them. I would also like to thank the anonymous reviewers for their support and advice.

I would also like to thank my mentors, colleagues, and friends for their support, particularly Yair Adiel, Yaron Ayalon, Zachary Braiterman, Michael Carroll, Michael Cook, Donny Cotton, Mehmet Darakçıoğlu, Jonathan Decter, Patricia Grieve, Najam Haider, M. Şükrü Hanioğlu, Amanda Izenstark, Jessica Marglin, Elias Muhanna, Farouk Mustafa, Jacob Olidort, James Robinson, Lawrence Rosen, Michael Satlow, Mark Sinyor, Lucette Valensi, Nancy Woyak, Muhammad Qasim Zaman, and Oded Zinger. I am immensely grateful to my colleagues in the History Department at the University of Rhode Island for their warmth and collegiality. I would like to thank my chairs, Timothy George and Rod Mather, for always ensuring that I had time to complete this project. I especially thank James Ward both for editing my work and for helping me to read some Hungarian texts that shed light on Halévy's early life. It was a joy to be able to connect with members of the Ḥabshūsh family. My thanks go out to Hanina Hibshoosh, who generously introduced me to them.

My research took me to Paris, Vienna, Jerusalem, and New York, and I built up a huge debt of gratitude to the many librarians and archivists who went out of their way to facilitate my explorations. I am very grateful to Stefan Sienell of the Austrian Academy of Sciences for his deep knowledge of the Glaser Collection, allowing me unfettered access to the archives, providing me with copies of much needed documents, and even giving me one of his unpublished papers.

I am also deeply grateful to the following librarians and archivists, without whom this project would not have been possible: Jean-Claude Kuperminc, Rose Levyne, and Guila Cooper of the Archives of the Alliance Israélite Universelle; Solange Roussier of the Archives Nationales; Marie-Claude Sabouret of the Musée de la Vie romantique; Ina Cohen and Jerry Schwarzbard of the Jewish Theological Seminary; the staff of the Institute of Microfilmed Hebrew Manuscripts at the National Library of Israel, and the librarians of Princeton University, Columbia University, and Brown University. I am very grateful to Emily Greene of the University of Rhode

Island Library. Without her assistance with interlibrary loan, I would not have been able to complete this project from Rhode Island.

I have also benefited from grants from the American Council of Learned Societies and the University of Rhode Island Council for Research.

I would like to thank my father, who gave me his love of scholarly endeavor and who read and commented on this entire manuscript. He is a constant source of inspiration to me. I would also like to thank my parents-in-law, Jerry and Sharon Muller, for the interest they have shown both in this book and in its dedicatees over their many years of development.

I can't even begin to express my debt to my wife, Sara. I am grateful to her not only for the erudite and transformative advice that she has given me on the manuscript, but also for her enthusiasm for the project itself. It has been wonderful to have a partner with whom I can share my scholarly enjoyments.

This book is dedicated to Hannah, Maya, and Daniel, with the hope that they will be blessed with the curiosity, empathy, love of learning, and enthusiasm of Ḥayyim Ḥabshūsh.

Alan Verskin
Providence, Rhode Island

A VISION OF YEMEN

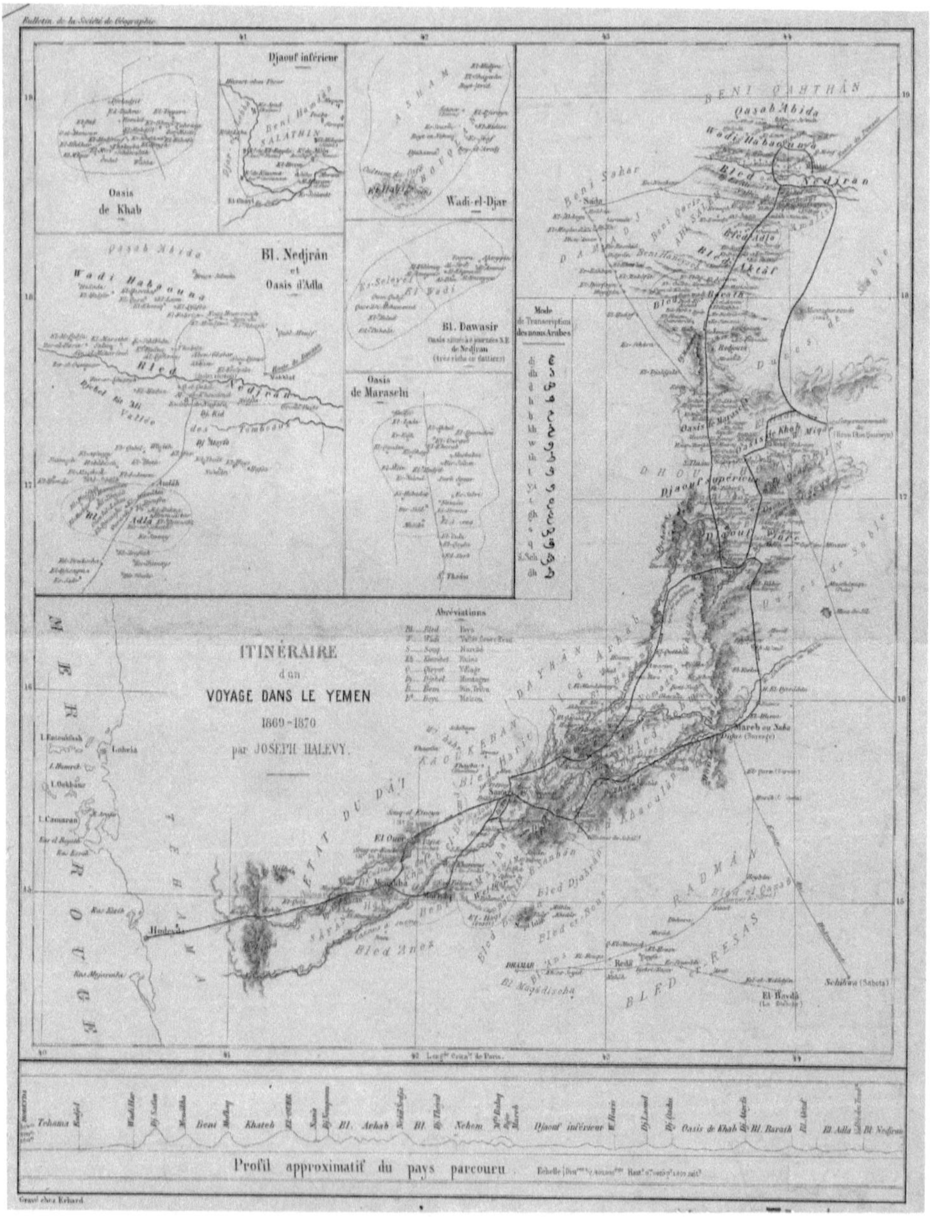

Map depicting Joseph Halévy's description of his journey.
Source: *Bulletin de la société de géographie* 6 (1873).

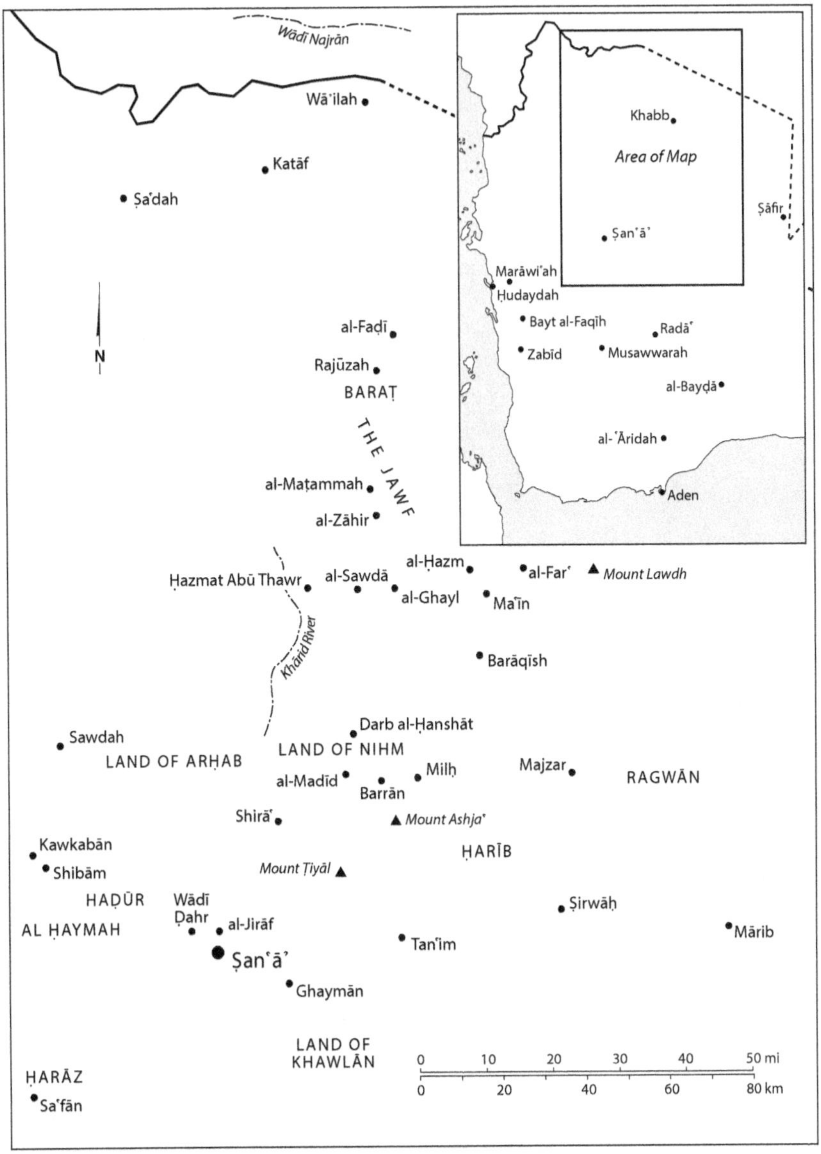

Map of locations mentioned in Ḥayyim Ḥabshūsh's *Vision of Yemen*.

PART 1

INTRODUCTION

ḤAYYIM ḤABSHŪSH AND THE EUROPEAN EXPLORERS

Toward the end of 1869, Joseph Halévy arrived in Yemen. To explain his presence, the pale, blond European claimed that he was a rabbi seeking alms for the Jews of Jerusalem. Although he bore impeccable letters of recommendation and demonstrated extreme erudition in Jewish wisdom, many local Jews wondered about his true purpose, on account of his near obsession with Yemen's ancient, pre-Islamic inscriptions. Because these were commonly used in magic, some suspected him of being a magician, a treasure hunter, or perhaps even a searcher for the lost Israelite tribes.[1] The European soon attracted the attention of Ḥayyim Ḥabshūsh, a young Jewish coppersmith from the city of Ṣanʿāʾ. Interested in magic and already a collector of ancient inscriptions, Ḥabshūsh was eager to learn from an adept and succeeded in gaining employment as Halévy's guide and assistant. For the better part of a year, the two journeyed across Yemen on a perilous quest to record the stone inscriptions of an ancient civilization. Their partnership kept them alive and ensured that their mission was a success, but their relationship soured and, by the time they returned to Ṣanʿāʾ in 1870, the two were estranged.

After Halévy returned to Europe, Ḥabshūsh attempted to contact him, still hoping to find in him a European friend whose influence could garner support for the Yemeni Jewish community. Halévy, however, did not respond. Ḥabshūsh also tried to contact other Europeans for the same reason and with as little success. Matters might have remained that way had Ḥabshūsh not met another strange traveler in Yemen many years later. Although Ḥabshūsh knew him as an enlightened Muslim jurist with a fascination for Yemen's pre-Islamic inscriptions, he was in fact another disguised European Jewish orientalist by the name of Eduard Glaser. When Glaser found out that Ḥabshūsh had served as a native guide to Halévy, he became interested in his story and urged him to commit it to paper, even though more than twenty years had passed since the journey. Ḥabshūsh assented, but he had in mind a much grander project than the one suggested by Glaser. He did not want to merely document the course of a scientific inquiry into archaeological ruins; he also wanted to describe Halévy's introduction to Yemen and its people. And it was not only the European's physical and intellectual journey that he wanted to recount but also his own. Ḥabshūsh welcomed European involvement in Yemen, even courted it, but he feared that orientalists would depict Yemen in a disdainful way that would not engage European readers' interest, let alone attract their support. He therefore endeavored to enchant them. He would take the orientalist's itinerary and build on it, turning it into a real-life tale of derring-do and adventure so as to portray not just a foreigner's discovery of Yemen but the journey of discovery and self-discovery of a native son. Thus was born Ḥabshūsh's *Vision of Yemen*.

A Vision of Yemen is composed of two main features: the cultural landscapes of Yemen and the complex relationship between Ḥabshūsh and Halévy, who navigate those landscapes. Sometimes the cultural landscape is the focus, with the travelers merely serving as a narrative framing device. At other times, Yemen is the background that throws the characters of Ḥabshūsh and Halévy into sharp relief. Whereas students of Yemen, the Middle East, Judaism, and the Ottoman Empire will find much of interest in the work's descriptions of history and culture, students of orientalism will find themselves drawn primarily to the Ḥabshūsh-Halévy relationship.

A Vision of Yemen is one of the earliest responses by a "native" to the phenomenon now known as orientalism, that is, the characterizations of the East produced by European artists, writers, and scholars.[2] These characterizations dominated first the European imagination of the foreign world and then, over time, came to greatly influence, if not overwhelm, Easterners' own self-perceptions. They sometimes also helped to retroactively justify, or to lay the groundwork for, imperialist interference and domination around the world.[3] Ḥabshūsh perspicaciously understood the danger of imbuing Joseph Halévy, an affiliate of the French Académie des Inscriptions et Belles-Lettres and later of the Sorbonne, with the power to shape the portrayal of Yemen and Yemeni Jewry for European audiences. He wrote in the hope of rebutting what he anticipated would be Halévy's negative descriptions of his land. In fact, although Halévy had apparently threatened to write such a description, his writings on contemporary Yemen were quite minimal. In them, he was indeed critical of practices that he viewed as superstitious or intolerant, but he also expressed gratitude to the Jewish community for its hospitality and singled out several individuals for praise.[4] Ḥabshūsh, however, had perceived in Halévy a scorn for the Yemenis and an indifference to their welfare, which he thinly masked with a façade of scholarly disinterestedness.

Ḥabshūsh did not object to foreign depictions of Yemen per se. Quite the contrary, he had a humanist's faith that to learn about others was to come to love them, to desire to see them prosper, and to relieve their suffering. Ḥabshūsh's own discovery of what were, in his eyes, the exotic inhabitants of the Yemeni hinterlands awakened in him a profound affection for them, a desire to help them, and, most of all, an urge to tell their stories. His anger at Halévy stemmed from his frustration at what he saw as a breakdown of this humanistic process. Halévy, he writes,

> filled the hearts of the inhabitants [of Yemen] with hope when he came to us in 1870, when we were in dire straits and on the point of being annihilated. The people imagined that his arrival and research would bring them the relief from adversity enjoyed by the rest of their coreligionists. They thought that he would strive on their behalf by informing charitable people of their plight in his letters. They did not know that he had already denied them in his heart and that their hopes were in vain.[5]

Ḥabshūsh never claimed to speak for all Yemenis, let alone for all "orientals" subject to increasingly intrusive European scrutiny. *A Vision of Yemen* is the distinctive product of an unusual author. Ḥabshūsh was a relatively prosperous Jewish man from the populous city of Ṣanʿāʾ who, nonetheless, took an interest in the experiences of individuals outside his community and social group. His *Vision of Yemen* is a witness to this. In large part it is a social history and ethnography describing a broad cross-section of society, including women, nomads, Muslims from all walks of life, and Europeans. Ḥabshūsh was also a litterateur, interested in playing with genre, language, and narrative. He tells trickster tales, composes desert poetry, and imparts folklore. He puns in both Hebrew and Arabic and peppers his writing with biblical allusions and occasionally Qurʾānic references. In the first part of *A Vision of Yemen* he experiments with a florid and grandiose style of Hebrew, chockful of allusions; the second part captures the cadences of the spoken registers of Arabic, at a time when the memorialization of dialect was not always considered in good literary taste. Both parts are punctuated with sly humor.

A Vision of Yemen offers a sophisticated exploration and analysis of some of the most sensitive and pressing issues of the period. Ḥabshūsh describes Muslim-Jewish relations, both symbiosis and persecution. He discusses the decidedly mixed blessings brought by Islamic revivals and Ottoman reform initiatives. He addresses the haughty attitudes of "enlightened" European Jews toward Yemeni Jewish customs, particularly ones involving sexuality and superstition. Ḥabshūsh also has his own prejudices. He has no compunction about describing his feelings of revulsion, discomfort, or smugness when he visits foreign and impoverished regions, where he witnesses unhygienic living conditions, or when he meets people whom he regards as simple, boorish, or otherwise shocking. Ḥabshūsh, however, also shows himself to be aware of the moral ambiguity of many of his own and his companions' actions, particularly where the fine line between self-serving and principled actions is difficult to discern. *A Vision of Yemen* is thus a thoughtful and self-reflective work that reveals the author's personality and his attitudes toward the people and societies with whom he comes in contact. Readers will likely find some of these attitudes praiseworthy and others reprehensible.

One of the most dramatic examples of this moral ambiguity appears in a wrenching anecdote featuring a not-at-all theoretical debate about abortion, polygamy, and honor killing.[6] Ḥabshūsh tells of how he and Halévy met an unmarried Jewish girl (*bunayyah*) who was waiting to be killed by her family for becoming pregnant after a rape. Such killings were not practiced by Ṣanʿānī Jews, but this family lived in Wādī Najrān, now located in Saudi Arabia, where Jewish practices closely mirrored those of local tribes. Ḥabshūsh pitied the girl and offered to perform an abortion so that the family could cover up the rape and allow the girl to live, an offer for which she was immensely grateful. When Halévy learned of this, he accused Ḥabshūsh of wanting to destroy a life and to shed innocent blood. Ḥabshūsh was shocked, for he could not understand to whose life Halévy was referring. When Halévy explained, Ḥabshūsh answered that, as a result of his "Arab upbringing" (*tarbiyatī al-ʿarabiyya*), he had never learned that destroying a fetus was murder, and he added that abortion was occasionally practiced in his native Ṣanʿāʾ.

Persuaded by Halévy's argument, he did not perform the abortion but instead offered to marry the girl, whom he found very beautiful, and in this way save both her life and the life of her unborn child. At first, the family objects for fear that he will not truly marry her but will instead run off with her and then, when she has no family to protect her, abandon her among strangers. Ḥabshūsh, however, assures them that he intends to be a proper husband. This proposal is happily accepted by all except Halévy, whose anger only worsened.

> "Do you not remember," my teacher angrily retorted, "that you left your house to serve God through our work, and now you want to involve me in other matters. Even if you leave her in the Jawf or elsewhere so that we can finish our travels, what will your family, your brothers, your sons, and your first wife say when you return to your house in Ṣanʿāʾ with a rival wife? Will this affair not be shameful and distressing for them? Will you not be forced to separate, not only from your first wife but also from your children? Will you not embroil your wife and children in conflict because of her? Such grief on her account! And your family will say, 'This is all the fault of the sage, Joseph Halévy.' But, oh people of Yemen, if you do not reverse this deed which you think is good but which is evil, I will not curtail my description of your vile deeds, either in the company of honorable people or in my book. I know that there are people among you who marry many women without considering the sin and misfortunes which befall them and their children."[7]

"How many humiliations and how much cursing I heard," Ḥabshūsh writes, "until I made up my mind and felt ashamed of myself" and "wholly and utterly abandoned the matter."[8] The two travelers depart, and we hear no more about the girl and her fate.

Ḥabshūsh's story of the girl captures the subtleties involved in the clashing of cultures, both in Yemen and beyond. The Najrānī Jewish family considers killing the girl a requirement of both Jewish and tribal law. Their position does not stem from hostility toward the girl; indeed, their concern for her can be seen in their fear that Ḥabshūsh means to take her and then abandon her without support among strangers. They support the killing because it seems lawful and natural to them, and they are shocked when they are told that Jewish law declares otherwise. How is it possible, they ask, for a good family to raise a bastard in their home? In contrast, the Jew from Ṣanʿāʾ and the Jew from Paris are shocked and horrified at the very notion of honor killing, a practice that they view as immoral, un-Jewish, and uncivilized. However, when an abortion or polygamous marriage is proposed to save the girl's life, the Najrānī Jews and the Ṣanʿānī Jew rejoice, but the Parisian Jew is horrified at the barbarity and impiety of the proposal. Ḥabshūsh thus shows his readers how cultural clashes are not simply binary. Moreover, although they involve complex ideological issues, they are not immune to personal factors. The debate may have been about religious ethics but, independent of this, Halévy wants his scientific mission to succeed and Ḥabshūsh makes no secret of his attraction to the girl.

A Vision of Yemen is therefore not just about a journey in search of antiquities. It is about the living and breathing societies of Yemen—some Jewish, some Muslim, some urban, and some pastoral. The work abounds with vivid descriptions of daily life, religious customs, and folklore, also providing one of the nineteenth century's subtlest analyses of Jewish-Muslim relations. Ḥabshūsh's portrait of his land is executed with great pride but also with honesty. Part travelogue, part anthropological account, part picaresque tale, it has been beloved by audiences both in the Middle East and in the West and has been transliterated into Arabic and translated into French, Hebrew, and Italian.[9] This translation is its first into English from the original Hebrew and Judeo-Arabic.

Ḥayyim Ḥabshūsh before and after the Journey

Ḥayyim ibn Yaḥyā Ḥabshūsh al-Futayḥī was born in 1839 in Ṣanʿāʾ to a respected family of Yemeni merchants and rabbis. Little is known about his life before his 1869 meeting with Joseph Halévy beyond that he was a coppersmith and was married with at least one child. However, his own narration in *A Vision of Yemen* gives us some insight into his personality. Ḥabshūsh tells us that, before Halévy's arrival, he had already developed an interest in collecting pre-Islamic inscriptions, which he refers to as Sheban (Sabaean) or Himyaritic inscriptions. Like many Jews, Ḥabshūsh associated these inscriptions with the biblical kingdom of Sheba (Sabaʾ) and with tales of King Solomon and the Queen of Sheba. Further, he believed them to have magical properties and supposed that Halévy's interest in them was also connected with magic.[10] When Halévy asked Ḥabshūsh to find and copy down all such inscriptions in Ṣanʿāʾ, Ḥabshūsh was able to do so quickly and with little difficulty because his prior personal interest had already made him familiar with their locations. Moreover, he was happy to copy them, even though this involved spending time in parts of the city where other Jews feared to tarry. When he was indeed confronted by Muslims about his presence there, he glibly improvised a cover story to justify his presence and safely copied the inscriptions.[11] Thus, according to his recollections, even before he met Halévy, Ḥabshūsh was a man given to the exploration of places beyond those affiliated with his own Jewish community. Soon after, when Halévy hired Ḥabshūsh to accompany him on a long and perilous trip through eastern Yemen, Ḥabshūsh readily agreed, drawn by both the prospect of being well paid and by "the opportunity to meet our brethren who dwell in the East."[12] We thus see that he already held certain qualities in common with the European orientalist: an interest in ancient civilizations, few qualms about risking dangerous situations or scruples about bending the truth to get out of them, and a desire to meet the Jews of remote lands.

Despite these preexisting commonalities, Ḥabshūsh describes Halévy's impact on him as a baptism into new modes of thought, the effects of which remained with him long after the two men parted. Ḥabshūsh would strive to keep up to date with intellectual developments in the European and Ottoman worlds by becoming a regular reader of their Hebrew newspapers. The only photograph of Ḥabshūsh that survives captures him carrying one of these newspapers, and their influence is evident in the European style of Hebrew in which he writes.[13] Halévy also influenced Ḥabshūsh by persuading him to abandon his belief in astrology, magic, and mysticism and to embrace a rationalistic form of Judaism.[14] As will be explained later, this dichotomy between rationalistic Judaism and its mystical forms had previously existed in the Yemeni Jewish community, but several Jews who had close contact with Halévy and Glaser would imbue this conflict with new meaning by spearheading an intellectual revolution among their coreligionists.

As a result of his encounter with Halévy, Ḥabshūsh's interest in the magical properties of inscriptions was transformed into a historical interest for the light they shed on the civilizations of the ancient Sabaeans and their successors, the Himyarites. Later, he further broadened this historical interest

Ḥayyim Ḥabshūsh. Hibshoosh Family Collection.

in another work, *Halikhot Tema* (The Ways of Yemen), a short collection of writings about Yemeni Jewish history based on both oral sources and a wide assortment of written material. Through friendships with Muslim scholars, Ḥabshūsh gained access to Islamic chronicles housed in the Great Mosque of Ṣanʿāʾ that were unavailable to other Jews.[15] *Halikhot Tema* describes centuries of Yemeni Jewish history, including discussions of Jewish messianic activity, the Yemeni adoption of the Sephardic liturgy, and the infamous nineteenth-century anti-Jewish legislation known as the Latrines Edict. It also contains an essay on the plight of elderly Jews and a letter written by the author to a society of London missionaries who were active in Yemen, asking them to stop distributing Bibles to Yemenis and instead to establish vocational schools for them.[16]

In *A Vision of Yemen* Ḥabshūsh depicts his young self as irrepressible, impetuous, and just a bit self-serving, a necessary defense for a person in a community subject to disempowerment and exploitation. He readily admits that he hoped to be well paid for his assistance to Halévy, that he was offended by his employer's miserliness and distrust, and that he was not averse to using trickery to gain what he believed he deserved. Although he depicts his older self as wiser and more sedate, the youthful themes resurface in some stories recounted about the older Ḥabshūsh. When, in the late 1880s, a special tax was imposed on the Jews to fund the renovation of the famous landmark gate of Ṣanʿāʾ, the Bāb al-Yaman, Ḥabshūsh was reportedly irritated that Jewish community leaders had not stood up to defend the Jews and negotiate to have the predatory tax lowered. Resolving that at least he would not be one of those to suffer financial loss, he approached the builders and persuaded them that such an important gate would require joints of polished copper. As a coppersmith, the work naturally went to him, and he was able to more than recoup what had been expropriated from him.[17]

A hint of Ḥabshūsh's combination of panache, erudition, and social activism can be seen in an 1875 petition on behalf of Yemeni Jews addressed to the British Jewish philanthropist Sir Moses Montefiore. The petition, which was signed by a wide array of eminent Jews, caught the attention of the philanthropist because it included an unusual signature written in a strange alphabet. His curiosity roused, Montefiore consulted an expert in Semitic languages, who identified the alphabet as ancient Sabaean and deciphered the text: "Ḥayyim Ḥabshūsh, the one who rouses the sleepers of France and awakens the slumberers of Europe,"[18] a phrase adapted from the liturgy of the Jewish morning prayers. By writing in Sabaean characters, Ḥabshūsh demonstrated his command of European turf by showing his comfort in a distinctly European cultural enterprise: the philology of dead languages, an impressive feat for anyone but especially for an "oriental." By calling to mind a phrase from the morning prayers recited by Jews all over the world, Ḥabshūsh appealed to Montefiore not on European grounds but on the basis of their common Jewish identity, which transcended geographic and cultural boundaries. But his message was a call to a particular form of action: European Jewry must wake up and help out their Yemeni Jewish coreligionists. In the space of a few words, Ḥabshūsh thus effortlessly established himself as a member of the European, the Jewish, and the Yemeni cultural communities.

Ḥabshūsh died in 1899 during a period of great famine and social instability. Over the next half-century the Jewish culture he had devoted so much of his life to defending and chronicling disappeared from Yemen. After his death, battles between local Yemenis and the occupying Ottoman forces resulted in the 1905 Siege of Ṣanʿāʾ, which killed about half the city's population.[19] The rise of Zionism in Yemen placed further pressure on an already weakened Jewish population. In 1938 Ḥabshūsh's 60-year-old son Yaḥyā was lynched, stoned to death in Ṣanʿāʾ by a mob inspired by public calls for the shedding of Jewish and Zionist blood.[20] Shortly after the establishment of Israel, almost the entire Jewish community of Yemen migrated there.[21]

One result of this dislocation was that Ḥabshūsh's legacy was taken up decades later by his great-nephew, Yehiel Hibshoosh. Yehiel was born in Ṣanʿāʾ in 1913 and immigrated to Palestine in 1930. There he helped to found Ezrat Aḥim, an organization devoted to assisting the growing numbers of immigrant Yemeni Jews. Yehiel was aware that the culture in which he had been raised stood at risk of being forgotten. He therefore self-published more than twenty books on Yemeni Jews and Judaism, distributing them to libraries around the world. His books include an investigation of religious schisms among Yemeni Jews, a record of a trip he made to Yemen as an elderly man in the 1990s, and even a book of Yemeni Jewish jokes.[22]

In his book on the history of his family, Yehiel includes several family stories about the exploits of his great uncle Ḥayyim, many of which are confirmed by other sources. Ḥayyim solves a murder,[23] battles false messiahs,[24] and prospects for gold.[25] An intrepid debunker of myths, he boldly pursues an alleged Lilith, the evil spirit of the night, to prove her to be a human.[26] Ḥayyim was also an expert in Islamic and tribal history and was recognized as such by Muslims, with whom he developed close relationships. Supposedly among these was the future ruler of Yemen, Imām Yaḥyā, who remembered Ḥayyim for his great wisdom long after the latter's death.[27] Ḥayyim's fierce independence and intellectual curiosity led some Jews to suspect him of heresy.[28] Ḥayyim brought Islamic books to the synagogue, which he would quietly read during prayer services, much to the consternation of the congregation.[29] He would also sit near the synagogue's bookshelf so he could easily retrieve fresh titles to stave off boredom. Ḥayyim nonetheless won many Jewish admirers, who eagerly sought out his opinions and sermons. Although Yehiel never met his great uncle and although his style tends toward the hagiographic, the book is colorful and engaging. Ḥayyim's boundless curiosity, energy, and confidence, already familiar from *A Vision of Yemen*, shine forth from Yehiel's book.[30]

Joseph Halévy

In Ḥabshūsh's narrative Joseph Halévy appears as an austere, authoritative, and deeply learned sage whose interest in antiquities all but overpowers any concern he might have for those around him and whose disdain for the Yemenis is palpable. In point of fact, however, Halévy, born in 1827, was little more than a decade older than his native guide, although he would outlive him by eighteen years, dying in 1917.[31] Moreover, his interest in ancient Yemen was not merely antiquarian but was intimately connected with his participation in some of the most pressing sociopolitical debates about race and religion that faced the Jews of his time. Indeed, before arriving in Yemen, he had already risked his life and reputation in the service of some of these causes.

That Ḥabshūsh lacked this insight into Halévy's beliefs and personal history is not surprising. Halévy was remarkably reticent, particularly about his own origins, and seems to have had a deep personal horror of notions of immutable ethnic identity.[32] Halévy was most likely a Hungarian Jew who

Joseph Halévy. *The Jewish Encyclopedia*, ed. I. Singer (New York: Funk and Wagnalls, 1904), 6:168.

participated in and fled the nationalist insurrection of 1848, eventually settling in the Ottoman town of Adrianople, now in modern Turkey.[33] Halévy's experiences in Adrianople as a stranger in his 20s exemplify many of the characteristics that initially impressed Ḥabshūsh.[34] When he arrived in Adrianople, he spoke neither Ladino nor Ottoman Turkish and, according to one source, his clothing and appearance resembled those of a Bulgarian Christian peasant.[35] However, he spoke such eloquent Hebrew and demonstrated such mastery of Jewish literature that he was assumed to be a rabbi and was given a teaching position. He soon learned the local languages, but his identity as a foreigner was clearly in evidence and he was thus often referred to as "the monsieur."[36] Although combative and sarcastic, his erudition and organizational talents were such that he soon became the director of the Jewish school at which he had been a teacher. In that capacity, he introduced many educational reforms, adding classes in French and Hebrew grammar to the curriculum and placing a heavy emphasis on European-style hygiene.[37]

His charisma was such that, within a few years of his arrival, all the Jewish schools of Adrianople merged under his leadership.[38]

In the course of building his school in Adrianople, Halévy forged ties with the Alliance Israélite Universelle, a Paris-based organization dedicated to assisting impoverished and oppressed Jews worldwide by "modernizing" them, largely through establishing Jewish schools based on the French model. For this reason, the Alliance is sometimes seen as the Jewish counterpart of the French "civilizing mission."[39] By 1905 the Alliance school system that Halévy had first introduced had supplanted the traditional education system in Adrianople, and the town became a major center for the Haskalah, the Jewish Enlightenment movement.[40]

Many in Adrianople supported Halévy's educational reforms, but he also met with considerable and sometimes violent opposition from those who claimed that he secretly aimed to convert Jewish children to Christianity.[41] Doubts about him were such that one source reported that a rabbi was sent to the bathhouse to check whether he was circumcised.[42] The last straw for the opposition was Halévy's attempt to prevent a local exorcism. In 1861 Halévy was excommunicated and driven out of the city.[43]

Halévy seems to have liked his position as an outsider and wanted to preserve it, even when his exile forced him to return to his native Europe. Rather than presenting himself as a European Jew, he chose to present himself as a native-born Ottoman Jew (even in government documents).[44] He played this role to perfection and was generally regarded, by French Jews and non-Jews alike, as an oriental Jew. His oriental mannerisms, and even appearance, were often commented on, both positively and negatively. Even the scholar and Jewish community leader Salomon Reinach, who knew world Jewry too well not to realize that Halévy had been schooled in Hungary, was convinced that he had been born in Adrianople as a result of a brief sojourn there by his parents.[45] Halévy took full advantage of being an Ashkenazi when in Sephardic society and a Sephardi when in Ashkenazic society. He seems to have believed that his identity as an outsider allowed him to act as a bridge between the Ashkenazic and Sephardic worlds. He composed Hebrew poems in the Andalusian meter for an Ashkenazic audience and taught a generation of teachers how to give a European-style education to Jewish children in the Muslim world.

Halévy spent much of the decade following his exile traveling.[46] He was commissioned by the Alliance Israélite Universelle to go to Morocco in 1861 to report on the status and needs of the country's Jews. His findings led to the establishment of the Alliance's most extensive educational project, a school system for Jews across Morocco.[47] The Alliance job, however, was short-lived, and Halévy had to spend several months wandering from town to town in Europe in search of work. At some point, he settled in Bucharest, where he became a teacher and then director of a Jewish school.[48] His efforts in combating Christian missionaries earned him prestige among Jews, which he used to leverage the founding of a branch of the Alliance for Romania.[49]

As in Adrianople, Halévy's educational reforms angered traditional Jews, as did his staunch objection to mystical practices. He was dismissed from his position as the Bucharest school's director once it became known that he rejected the *Zohar*, a key text of Jewish mysticism.[50] Halévy lived in Bucharest from 1862 to 1867, although this period was punctuated by several long absences as a result of his travels on behalf of the Alliance. One such mission involved a trip to investigate the receptivity of German Jews to Alliance schools. Lest one think that his critical eye lit only on "oriental" Jews, it is worth noting that Halévy described the general spirit of German Jews as one of "dreaminess and impracticality," and he dismissed the thought of Samson Raphael Hirsch, the intellectual founder of neo-Orthodoxy, as no better than "Polish Hasidism."[51] Halévy's distaste for Ashkenazic Hasidism can also be seen in his compliment to the Sephardic Jews of Turkey, of whom he wrote, "The fanaticism . . . which causes such devastation within the communities of northeastern Europe is thankfully unknown among those exiled from the Iberian Peninsula."[52]

In 1867 Halévy undertook a mission to Abyssinia (modern-day Ethiopia) that made him famous. The journey stands in curious contrast to the one he made to Yemen just two years later and perhaps provides a partial explanation as to why he behaved in the unsympathetic manner described by Ḥabshūsh. Beginning in the 1850s, European Jews became aware of the existence of their Abyssinian coreligionists through the reports of Christian missionaries who had first made contact with them and targeted them for conversion. In 1864 Rabbi Azriel Hildesheimer of Eisenstadt circulated a letter outlining their plight and calling for intervention. A few weeks later, Halévy responded in *Ha-Magid*, a Hebrew newspaper based in what is now Poland, passionately volunteering himself to make contact with them and detailing his credentials.[53] In a subsequent letter to the Alliance, written in eloquent Hebrew, Halévy pleaded his case.

> (1) For many years, I have had a great longing and desire for this journey. On a distressful day in 1848,[54] I swore an oath to the God of Israel to travel to Abyssinia to improve the situation of our brethren there in any way I could. From then until now, I have not ceased to prepare myself for that journey. Only concern for the welfare of my home and children has hitherto stopped me. . . .
>
> (2) I have been a voyager from my youth. I have traversed the northern glaciers, the Egyptian summer has smote me, and the days and years have shot arrows at me, but thankfully my health is strong and I have known no sickness or illness.
>
> (3) I have acquired knowledge of many ancient languages. I understand English, Turkish, Arabic, Abyssinian (Geʿez), and Amharic to the extent that I can not only easily express my ideas in them without the aid of a translator but also, once I have spent a few days among these people, can preach in their congregations in these languages.
>
> (4) From my youth, I have studied the science of our holy Torah and the wisdom of the Talmud and midrash. I also entered the temples of natural science, mathematics, and algebra. I have knowledge of geography, world history and, most important, everything touching upon the history of our people and the ways of our sages in all their denominations.
>
> (5) I am very experienced in polemics with Christians. I know the Gospels almost by heart, and the beliefs of the various Christian denominations are very familiar to me. Praise be to the God of Israel, I have the capacity to shut the mouths of the missionaries and demolish the walls of their faith to their foundations! I hope that I will stymie these British envoys to the land of Abyssinia and rescue the prey from their hands.[55]

Halévy's candidacy was supported by several prominent rabbis, including the famous Ashkenazic reactionary Meir Loeb (better known as the Malbim), who praised his great learning, and Yakir Giron, then the chief rabbi of

Constantinople. Two years later, the Alliance agreed to fund the journey and, by 1867, Halévy was in Abyssinia.[56]

In Abyssinia Halévy traversed hundreds of miles of rough terrain, much of which was engulfed by war and in which the emperor had taken to imprisoning European missionaries and other suspicious foreigners.[57] Although Halévy could have traveled under the protection of the British army, he opted to travel independently. Riding a camel and brandishing a rifle, he disguised himself as a rhinoceros dealer.[58] While on the road, he let no time go to waste. He read Zoroastrian texts with a Parsi from Malabar, studied the religious ceremonies of the Indians, and learned Chinese and Hindi from workers in the British army whom he met along the way.[59]

After several weeks, Halévy finally encountered an Abyssinian Jewish community. When he told them he was their coreligionist, they at first shied away from him, suspecting that he was yet another Christian missionary. "What! You a Falasha!* A white Falasha!" they challenged. "You are laughing at us! Are there any white Falashas?"[60] Halévy claimed to have responded:

> Oh, my brethren . . . I am not only a European; I am, like you, an Israelite. I come, not to trade in Abyssinia, but to inquire into the state of my coreligionists in conformity with the desire of a great Jewish Association existing in my country. You must know, my dear brethren, that I am also a Falasha! I worship no other God than the great Adonai, and I acknowledge no other law than the law of Sinai![61]

Halévy thus attempted to persuade the Abyssinian Jews that Israelite identity was a matter of religion rather than of skin tone. It was devotion to God and the Mosaic precepts that constituted their shared religious community, not physical appearance. Halévy speculated that European and Abyssinian Jews may have shared descent, but it was the idea of ancestry rather than its actuality that was important: "Among no nation do we find the feeling of brotherhood so powerful as among the Hebrew race. At the sound of the magic word 'Israel,' distances are forgotten, all differences of color, lan-

* Abyssinian Jews call themselves the Beta Israel. Halévy, like other Europeans of his day, referred to them as Falashas. Although Halévy he did not use the term with the intent to be derogatory, the term originated in Abyssinia as a pejorative exonym and is to be avoided. See Steven Kaplan, *The Beta Israel (Falasha) in Ethiopia* (New York: NYU Press, 1992), 9–10.

guage, and costume vanish, and the idea of a community of origin joins all hearts together."[62] For Halévy, "Hebrew race" referred to a concept of Jewish peoplehood. He understood the concept of race as something fluid, international, and multi-ethnic and not simply limited to heredity. Halévy was able to persuade the Abyssinian Jews to adopt this flexible concept of Jewish peoplehood, and he was welcomed into their community with great warmth, which he clearly returned. Unlike the missionaries who preceded him, he did not, for the most part, try to alter their religious observances, and, also unlike the missionaries, his accounts of their practices are generally regarded as reliable.[63]

Upon his return to France, Halévy pleaded with the Alliance to support the Abyssinian Jews. He described them as an "industrious and intelligent people with a promising future." After a moving account of their sufferings, he demanded that European Jews come to their aid.

> [These Abyssinians] are Jews by virtue of their ardent faith and their study of the law and the words of the prophets, which they read in their temples and teach to their children. Their complexion is different from ours, but their good faith and virtue must make us proud of our kinship with them. They practice all the Mosaic rites insofar as they are able and submit without complaint to the privations that the law requires of them. They would rather suffer a thousand deaths than break their covenant with the Lord.[64]

Despite years of effort, however, Halévy was unable to persuade the Alliance to deliver aid to the Abyssinian Jews. The experience left him deeply embittered.[65] Still worse, Halévy had brought a young Abyssinian Jew to Europe who he had hoped would be educated in an Alliance school and would return to his homeland as a teacher. Officials at the Alliance, however, denied the man's Jewishness and dispatched him to Alexandria, where he fell ill and died. To make matters worse, the Alliance accused Halévy of deliberate fraud in claiming that the man was a Jew.[66] It was not until 1904 that Halévy succeeded in organizing a mission, led by his student Jacques Faitlovitch and funded by Baron Edmond de Rothschild, to deliver aid to the Abyssinian Jews.[67] When the Alliance learned of the mission, it financed a countermission that argued against investing in Abyssinian Jews, largely by claiming that they were of an inferior race.[68]

Thus, when Halévy returned from Abyssinia in 1868, his relations with the Alliance were fraught. Fortunately for him, however, he would be granted a respite from his employer. Although he had no formal university education, his writings on Abyssinia had brought him to the attention of the celebrated French intellectual Ernest Renan and the French Académie des Inscriptions et Belles-Lettres. Renan was organizing an ambitious project to collect all the world's Semitic inscriptions and needed someone to travel to Yemen to explore its great pre-Islamic Semitic civilizations. Travel through Yemen was unusually dangerous in the nineteenth century. Local Yemeni historians referred to the period as "the time of corruption" to indicate that civil unrest had reached epic proportions. Their chronicles are filled with descriptions of rampant banditry, violent tribal wars, and leadership disputes.[69] Strangers in those troubled times, even those native to Yemen, were viewed with great suspicion and hostility.[70]

Amid such unrest, it was vital for foreigners to blend in, and it was for this reason that, although Renan was uninterested in contemporary Yemenis, whether Muslim or Jewish, Halévy's connections with the traditional Jewish world worked in favor of rather than against his appointment. Whoever was sent to Yemen, Renan reasoned, needed to be accepted by local hosts and guides. For a Yemeni Muslim, accompanying a European across Yemen was difficult. A Muslim could travel with safety only as far as his tribal connections extended, because crossing into the territory of a rival tribe was fraught with danger. In contrast, because Jews were not perceived as security threats, they could cross tribal borders in relative safety and secure food and lodging from their coreligionists. Following this logic, Renan deduced that Yemen could be traversed only with the assistance of Yemeni Jews. Because a foreign traveler had to gain the cooperation of these Jews, Renan thought that it would be best to send a rabbi. Only someone with such credentials could win the support of the local Jewish community and thereby negotiate Yemen's complicated web of tribes.[71]

Renan's first choice for the journey had been Jacob Saphir, a Jerusalemite rabbi with no secular credentials whatsoever but whose Hebrew-language account of his travels in Yemen Renan had appreciated.[72] Saphir, however, had declined the mission, opening the way for Halévy. Because Saphir's journey had been a success, Halévy adopted a similar plan and went disguised as a Jerusalemite rabbi collecting alms.[73] Even with the protection of the Jewish community, the journey was difficult. Travel in Yemen required immense courage and physical stamina. Many of the locations on his itinerary had never been visited by Europeans, and the death toll of those who had visited the country was high.[74]

Halévy was thus in an awkward position. To succeed, he required the cooperation of Yemeni Jews. However, unlike his journey to Abyssinia, his mission was a scholarly project on behalf of the French Académie, not a humanitarian mission on behalf of the Jewish community. Ḥabshūsh would blame Halévy for neglecting his humanitarian responsibilities to Yemeni Jews, but Halévy was likely restricted in what aid he could bring them after the Alliance had so humiliatingly denied his public pleas on behalf of Abyssinian Jews. Instead, in Yemen, Halévy seems to have largely contented himself with fulfilling the narrow role provided to him by Renan. In contrast to his extensive writings on Abyssinian Jews, he barely reported about his encounters with Yemeni Jews, let alone advocated on their behalf. Nor was he spurred to action after he was publicly criticized for this neglect in an editorial published in a Jewish newspaper.[75] Having felt betrayed by the Alliance after his mission to Abyssinia, he would not risk a repeat in Yemen.

Semites, Anti-Semitism, and the Journey in Search of Archaeological Remains

Why was Halévy willing to risk life and limb to collect Semitic inscriptions in Yemen? Why did Ernest Renan, one of the most prominent figures in the French literary world, regard his project to collect all existing Semitic inscriptions as his life's crowning achievement?[76] For both scholars the inscriptions had a personal and social value. Renan came to propound a theory that the grammar of languages shaped the thoughts of those who spoke them. It was on these grounds that Renan privileged Aryan civilization, claiming that Semites were trapped by the grammar of their language in a monotheism that denied them a creative impulse. For Renan, this meant that the Semites were incapable of creating myths or writing epics, incapable of abstract philosophical thought, and also bound to political systems of absolutist government.[77] It is important to note that, for Renan, there was a path by which Semites could be freed from their inferiority. Because he believed that race was primarily linguistically defined, Semites could escape their predicament by learning Aryan languages. On this basis, he once remarked, "Fanaticism is impossible in French. . . . A Muslim who knows French will never be a dangerous Muslim."[78] Here, Renan was referring to Muslims, but he might just as easily have been referring to Jews. For Renan, Jews were a religion, not a race. He respected and had good relations with many French Jewish intellectuals, whom he regarded as an integral part of the French "race."[79] However, although Renan believed that the difference between Semites and Aryans was linguistic, not biological, he was dismissive of the Jewish intellectual tradition because it had been largely composed in Semitic languages.[80]

Renan's views of Semitism motivated a generation of Jewish scholars to mobilize in defense of their tradition.[81] Many responded by attempting to demonstrate the creativity of not just the Hebrew literary corpus but also that of other Semitic civilizations. In nineteenth-century France the old tradition of distinguishing between Jews and European Gentiles on the basis of theology was dwindling in the face of modern post-religiosity and was giving way to a new form of categorization. Jews and Gentiles were replaced with Semites and Aryans. This began as a linguistic categorization, put forward by secular European intellectuals, when language was thought to determine culture and even character; but in time it would harden into a biological, racial science. Halévy appears to have recognized the dangers of the new category of "Semites" and spent much of his life encouraging European Jews to ignore skin color and race, and embrace their coreligionists throughout the world. He also sought to prove, particularly to those outside the Jewish community, the glory and creativity of the civilizations produced by writers of Semitic languages, including those he explored in Yemen with Ḥabshūsh.

Halévy's desire to defend Semitic culture turned into a lonely half-century battle to prove that the Sumerian language was Semitic and not Indo-European. The stakes were high. At the time, scholars believed that the Sumerians had originated Mesopotamian civilization and had then passed it on to others. If it could be shown that the Sumerian language was Semitic, the Semites could be credited with this momentous and innovative contribution to world civilization. If not, Semitic civilization was merely imitative of that of the non-Semitic Sumerians. Halévy continued to argue that Sumerian was a Semitic language, even when he was presented with overwhelming evidence to the contrary and even when maintaining this position jeopardized his academic employment and led to his ostracization.[82] Why did he persist? Jerrold Cooper, in his study of the Sumerian debate, suggests that

> Halévy had intimations of an evil that . . . [his contemporaries] would not have imagined possible. The genius and tragedy of Halévy was to perceive and strongly feel that the very existence of the Sumerians provided ammunition and comfort to the most base antisemitism. Trapped himself by the racial assumptions of his times, he unwittingly sacrificed a scholar's dearest possession, his objectivity, in a lifelong battle against a people and a language dead some four thousand years.[83]

During Halévy's lifetime, what were once linguistic delineations of Semitism became inextricably intertwined with notions of "national character" and biology. Within twenty-five years of Halévy's death, the denigration of Semitic civilization in scholarly journals was used to justify the logic of genocide.

When Halévy reached Yemen in 1869, the Sumerian debate still lay about five years in the future, but it was European debates on Aryanism and Semitism that had brought him there. He had come to Yemen as a defender of Semitic cultures, of which he viewed himself a part.

Halévy entered Yemen through Aden, a convenient embarkation point, as the city was governed by the British. To avoid political unrest, he took a circuitous route to Ṣanʿāʾ, where he was delayed for two months because of a serious illness. Once healed, he considered two routes to Mārib. The easiest ran directly from Ṣanʿāʾ to Mārib and would take advantage of salt caravans with the same itinerary. The second, more difficult route involved traversing the Jawf region. Although ancient Greek sources indicated that a rich civilization had once flourished there, no European had visited the region since the failed Roman invasion in the first century BCE.[84] Halévy's contacts in Ṣanʿāʾ tried to warn him away from the Jawf. Only its nomadic tribes, who had a reputation for inhospitality and violence, knew the geography of its mountains, flatlands, and desert. A reliable guide would be essential for the success of any such voyage, and there was little chance of finding one. Nevertheless, this was the route that Halévy chose—the lure of the ancient civilization that he hoped to find there was simply too great. His decision was a good one, despite several brushes with death, including getting lost in the desert and being imprisoned by hostile tribes. Once he reached Mārib, his stay was cut short by an Indian antiquities dealer, who viewed him as a competitor. The rival dispatched men to harass Halévy, seriously limiting his ability to transcribe inscriptions.[85] He thus collected fewer transcriptions from Mārib than he would have liked.

When he returned to France in 1871, Halévy was fêted as one of the greatest explorers of his age. At the Institut de France, Renan lionized Halévy for entering lands that no European since Aelius Gallus, a Roman consul in the age of Augustus, had dared to tread. Many years later, this feat of exploration was to earn Halévy France's Legion of Honor.[86] Halévy's journey was indeed remarkable. He had discovered six ancient cities, including the splendid ancient capital of Qarnaw, and had transcribed an astonishing 685 inscriptions.[87] Decades later, many of these achievements remained unrivaled. As late as 1920, some fifty years after his voyage, the British Admiralty's *Handbook of Arabia* still relied on Halévy as its authority on conditions in northern Yemen.[88] Halévy's trip to Najrān, now in Saudi Arabia, was not repeated by a European until 1936, when H. St. John "Abdallah" Philby was able to reach the area with the personal help of the

48. — 7.

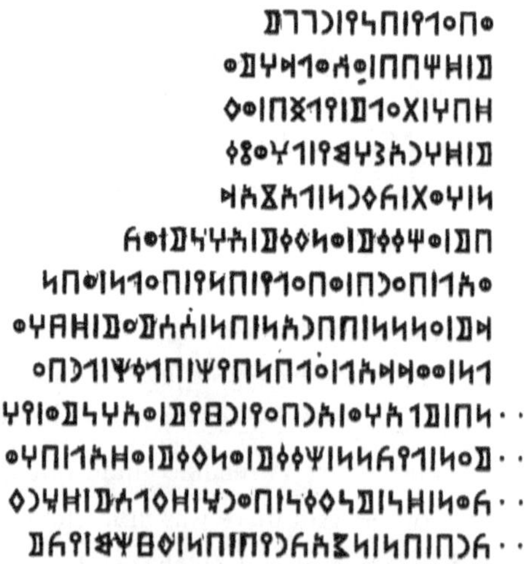

Inscriptions from Ṣirwāḥ. Joseph Halévy, "Rapport sur une mission archéologique dans le Yemen," *Journal Asiatique* 6 (1872): 110.

Saudi king. Nearly a century later, the noted Egyptian archaeologist Ahmed Fakhry affirmed that the scope of Halévy's voyage remained unrivaled even in his own time.[89]

The attitude of Yemeni Jews to Halévy was less celebratory. Halévy had arrived in Yemen disguised as a rabbi collecting alms for the poor of Jerusalem and bore letters of introduction that indicated his commitment to aiding Yemeni Jews. The collection of such alms was a widely attested and age-old custom (one mentioned rather frequently, for example, in the New Testament). Its primary purpose was not to transfer wealth from the rich to the poor but rather to provide an opportunity for Jews to pay their dues and, in return, to receive the spiritual satisfaction of supporting and being members of the greater Jewish community. The Jewish community of Jerusalem, whose emissaries traveled throughout the Jewish world, was a point of connection between Jews of different lands.[90] By fostering this connection, Jews hoped to receive material support, in their hour of need, from Jews across the globe. For this reason, poor Jewish communities, like those in Yemen, gave collectively while still seeking aid from their brethren abroad. Believing Halévy to be a Jerusalemite emissary, the Yemeni Jews placed high hopes in his ability to help them. Their hospitality, one of the most highly prized virtues in Yemen, was fully on display throughout Halévy's journey. People of all kinds—rich and poor, men and women—deprived themselves of what they had to provide for their guests. They did not realize that, although Halévy would make use of them when it suited him, he had no intention of reciprocating their favors. Their hopes continued even after Halévy left Yemen, because, as the community expressed itself in a letter to the Anglo-Jewish Association, they felt that he would be a witness to their suffering and pitiable situation.[91]

The arrival of Eduard Glaser in Yemen some twenty years later, asking for an account of Halévy's journey, gave Ḥabshūsh the opportunity not only to point out his own role and his community's role in Halévy's celebrated achievements but also to turn the tables on his orientalist companion. If Halévy had exploited his Yemeni Jewish connections to launch an investigation of the ancient Sabaeans, Ḥabshūsh would exploit Halévy's investigation of the Sabaeans to draw the attention of the world to the living people of Yemen.

Eduard Glaser. Archiv der Österreichischen Akademie der Wissenschaften, Vienna, Glaser Collection 13/6.

Eduard Glaser and the Commissioning of A Vision of Yemen

Eduard Glaser, the scholar who commissioned *A Vision of Yemen*, bore a curious resemblance to both Ḥabshūsh and Halévy. Like Ḥabshūsh, he devoted his life to Yemen and its people, both Muslim and Jewish. Like Halévy, he was born a European Jew, became a talented linguist and Semiticist, and managed to alienate most of the academy. And, like both Ḥabshūsh and Halévy, he had an adventurer's talent for disguise. But, unlike either, his guise was that of a Muslim scholar, and he came to inhabit it so fully that he felt conflicted about whether he was in disguise at all. Moreover, although he never found a home in the European academy, he maintained warm and mutually respectful relationships with his Yemeni acquaintances throughout his life.

Glaser's Yemeni Muslim friends were deeply impressed by him. The Egyptian archaeologist Ahmed Fakhry, who visited Yemen half a century after Glaser, remarked that a positive image of him lived on in the stories told about him. He was most beloved, Fakhry said, by the Ashraf tribe, whose chief, Sharīf Muḥammad, had named his son Ḥusayn after Glaser, whom he regarded as a close friend.[92] Despite the Muslim identity that he assumed, Glaser also developed close relationships with Jews, including the prominent Jewish leader and scholar Yaḥyā Qāfiḥ, who was the only Yemeni aware of his true identity. When Glaser returned to Europe, he continued this friendship by sending Qāfiḥ scientific instruments, Hebrew books on the natural sciences, and anti-Kabbalistic polemics.[93]

Finally, like Ḥabshūsh and Halévy, Glaser was concerned about Jewish communal safety, but he proposed his own unique solution to the problem. He believed that part of Yemen could become the Jewish safe haven for which the newly emerging Zionist movement was so desperately searching.[94]

Born in 1855 to a family of impoverished Jewish farmers in the small Bohemian village of Deutsch-Rust, Glaser left home as a teenager against his parents' wishes in search of a better education. He enrolled in a Prague high school, and it was there that he decided that he wanted to be a traveler, apparently after reading reports about Dr. David Livingstone's famous voyages.[95] After graduating from high school, he went on to complete a degree in sciences at the Polytechnic in Prague, but he was already studying Arabic on the side. In 1877, after a year of army service, Glaser enrolled at the University of Vienna, where he studied Arabic and astronomy.[96]

In Vienna Glaser met David Heinrich Müller, a distinguished scholar who rose to become dean of philosophy at the University of Vienna while also serving on the faculty of a local rabbinic seminary. It was Müller who inspired Glaser to learn the Semitic languages of ancient Arabia. Despite Glaser's intellectual debt to Müller, the two soon fell into conflict. In 1881 Müller chose another of his students, Siegfried Langer, to travel to Yemen for research, leaving Glaser feeling snubbed. In 1886 Glaser dramatically expressed his resentment in a vicious and lengthy self-published review of Müller's work.[97] Glaser's propensity for such feuds left him widely disliked in the scholarly community. For instance, the Swedish orientalist Carlo de Landberg heaved a sigh of relief when Glaser passed away, foreseeing for his profession "a period of calm and impartial collaboration." Glaser, he said, "saw persecutors and rivals everywhere. With his petty spirit and often venomous pen, he laid a troublesome burden on our studies, because no one was safe from his evil tongue."[98]

Glaser's clash with Müller denied him a doctoral degree and barred him from a university position. Despite this setback, Glaser devoted his life to the study of Yemen but was compelled to undertake this with little institutional support. To finance his first trip to Yemen and gain fluency in Arabic, he spent nearly two years working at Austrian consulates, first in Tunis and then in Egypt (1881–1882). Later, always short of funds, he supported himself by selling manuscripts, artifacts, and transcriptions and occasionally by writing for the German press.[99] Glaser's interest in Yemen cannot be explained as an attempt at self-advancement. Expertise in Yemen could not promise a successful career, as the region was of little interest either to European politicians or to academics. Even Halévy, who had devoted so much of his scholarship to the study of Yemen, achieved academic employment on the basis of his knowledge of Abyssinia. Glaser, though aware of this, devoted himself to Yemen even when other more lucrative opportunities were available.[100]

Glaser's diaries offer glimpses of what led him to devote himself to Yemen. In one passage, he writes:

> Whenever I find myself among [its] ruins or when I decipher an inscription, I feel like a necromancer. My entire body quivers with an indefinable feeling like a dull sepulchral tone, an eerie and sublime spirit's call, a trumpet pro-

> claiming the approval of redeemed Minaic kings, the ghosts of the dead, the skeletons of the forgotten. Surrounded by this world of spirits and ghosts, I often forget the present, my own self, and I become a ghost. The spirit world is a great dance, and he who sticks his nose into it once is drawn with its magical power into the dizzying circles of the underworld.[101]

In his diaries Glaser thus admits to experiencing Yemen not only as a scientist but also as a mystic. Interestingly, this sentiment is absent from his publications, which belong to that form of German orientalism described by one scholar as "narrowly-focused, philologically-exacting and historically-minded."[102] It appears, then, that Glaser understood his academic and personal pursuits as quite separate, a model of scholarship different from the one embodied by either Halévy or Ḥabshūsh.

In addition to his fascination with Yemen's ancient history, Glaser also felt a deep love for the Yemeni people, which he often expressed in his diaries. His relationship with them was complicated, because his trips were predicated on a degree of subterfuge. He was able to travel freely by disguising himself as a *faqīh*, a learned Muslim scholar, although he had never so much as converted to Islam. He chose to assume this identity after consulting with the famous Ottoman field marshal Osman Nuri Pasha, who considered it essential for Glaser's survival. Glaser went by the alias Ḥusayn ibn ʿAbdallāh al-Birāqī. The name al-Birāqī was Glaser's arabicization of Prague, but he told anyone who asked that it was a small town in the heart of Arabia.[103]

Although, by all accounts, Glaser played the *faqīh* to perfection, his diaries reveal that he also wished to transcend the charade. In an extended meditation about Islam, he reveals that he was often uneasy with the subterfuge and set limits on it. For example, he prayed in a mosque only twice and gave the Friday sermon once, and then only under circumstances of life-and-death necessity. Moreover, he discovered a deep affinity with Islam and with Yemeni Muslims in particular. He found Islamic religious obligations to be "reasonable" and felt that Yemeni Muslims were more sincere in their faith than Europeans. He was particularly impressed with Islamic toleration of other religions, remarking that "the most fanatical Muslim is still more tolerant of other faiths than the most enlightened adherent of other religions." Europeans, he said, would benefit from becoming "better acquainted with these people—not from the high horse of politics or technological progress, but from the intimate traffic of daily life." Glaser was transformed by the disguise that he assumed. "Although I was not a real *faqīh*," he concluded, "my role as a *faqīh* was not entirely feigned."[104] Glaser's close friends confirmed the claim. Over his grave in the Jewish cemetery of Munich, they placed a marker that bears an inscription in both German and ancient Minaic. The German inscription is prosaic.

> Here lies
> Dr. Eduard Glaser
> Explorer of Arabia
> Born 30 March 1855 in Deutsch-Rust
> Died 7 May 1908 in Munich

In contrast, the Minaic inscription reads: "The funerary monument and grave of Ḥusayn ibn ʿAbdallāh al-Birāqī, the great traveler. May the Lord of the Heavens grant peace to his heart and well-being to his hand."[105] By referring to Glaser by the Islamic name that he used in Yemen, the inscription affirms the importance of the Islamic identity that he adopted.

During the 1880s and 1890s, Glaser made four lengthy trips to Yemen.[106] His ability to travel and remain there for long periods was dependent on good relations with both the Ottomans and the Yemenis. The Ottomans gave Glaser permission to engage in his scholarly explorations of Yemen in exchange for his political services. As early as 1883, Glaser accompanied Ottoman forces on maneuvers, helping them to negotiate with local tribal leaders.[107] It was his close relationship with the Ottomans that garnered him two months in the ancient Sabaean capital of Mārib, which was particularly rich in inscriptions. The few Europeans who had reached the town before him, in contrast, had spent but a few days there. Although Glaser performed a variety of services for the Ottomans, he seems to have earned from them only permission to travel, not money.[108] Glaser generally thought highly of the Ottomans.[109] He believed that with their technological resources and expertise, they could dramatically improve the lives of Yemenis through mutually beneficial development projects. He was not averse to other empires doing likewise, but he believed that the Ottomans were best placed to make an impact because of their already heavy investment in the country. That being said, in his diaries Glaser often criticized Ottoman officials for their high-handed and disrespectful treatment of Yemenis.[110]

On his final trip to Yemen, rather than collect all the inscriptions himself as he had previously done, Glaser trained teams of locals, including Ḥabshūsh, to help him. In a letter to a friend, he proudly described his new and pathbreaking methodology.

> I have trained ordinary Bedouins to print off and copy inscriptions. I had a whole body of such assistants, furnished with metal box, paper, lead pencil and brush, getting material down according to all points and tracing it off, correct to the last detail, in regions where no European will ever tread. . . . I have gone into everything very carefully with a view to its scientific value, and I can truly say that my results are at least as good . . . as those of my three previous expeditions.[111]

By pioneering this method, Glaser was able to record hundreds of inscriptions, many of which have since been destroyed.

It was during this final trip, with its unorthodox trust placed in the "natives," that Glaser and Ḥabshūsh became friends. What precipitated this is not entirely clear, although it seems that Glaser's experiences with his Yemeni protégées likely primed him to give serious consideration to his predecessor's protégé. Less charitably, given Glaser's harsh criticisms of Halévy's scholarship and his propensity for squabbling with fellow orientalists, it is possible that he cultivated a relationship with Ḥabshūsh to seek out potentially damaging information on a rival.[112] It is also not clear precisely what Glaser revealed about himself to Ḥabshūsh. It is evident that Ḥabshūsh believed Glaser to be a European who knew Hebrew well. However, it also appears that Ḥabshūsh was under the impression that Glaser was *not* Jewish.[113]

Ḥabshūsh acknowledges Glaser's role in the shaping of *A Vision of Yemen*. It was Glaser, he tells us, who asked for an account of Halévy's travels. And it was Glaser who bade him to stop writing in Hebrew partway through the book and switch to Judeo-Arabic. Nonetheless, Ḥabshūsh makes clear that he has his own modus operandi. He acceded to Glaser's request because he judged Glaser to be a "sincere" person and saw him as a friend. He would acquiesce to his request to write the travelogue, but he would also include matters that did not pertain to Glaser's request.[114]

The Reception of the Native Guide's Narrative

Halévy and Ḥabshūsh's accounts of their journey through Yemen bear many similarities, but they also diverge in many respects. Some of these differences are accounted for by the fact that Ḥabshūsh wrote *A Vision of Yemen* nearly a quarter-century after his journey and openly acknowledges that there are gaps in his memory.[115] Other differences seem to reflect not just random memory lapses but a desire to reshape past events. These inconsistencies have led to much debate among scholars. Did Ḥabshūsh play as central a role in Halévy's accomplishments as he claimed? Are his descriptions of Halévy's character reliable?

Ḥabshūsh's portrait of Halévy in *A Vision of Yemen* is at once critical and admiring. Although appreciating the difficult position of foreigners in Yemen, Ḥabshūsh faults Halévy for his posture of cold indifference or outright disdain for those he meets. Sometimes Halévy remains aloof, pretending to neither see nor hear those around him, although, Ḥabshūsh wryly observes, he certainly absorbs it all and records it in his notebook.[116] At other times, Halévy vents his rage at those who displease him.[117] These flaws notwithstanding, Ḥabshūsh esteems Halévy's rabbinic learning.[118] It was on account of this learning, he says, that Yemeni Jews had privileged him with a social intimacy seldom experienced by European travelers and that some, like Ḥabshūsh himself, had been persuaded by him to reject magic and mysticism. Even this persuasion, however, seems to have involved displays of righteous indignation rather than the building of enduring relationships with local Jews.[119] This description contrasts sharply with Halévy's behavior in other parts of the world. Whether in the Ottoman Empire, Europe, or Abyssinia, he seems to have quickly learned the local language, insinuated himself into his host society, and made a considerable impact on it. Ḥabshūsh's description of Halévy's opposition to mysticism and magic are consonant, however, with his behavior in Adrianople, where he protested the performance of an exorcism, and in Bucharest, where he argued against the *Zohar*. Ḥabshūsh's portrait of Halévy as largely disengaged is perhaps supported by Halévy's relative silence about his experiences of Yemeni Jews in comparison with those of Abyssinian Jews.

Ḥabshūsh's other criticisms of Halévy take direct aim at Halévy's reputation as a scholar and explorer. In Ḥabshūsh's eyes, Halévy is not a selfless adventurer who, for the sake of broadening human understanding, painstakingly transcribed ancient inscriptions at great risk to his life. Rather, he is an entitled European, with a proclivity for deception, who left his most difficult and perilous work to Yemenis. Although sometimes praising Halévy's bravery and ability to undergo privation without complaint, Ḥabshūsh also claims that Halévy made dangerous demands of him that indicate his thoughtless ignorance.[120] Further, Ḥabshūsh is clear that it is he and not Halévy who takes the greatest risks and expends the most effort. For example, in the Jawf, where the two stayed the longest, Halévy barely stirred from the house of his Jewish hosts while Ḥabshūsh climbed mountains and braved hostile tribes in order to do his bidding.[121] Ḥabshūsh further claims that it was he and not Halévy who had executed the vast majority of the transcriptions and even that Halévy had not so much as visited many of their locations.[122]

Although *A Vision of Yemen* had not yet been written, these damaging allegations made their way to Europe shortly after Halévy's return. They began to surface in 1872, when the scholar Baron von Maltzan denounced some tablets sold by Ḥabshūsh as forgeries by showing that their texts were haphazardly drawn from transcriptions published by Halévy.[123] The incident, which received considerable attention because some of these forgeries had already made their way into the British Museum, raised the question of why Ḥabshūsh's forgeries resembled Halévy's inscriptions. Some believed, following von Maltzan, that Ḥabshūsh had somehow surreptitiously copied transcriptions made by Halévy. Others believed the reverse—that Halévy had taken the inscriptions from Ḥabshūsh and then falsely claimed to have discovered them himself.

The damage to Halévy's reputation is reflected in a letter by William Prideaux, a British scholar of Arabian antiquities. Prideaux was puzzled by the relationship of Ḥabshūsh's texts to Halévy's: "If Halévy newly publishes the inscriptions exactly as they are on the [forged] plates, I should quite as soon suspect him of copying from the Jew [i.e., Ḥabshūsh] as the Jew of copying from him. Halévy's character is, as you know, indifferent."[124] Halévy, when questioned about the forgeries, tersely responded that the forgeries were based on his own transcriptions, which had been stolen by the forger, whom he described as "my guide from Ṣanʿāʾ."[125] Halévy's admission gives away remarkably little. In his publications not only does he not acknowledge Ḥabshūsh by name, but he also does not even indicate that he was accompanied by a single guide throughout the journey. Sometimes he seems to be alone, sometimes accompanied by a variety of different guides. His admission of Ḥabshūsh's existence can therefore not be viewed as an unqualified confirmation of Ḥabshūsh's claim that he accompanied Halévy throughout his journey. Interestingly, in his report of his journey, Halévy does briefly describe his guide from Ṣanʿāʾ, whom we can perhaps identify as Ḥabshūsh. The guide, he says, was put into such good humor by having successfully killed a poisonous snake with his stick that he loquaciously told him his life story, as well as "a thousand infantile anecdotes that puerile people rehash with inexhaustible pleasure."[126]

S. D. Goitein's publication of an edition of *A Vision of Yemen* in 1941 reopened this nineteenth-century debate. Had Ḥabshūsh really accompanied Halévy throughout his journey, tasked with transcribing inscriptions, or was he merely Halévy's "guide from Ṣanʿāʾ," one guide among the many locals to whom Halévy had appealed for route guidance? Goitein, perhaps reinforced by stories about Ḥabshūsh's travels still told by Yemeni Jews, believed Ḥabshūsh's claim that he had accompanied Halévy. In Goitein's view, Halévy had omitted his name only because he, "like many other travelers of his century, did not consider the services rendered by a native worthy of record in a scientific report."[127] Perhaps Ḥabshūsh himself alludes to this when he describes his role as that of "one who sees without being seen."[128]

Others, like the British explorer H. St. John Philby, expressed outrage that Ḥabshūsh's claims were given credence. He dismissed Ḥabshūsh as inflating his own role in Halévy's saga, just as "many an Arab of today is prone to exaggerate and trade upon an alleged share in the exploits of Colonel Lawrence."[129] Thus, according to Philby, *A Vision of Yemen* should be viewed as a work of fiction. At best, he concluded, the work, "though garrulous, loosely composed, and lacking in scholarly exactitude, is of considerable interest as a record of the author's own journey or journeys in country already covered by a more observant traveler, who had evidently inspired him with zeal for profitable exploration."[130] This line of thinking has more recently been revived by an Italian geographer, who suggests that Ḥabshūsh distorted his account of the journey to please Glaser by belittling Halévy.[131] Like Goitein, I am inclined to believe Ḥabshūsh's claim because of the considerable agreement between Halévy's and Ḥabshūsh's accounts. However, the question cannot be definitively resolved on the basis of the available evidence. Ultimately, the value of *A Vision of Yemen* must lie mainly in its cultural descriptions of Yemen and in its reflections on the Yemeni-European encounter.

Politics, Scholarship, and Personality

The figures of Ḥabshūsh, Halévy, and Glaser present a series of challenges for critically minded students of the encounter between East and West during the age of European imperialism. The first challenge is their problematization of the concept of "insiders" versus "outsiders." Halévy is at once an insider and an outsider. His deep knowledge of the Jewish tradition leads some Yemeni Jews to embrace him as a source of religious authority, even as the foreign cultural norms that he embodies alienate them. Glaser too was not solely an outsider. His disguise transformed his own sense of identity and radically changed the nature of his interactions with Yemeni Jews and Muslims. For his part, Ḥabshūsh a born and raised native of Yemen, experiences his land as both an insider and an outsider. He regards some Yemenis as foreign and exotic and struggles to come to understand them. Then, at the end of his narrative, he describes how his appearance and form of conversation have been so transformed by his journey that he is no longer recognized by other Jews as a native of his region. He then assumes the identity of a person from the region that he has visited, an identity to which, he comes to believe, his ancient ancestors were connected, and the reader is left to wonder whether, like so many European orientalists, he has "gone native."[132] Ḥabshūsh's *Vision of Yemen* is thus an attempt to capture both the foreign and the familiar, and the neat dichotomies between "native" and "stranger" and between anthropologist and auto-ethnographer are blurred.

A second challenge to consider is the extent to which a person's emotional affinities predictably correlate with the embrace of a particular political position. One might assume, for example, that those who embraced Yemeni culture would reject imperial involvement, or that those who embraced imperial involvement had the interests of a particular imperial power at heart. But the line between emotional affinity and political position is not so straightforward. Ḥabshūsh, though positively disposed toward Yemen and resentful of both Halévy's haughtiness and British missionary work, encouraged European involvement in improving the "plight" of Yemen. He also welcomed Ottoman imperial rule, despite the counterproductive backlash against Jews that followed in the wake of its reformist decrees. At one point, Ḥabshūsh even compares the Ottoman sultan to the sun and his officials in Yemen to moons. He exonerates the sultan from his officials' wrongdoings on the grounds that "some of the moons . . . are darkened on account of their distance from the rays of the sun."[133]

Glaser's political views were even more complicated. He seems to have been on intimate terms with many Yemeni Muslim leaders and to have thought highly of them and their religion, yet he also believed that Yemen was being neglected and that someone ought to invest their energy and settler-colonial ambitions in it. In Yemen he made no secret of his approval of Ottoman rule and actively advised the Ottomans on how to increase their power over the country. However, he also reached out to other external powers, urging them to do the same. At various points, he unsuccessfully attempted to persuade the governments of Russia[134] (the enemies of the Ottomans) and Austro-Hungary,[135] and even German Jews,[136] to establish colonies there. Neither Glaser nor Ḥabshūsh appeared to view advocating outside intervention in Yemen as inherently contradictory to their criticisms of European or Ottoman high-handedness. Of the three adventurers, it was Halévy who had the greatest distaste for Yemeni culture, yet it was also Halévy who never sought to see it "improved" through social or political interference.

The examples of Ḥabshūsh, Halévy, and Glaser exemplify the complexity of the relationship between academic scholarship and the contemporary ideological struggles in which academics participate. These three scholars were indeed products of their time. Their geographic origins and blood ties, as well as the politics that affected their own ethnic groups, profoundly affected their individual intellectual trajectories and their attitudes toward and evaluations of others. However, it did not predetermine them. To a remarkable extent, each of the scholars charted a unique course for himself. Halévy would not allow himself to be part of the mainstream. In the East he became a Westerner, a "Monsieur"; in the West he was an Oriental. He doggedly fought against the rising tide of Semitism and its corollary, anti-Semitism.

On a religious mission to Abyssinia, he pretended to be a trader. On a secular scientific mission to Yemen, he pretended to be a rabbi. Although an educator employed by the anti-Zionist Alliance Israélite Universelle, he founded the Parisian chapter of an early Zionist organization.[137] The easy path was rarely taken.

Ḥabshūsh also defied intellectual predetermination. He made his own way, leaving the life of a scion of a prominent Jewish family to embark on a dangerous and difficult trip. He approached Halévy and chose to become his disciple, despite the psychological pain it entailed in requiring him to jettison his beliefs in magic and mysticism. But he was not content to be a blind follower. He criticized the man whom he called his "master" and dedicated an entire book to chastising him. He too paved his own path as a scholar and activist. Glaser, for his part, rejected or alienated almost every family member, mentor, or academic circle that would have him. His own gravestone stands as testament to the uneasy and uncomfortable position he carved out for himself.

Finally, the stories and figures of Ḥabshūsh, Halévy, and Glaser are striking for one more commonality they share: their glorious failures. Ḥabshūsh, Halévy, and Glaser were defensive egoists and also selfless idealists. Their goals were lofty, and their efforts to achieve them were intense and unflagging. Their talents were extraordinary. And yet they failed, perhaps inevitably, to achieve most of what they set out to accomplish.[138] Glaser's plans came to naught. Although he was loved and respected by many Yemenis, his political achievements were minimal and the scholarly recognition that he deserved came only posthumously. Halévy too would fail in many of the efforts that he cared about most. The Jews of Abyssinia did not become a recognized and respected part of the Jewish community until decades after his death. Even though Halévy's identity as an outsider seems to have been of some benefit to him in the Jewish world, his isolation in the academic circles of Europe had a different effect. Perhaps the greatest symbol of this isolation was his journal, the *Revue sémitique d'épigraphie et d'histoire ancienne*. Founded at his own expense in 1893, the journal ran for over twenty years and covered the entire field of Semitic studies. As one orientalist wrote, Halévy was not only its sole editor but also almost its sole contributor.

> Each number of the periodical contained from 150 to 200 closely printed pages, and if one considers what it means to fill this amount of space every three months—for the *Revue* and Joseph Halévy were absolutely synonymous, with only occasional contributions from other pens—one will realize the vast resources and enormous learning as well as the indomitable energy of this man which enabled him to carry on such work until he was in sight of four score years and ten.[139]

The journal was at once a blessing and a curse for Halévy. It gave him great freedom to share his research and wage his numerous battles, but this freedom from oversight also contributed to his isolation and marginalization, and his writings became increasingly idiosyncratic. He wrote by and for himself.

For all of Ḥabshūsh's pains, his boldness, his brilliance as a raconteur, and his affection for his community, *A Vision of Yemen* never had the impact he wanted it to have. It was supposed to be read to make people care and work to better the life of the Yemeni people, especially its Jews. However, when it was finally printed nearly half a century after it had been written, its call for aiding Yemeni Jews through local change was no longer relevant. By 1950, less than a decade after its publication, most of these Jews had left for Israel, caught up in international events and movements over which they had little control. The value of *A Vision of Yemen*, therefore, lies not in its practical impact but in the lost world that it vividly captures and in the hope and passion that went into its writing.

THE PEOPLE AND POLITICS OF YEMEN

Ḥabshūsh's 1869 journey through Yemen with Halévy was his own introduction to his land's astonishing diversity. For the first time, he journeyed far beyond his native Ṣanʿāʾ, passing through mountains, forests, fertile farmlands, and desert and meeting with the communities, some rural, some urban, and some nomadic, that populated them. In *A Vision of Yemen* Ḥabshūsh explores how each of these communities was influenced by their environment, the varying and sometimes competing cultural and religious authorities, and external pressures.

Religious and Tribal Identity

The most basic lines of demarcation in Yemen were religious. A Jewish presence in the country dates back at least 2,000 years, and there were even brief periods when parts of the land were ruled by Jewish kings.[1] By the nineteenth century, Jews were scattered across Yemen, often with only three or four Jewish families per village, although a larger population lived in the Yemeni capital of Ṣanʿāʾ. It is estimated that, in Ḥabshūsh's time, Jews accounted for roughly one-fifth of Ṣanʿāʾ's population and that, at the beginning of the twentieth century, Yemen had 60,000–80,000 Jews out of a total population of 3–4 million.[2] Islam came to Yemen in the seventh century CE. Many denominations of Islam were represented in Yemen, but by the nineteenth century most Muslims belonged to the Zaydī denomination, a form of Shiʿism. In theory, Zaydīs were led by a single religiopolitical leader known as an imām. In the nineteenth century, however, disputes concerning succession and general political weakness led to the existence of multiple claimants to the imamate and sometimes to the office being widely ignored. There was also a large population of Sunnī Muslims in Yemen, most of them adherents of the Shāfiʿī rite. Ottoman officials were also an important Sunnī presence in nineteenth-century Yemen. From 1872 they were a major presence in the capital city of Ṣanʿāʾ, from which they ruled, but they also exercised varying degrees of authority throughout the country. The port city of Aden had for more than two centuries been of interest to European trading empires and was then ruled by the British. Its population boasted a large variety of people from around the Indian Ocean. On account of trade, contacts between Ṣanʿāʾ and Aden were frequent, and both cities had substantial Jewish populations.

In addition to religion, other forms of communal affiliation and cohesion were important. Yemen was a socially stratified society governed by a system of tribal law known as the Ṭāghūt.[3] Tribal identity was based on an ideal of honor (*sharaf*) stemming from a belief in shared descent.[4] It was this idea of honor that allowed for all people to be divided into two main categories: tribesmen who possessed the quality of honor and nontribesmen, often referred to as "weak" (*ḍaʿīf*) people, who did not.[5] "Weak" here does not mean physical weakness. Rather, it merely means that, because such people could neither make war nor enforce peace by providing protection, they were not players in the game of tribal honor and its opposite, disgrace (*ʿayb*).[6]

"Weak people" in Ḥabshūsh's time came in all stripes. There were *sayyids* (descendants of Muḥammad), like the caste of the Hujar, who lived in sacrosanct communities and whom tribesmen viewed as their spiritual superiors. Such weak individuals might even be called on to adjudicate disputes between tribesmen, or they might be sought out as teachers and healers. Although they were protected and were often paid for their services, their superiority was not always realized on a practical level, because tribesmen still held effective political control.[7] Socially inferior weak people included traders, craftsmen, merchants, barbers, butchers, lower caste groups like the Qarār, and, importantly, Jews.[8] Under tribal law, Jews did not possess a special designation on account of their religious status—they were simply one kind of weak people among many. Tribesmen were honor-bound to protect the weak, because their effectiveness in doing so was seen as a witness to their power to defend their people and land. Indeed, having many weak people under one's protection was a sign of great prestige. In addition, tribes also received tangible material benefits from those they protected. For example, in return for a tribe designating a town or market as a *hijrah* (i.e., an area that received their guarantee of protection), the tribe would receive a regular tribute. Through this institution, tribes were able to maintain economic development.[9]

In Yemen, tribal law provided an important layer of identity in addition to religious affiliation. Though not grounded in Islamic norms, most nineteenth-century Yemeni Muslims preferred to regard tribal law as complementing rather than contradicting Islam.[10] Nonetheless, as Ḥabshūsh shows, the two legal systems conceived of relations with Jews quite differently, and Jewish quality of life markedly differed depending on whether Jews were regulated by Islamic or by tribal law.[11] The deep social and religious implications of tribal law and identity, for both Jews and Muslims, are explored in detail in *A Vision of Yemen.*

Foreigners in Yemen

Since medieval times, European merchants have plied a vigorous trade in Yemen's coastal towns. By the seventeenth century trade had become so great that Western diplomatic trade representatives crowded the ports of Aden, Hodeida, and Mocha. Ottoman, Portuguese, and British intelligence operatives also journeyed to the Red Sea coast to monitor the lucrative India trade route. However, imperial interest in Yemen was curbed by geography. The approach from the Red Sea involved navigating hazardous coral reefs, which were also known to harbor pirates.[12] The land route was also perilous. Yemen was shielded from the north by the largely impassable Empty Quarter, the world's largest sand desert. Perhaps these difficulties could have been surmounted if Yemen, beyond the coastal towns, had possessed resources of interest to the great powers, but, as one British explorer put it, Yemen was a land "so naked that none covets it."[13] Thus, although Europeans were heavily represented along Yemen's coast, few made their way into the interior. Only the Ottomans, in order to gain hegemony over the Muslim world and control over the holy cities of Arabia, dared to venture there and then only at great cost. A popular Yemeni saying describes Yemen as "the graveyard of the Turks," and the great toll on Ottoman troops became fodder for mournful Turkish folk songs.[14]

In the nineteenth century the Ottomans attacked Yemen, and by 1872 they controlled its central lands, including Ṣanʿāʾ. The Ottomans occupied Yemen when their empire was undergoing dramatic political reform. These reforms, known as the Tanẓīmāt, were undertaken to allow them to keep pace with

European commercial, technological, and military growth. The Ottomans regarded Yemen as particularly "backward" and "savage" relative to other parts of the empire.[15] Although fewer reforms were implemented there for this reason, the Ottomans nonetheless believed that their purpose in Yemen was that of a "civilizing mission." They attempted to achieve this goal through centralization, the modernization of transport and agriculture, and the development of a bureaucracy through education.[16] One of the goals of the Tanẓīmāt reforms was that of fostering a more robust Ottoman identity and patriotism. They formally abolished older forms of sectarian corporate identity and promoted the Ottoman sultan as the ruler, representative, and protector of all Ottoman subjects, regardless of religion. In Yemen this effort included the abrogation of several laws whose purpose was to socially reinforce the hierarchical relationship between Muslims and Jews.[17] These Ottoman reforms were to have drastic, if unintended, consequences for Yemeni Jews, regardless of whether they lived under tribal or Islamic law. Some Muslim Yemenis, because of this loss of social hierarchy, attacked Jews in retaliation, and, as Ḥabshūsh explains, Ottoman laws had the effect of impoverishing many of the tribes, with the result that they sought redress from the Jews.[18]

Nonetheless, despite the mixed blessings of Ottoman rule, Ḥabshūsh's overall opinion of it was favorable. His reasons for this judgment were clear. He credits Ottoman-facilitated commerce for bringing food to famine-stricken Yemen and for access to money with which to buy it. He even has an extended monologue about how it is a mistake to view Ottoman-era inflation of the cost of living as an evil, because it is a natural consequence of increased prosperity and incomes that have risen faster than expenses.[19] Moreover, the Ottomans brought stability to Ṣanʿāʾ. As a result of their influence, the Jewish quarter expanded and permission to build new synagogues was granted. As Ḥabshūsh frequently observes, life in Ottoman Yemen in the 1890s was vastly better than the Zaydī-dominated Yemen that Halévy had seen. Not all Jews agreed with this assessment and approved of Ottoman rule. Traditionalists feared the modernity that it brought. Many officials, they said, befriended Jews and spread reformist doctrines, making Jews lax in their religious observance.[20]

By and large, most foreigners who ventured beyond the coast into central Yemen were Ottomans. The few Europeans who made this journey, usually with little institutional support, had diverse motives, including interests in biblical studies, inscriptions and objets d'art, and botany.[21] For Halévy, the most significant of these was the French traveler Thomas Arnaud, the only European to see the Sabaean capital of Mārib before him. Arnaud claimed that his interest in "the East" stemmed from a disenchantment with Europe.

> There are periods in life when one senses—and without knowing why—that everything which had been smiling on you is growing cold. . . . That happened to me. . . . I felt myself close to that difficulty of living that in a certain way pushes a man out of himself and causes him to feel the need for renewal. . . . I was hoping for other people, other horizons, other events, and I said . . . "Our Europe is only a molehill. The Orient alone is great, the Orient alone is splendid."[22]

Arnaud's sojourn in the "Orient" began with a stint as a pharmacist for Muḥammad ʿAlī, the ruler of Egypt. It was ʿAlī's invasion of Yemen on behalf of the Ottomans in the 1830s that first brought Arnaud there, but, after the venture failed, Arnaud deserted and joined the imām of Ṣanʿāʾ. The Frenchman found Yemen agreeable and became steeped in an Arab culture with which he increasingly identified. In his diary he expressed the hope that, "freed from the . . . Ottomans, the great Arab family . . . so gifted with intelligence and vitality, would resume its history, once so brilliant, and in place of that ruin of an empire that is collapsing on the banks of the Bosphorus, would again spring to life . . . and astonish Europe."[23] It was the pre-Islamic inscriptions that Arnaud brought back to France that piqued French scholarly interest in Yemen and set the stage for Halévy's voyage two decades later.

Jewish travelers came to Yemen for diverse reasons.[24] For centuries emissaries from the impoverished Jewish communities of Palestine had been sent to Yemen to collect alms and give spiritual guidance.[25] The most famous of these was Jacob Saphir, who traveled to Yemen in 1859 and provided Europe with its first descriptions of the daily life of Yemeni Jews and a portrait of their literature. Although Saphir was critical of certain aspects of what he saw, he was deeply impressed with the religious fervor of Yemeni Jews and believed that their Judaism, because of its relative isolation, was more authentic than that of other Jewish communities.[26]

Some European Jews traveled to Yemen in search of the lost tribes of ancient Israel.[27] Perhaps as early as the ninth century, rumors circulated that one such tribe had established a large and independent Jewish kingdom in Arabia filled with great scholars and mighty warriors.[28] Searches for this legendary tribe periodically brought Jewish travelers to Yemen. For example, in 1833 a disciple of the Vilna Gaon, a famous European rabbi, arrived in Yemen in search of the lost tribes. The rabbis of Ṣanʿāʾ were enthusiastic about his mission and even provided him with a guide. Despite the failure of his mission, their hopes continued and were still alive when Halévy arrived. Indeed, many Yemenis, including Ḥabshūsh, believed that Halévy had come to Yemen in search of them.[29] After their journey together, however, Ḥabshūsh concluded that these tribes were mythical.

Other European Jews came to Yemen for trade. Jacob Saphir's reports of Yemeni manuscripts brought several dealers in search of them. Shortly after Halévy left Yemen, Moses Shapira succeeded in plying a vigorous and, according to Ḥabshūsh, unscrupulous trade in Hebrew manuscripts.[30] Others, such as Moshe Ḥanokh ha-Levi, plied a similar trade but became integrated in the local community and were viewed positively.[31] Christian missionaries also came to Yemen, most sent by the British Society for Promoting Christianity Among the Jews.[32] Although they did not win many converts, their Bibles were widely distributed. Indeed, Ḥabshūsh reports that he discovered a Hebrew translation of the New Testament among the relatively isolated Jewish community of Najrān, some 250 miles north of Ṣanʿāʾ.[33] The most prominent of these missionaries were Joseph Wolff and Henry Stern. Both were originally born into German Jewish scholarly families, had great familiarity with Jewish tradition, and were able to speak Hebrew. Both also had an interest in discovering the lost tribes and in purchasing manuscripts. Thus, by the time Halévy arrived in 1869, Yemeni Jews already had some knowledge of the various kinds of European Jews.

Muslim-Jewish Relations under Islamic Law

Discussions of Muslim-Jewish relations occupy an important place in *A Vision of Yemen*. Ḥabshūsh shows how they vary across time and locale in response to both local and external pressures. We hear of intimate relations between Muslims and Jews, stories of Muslims sacrificing their lives for Jews, and descriptions of Muslim persecution of Jews. One of Ḥabshūsh's recurrent themes is that, as a general rule, Jews governed by Zaydī Islamic law in the Ṣanʿāʾ region fared worse than Jews who lived in the highlands under tribal law. To understand the distinction that he is drawing, I outline the provisions of Islamic law and then those of tribal law that apply to Jews.

Scholars of Islamic law locate the requirement of religious toleration in a Qurʾānic verse stating that non-Muslims who are "People of the Book," defined elsewhere as Christians, Jews, and "Sabians" (*Ṣābiʾūn*), are entitled to practice their religion in exchange for paying a special poll tax (*jizyah*) and being humbled.[34] The implications of the verse were later developed in a pact (*dhimmah*) that detailed the legal disabilities that non-Muslims had to accept in exchange for toleration.[35] Bernard Haykel, a scholar of Yemeni Islamic law, explains that the "pact imposed on *dhimmī*s regulations whose aims were to abase and humiliate them as well as to distinguish them from Muslims."[36] Some regulations, such as the poll tax on non-Muslims, were almost universally present in pacts across the Islamic world; others were subject to local variation. One typical Yemeni Zaydī pact includes the following stipulations regulating Jews:

> They are obliged to adopt a dress by which they are distinguishable and wherein lies humiliation consisting of side-locks, wearing a badge, and the cutting of the middle of the forelock.
>
> They are not to ride astride on saddles but are to ride sidesaddle.
>
> They will not perform religious rites except in their synagogues.
>
> They will not make a new synagogue but can renovate what has fallen into ruin.
>
> They are not to dwell anywhere but in their quarters, except by permission of the Muslims for the sake of some public good. . . .
>
> They are not to ride horses or build their houses higher than those of Muslims.
>
> They must sell a Muslim slave that they own or have bought.[37]

Despite their discriminatory nature, such pacts nonetheless provided a space for Jews in Islamic society and protected them against forced conversion. Moreover, although the poll tax on Jews was burdensome, it also provided a powerful financial incentive for the ruler to honor the pact. On the other hand, particularly when rulers ignored the pact in order to grant privileges to their Jewish subjects, the pact could become a source of future instability. For example, a synagogue built with the permission of one ruler in violation of the pact might subsequently be torn down, perhaps even generations later, by those seeking to honor the original terms of the pact, often with additional serious repercussions for the Jewish community.[38] Further, although violations of the pact were usually prosecuted on an individual basis, it was possible to hold the community collectively responsible for violations, because the pact was concluded between the ruler and the Jewish community as a whole. Zaydī law stipulates, for example, that the pact can be nullified if there are *dhimmī*s who promote sedition (*fitnah*) among Muslims or commit highway robbery.[39] Under such circumstances, an entire Jewish community might forfeit Muslim commitments of toleration, paving the way to forced conversion, enslavement, execution, or exile.

Yemeni Jews faced an additional precariousness not usually faced by other Jewish communities of the Muslim world. As early as the twelfth century, Muslims debated the legality of Jewish residence in Yemen, with the result that some jurists were uncertain whether it had been legal for rulers to conclude any *dhimmah* pacts whatsoever with local Jews. Their arguments relied on reports that the Prophet Muḥammad had demanded that no religions other than Islam be practiced in the Arabian Peninsula.[40] Although jurists universally accepted the authenticity of these reports, they debated whether this area included Yemen or whether it applied only to the Ḥijāz region of Arabia, which had been the site of the prophetic mission. These juristic discussions occasionally led to forced conversions of Jews, but until the seventeenth century they had never led to mass expulsions.[41]

The seventeenth century, however, was tumultuous for both Jews and Muslims—a time of plagues, famine, and war against the Ottomans. The Jewish response to these events was growing communal support for a messianic movement. In 1667, seeing the movement as a cause of civil unrest, the Yemeni ruler Imām al-Mutawakkil canceled his pact with the Jews, justifying his actions thus: "If [we assume that] those [Jews] indeed possessed a pact, then they have [certainly] violated it, because they have frightened the Muslims to such an extent that some of them have abandoned traveling for fear of what they have said. . . . No one doubts their attempts to lead the Muslims into sedition."[42] On the basis of this reasoning, al-Mutawakkil considered either killing or enslaving the Jews and opted for the latter. As a symbol of their new status, Jews were initially banned from covering their heads in public. However, after entreaties, they were allowed to do so with shabby cloths, provided that these did not resemble proper headgear. The intent of the edict was humiliation, because being bareheaded was considered undignified by Muslims and Jews alike.[43]

A decade later, al-Mutawakkil decided that his measures against the Jews had been insufficient. Motivated by the growing juristic consensus that Muḥammad's prohibition of non-Islamic religions in Arabia also applied to Yemen, he ordered the expulsion of the Jews. Although al-Mutawakkil died before implementing the decree, it was executed in 1679 shortly after his death.[44] Jewish prayer was banned, and synagogues were either destroyed or converted into mosques.[45] Once their property had been confiscated, the Jews of the Ṣanʿāʾ region were deported to the small town of Mawzaʿ in southwestern Yemen. There they were encouraged to leave the country by sea from the port of Mocha. Because few ships were available, most remained in Mawzaʿ, where many died of starvation and disease brought about by crowded living conditions.

Because their exile created economic havoc for Muslims in Ṣanʿāʾ, the Jews were allowed to return a year later. The scars of the experience, however, were lasting. Many who survived converted to Islam. Lands that had been confiscated were not returned, and there seems to have been a consequent shift in Jewish professions from agriculture to the handicrafts. Much Yemeni Jewish literature was lost, abandoned during the flight.[46] The exile also had an effect on how Muslims perceived the permanence of the Jewish community. After the Jews returned, there were several attempts to re-expel them. The first major attempt occurred in 1725 but was thwarted by a Jewish family close to the ruler. The second attempt, in 1762, coincided with that family's fall from favor. Although the Jews were not expelled, twelve of the fourteen synagogues in the Ṣanʿāʾ region were destroyed. It took thirty years before Jews, in exchange for a large fee, were allowed to restore them.[47]

The return of the Jews after their exile to Mawzaʿ coincided with new laws, either unique to Yemen or highly uncommon elsewhere in the Islamic world, to distinguish and humiliate them. During the eighteenth century, for example, the Latrines Decree was implemented. In many parts of the Islamic world, Jews took on sewage removal. The Latrines Decree, however, broke with Islamic tradition by imposing this work as a humiliating obligation. Although levied on the Jewish community as a whole, Jewish leaders were usually able to negotiate their own selection of workers. It was thus mostly indigent Jews, dependent on communal charity, who had to perform the unpleasant task. On some occasions, however, the authorities forced Jewish dignitaries to do it.[48] Some Islamic jurists questioned the edict on the grounds that it was a forbidden innovation in divine law. Muḥammad al-Shawkānī, an influential jurist and chief judge of the Zaydī state, disagreed.

> The Lord, may He be lofty and exalted, has reported in His Book that humiliation is permanently affixed to the Jews, permanently adhering to them as long as they exist, encompassing all persons at all times, in all conditions. By this [humiliation] is not meant some innate or essential characteristic, rather what is intended is to have mastery over them. . . . Indeed, what is meant is the abasement which results from any reason which God has not prohibited. Obliging them to collect excrement results in the abasement that is pitched upon them, and everything that results in the abasement that is pitched upon them is permissible, therefore obliging them to collect it is permissible.[49]

Al-Shawkānī's judgment prevailed. The decree became so popular that, when the Ottomans annexed Yemen in the nineteenth century, they were unable to abolish it. Indeed, under their rule the practice even spread to areas in which it had been previously unknown.[50]

Another law, unique to Yemen, was the Orphans' Decree. It mandated that Jewish minors who had been orphaned be permanently taken away from their families and community and be forcibly converted to Islam. Although regular enforcement began only in the eighteenth century, the decree was discussed in legal sources in the late fifteenth century, and there is some evidence of its sporadic implementation in the late seventeenth century.[51] The decree was abolished by the Ottomans in 1872 but was renewed once the Ottomans withdrew in 1918. Reflecting general consensus and the view of Ḥabshūsh, one modern scholar notes that the Orphans' Decree "has been preserved in the collective memory of Yemeni Jews as the single most threatening and oppressive act against their community . . . causing more harm and distress than any other arbitrary governmental order."[52] Such policies led the Ottomanist Jane Hathaway to remark that, compared with other Muslim societies, "Yemen has gained a poor reputation for treatment of its ancient Jewish minority."[53]

Muslim-Jewish Relations under Tribal Law

Whereas Jews of the Ṣanʿāʾ region were governed by the Islamic laws, the Jews of the highlands were governed by tribal law. Like Islamic law, tribal law also regulated Jews, but it conceived relations with them differently. Whereas the *dhimmah* pact established a relationship that denied non-Muslims privileges on the basis of their rejection of Islam, tribal law established a relationship with non-Muslims on the basis of noblesse oblige. According to tribal law, because Muslim tribes were powerful, the demands of honor obliged them to protect the weak, including the Jews.

It was as "weak people" that Jews were granted a place in the tribal world. Little legal significance was attached to their religious status; instead, the laws that were applied to them were the same as those for other weak people, many of whom were Muslims. Having their status determined by criteria unrelated to their Judaism led to Jews enjoying several privileges denied to them by the Islamic *dhimmah* pact. For example, under tribal law Jews could carry weapons (and could even fight on behalf of their patrons), ride any kind of mount seated as they pleased, and build their houses to any height (i.e., they could be taller than Muslim houses).[54] Further, whereas Ṣanʿānī Jews, regardless of their wealth, dressed in rags and were prohibited from wearing turbans, Jews of tribal regions often dressed much like Muslims. Ḥabshūsh comments that, when traveling in the Baraṭ region, he was astonished to find that he was often unable to distinguish Jews from Muslims by sight.[55] In another passage he describes a tribal patron who required his Jewish clients to appear before him in great finery, as this reflected well on his ability to protect them.[56] This same idea of concern for the well-being of Jewish clients is evidenced when Ḥabshūsh, in a remarkable aside, relates that one Muslim tribe paid the Islamically mandated *jizyah* for its Jewish clients, when the sum the Ottomans demanded was more than they could raise.[57] Thus, in contrast to the *dhimmah* system, which was based on a concept of religious hierarchy, the tribal system took the form of patron-client relations. This type of arrangement with Jews was uncommon, although not unknown, in other parts of the Islamic world.[58]

Jewish relations with the tribes were usually stable. According to tribal law, patrons were to take their responsibilities to their Jewish clients seriously and to view their bond to them as something akin to a blood contract.[59] To violate the rights of a Jewish client was regarded as a great disgrace and an affront to the tribesmen under whose protection the weak person lived.[60] Indeed, as Ḥabshūsh notes, tribes sometimes went to war because a Jew had been attacked and thus tribal honor besmirched.[61] In return for protection, a Jew would honor his patron with gifts, consult him on important life events, and perform work for him.[62] Abandoning one patron for another was possible but brought great disgrace on the patron, because it implied that he lacked power as a protector.[63] Ḥabshūsh describes the worry of one tribesman that his Jewish clients would leave him: "If they were to flee from us, we would be a laughingstock before all the tribes."[64]

One of the illuminating differences between the treatment of Jews under Yemeni tribal and Islamic law has to do with the penalties imposed for the spilling of blood. Jews were regarded as social inferiors according to both Islamic law and tribal law. This meant that, in some sense, Jewish deaths were deemed less significant than Muslim deaths. In tribal law, as Ḥabshūsh explains, this had a number of consequences. For one, it meant that in a situation that called for "an eye for an eye" (i.e., retaliation in kind), inferiors were exempt from being retaliated against when they committed a crime. There was no point in taking their life, because their life had less value, and it was even considered disgraceful to do so. By contrast, the life of someone who possessed "honor" had value, and under certain circumstances tribal law required that life to be taken in retaliation. Ḥabshūsh explains:

> [According to tribal law,] if a slave, woman, child, Qarārī, or Jew kills someone, retaliation is not visited upon them but rather upon their family or patrons [depending on the circumstances]. This is because [the murderer, as a weak person, has] no value. However, if a tribesman kills one of these people, his offense is very great. For this reason, if one side in a war is weak, they

> send their women and children ahead of them to fight. Since it is not possible for their opponents to fight them, they accept defeat. It is a matter of great disgrace for them to kill such people, regardless of whether or not they are deserving of death. The killing of tribesmen, however, is a point of pride.[65]

Similarly, in tribal law, the monetary penalty for killing a Jew or other weak person was higher than the penalty for killing a person who had honor. According to both tribal and Islamic law, one of the consequences of homicide was that the perpetrator, or sometimes his or her family, would have to pay compensation to the heirs of the victim. This compensation was known as the bloodwite. The amount of compensation owed depended on the victim's religion, sex, and status as a free person or a slave. Because Jews were regarded as weak and because it was a matter of disgrace to kill them, Ḥabshūsh tells us that the tribes set the bloodwite for the death of a Jew at quadruple the amount set for the death of a Muslim tribesman.[66] By contrast, in classical Islamic law the bloodwite for killing a non-Muslim was lower than that for killing a free Muslim male, although how much lower was the subject of debate among the legal schools.[67] This meant that the financial disincentive for harming Jews was higher under tribal law than under Islamic law. The result of these factors was that tribal law provided an environment in which Jews could live in relative security.

Relations between Muslims and Jews, however, did not always follow either tribal or Islamic laws. Local factors sometimes trumped the law, and, in addition, everyday interactions encompassed many matters that the law did not cover. Bat-Zion Eraqi Klorman discusses how popular Muslim beliefs in the magical powers of Jews shaped interfaith relations in Yemen. Many Muslims, she says, saw Jews as "mysterious beings, possessing supernatural powers that could cause either good or evil." Muslims were both attracted to and fearful of the "otherness" of Jews. Jews were simultaneously "needed and respected" and "feared and disliked," intimately connected with Muslim society, yet still regarded as outsiders. To mediate relations with Jews, a "popular Muslim-Jewish syncretistic religion" was formed.[68] Although belief in the magical nature of Jews did not make its way into tribal law, it often determined when and how that law was implemented. Ḥabshūsh tells us at the beginning of his work that, as a result of his encounter with Halévy, he has disavowed magic. Nonetheless, he feigns knowledge of magic at several points in his negotiations with both Muslims and Jews. In Ghaymān, for example, he is able to mobilize the entire village to assist him in his excavations by leading them to believe that he has access to magical knowledge that could procure treasure.[69]

Nineteenth-Century Crises

Ḥabshūsh opens his book by remarking that, when Halévy arrived in Yemen, his community was "in dire straits and on the point of being annihilated."[70] Ḥabshūsh was not alone in this gloomy assessment of his age. Yemeni Muslim chroniclers often refer to the nineteenth century as "a time of corruption."[71] Corruption came in many forms. A series of natural disasters ravaged much of Yemen, including Ṣanʿāʾ, its most populous city and Ḥabshūsh's home. In 1827 a plague of locusts unleashed severe famine. In 1836 an earthquake in Ṣanʿāʾ killed many.[72] Civil unrest overtook the country. Local tribal leaders battled among themselves, and bandits controlled the roads. In the words of one local chronicler, there were "enough conflicts and battles to fill books and empty ink-wells."[73] Ṣanʿāʾ itself came repeatedly under siege. For centuries Zaydī imāms had maintained order in the city, but, after the death of Imām al-Mahdī ʿAbdallāh in 1834, no clear successor emerged. Instead, battles between groups championing rival imāms left the region divided and unstable. With no one able to project power, Yemen came to be controlled by a dizzying array of tribal groups, some Sunnī, others Shīʿī. The instability produced an economic crisis, which included the collapse of the coffee trade, one of Yemen's main sources of income. Sensing weakness, the great powers began to encroach, the Ottomans from the north and the British from the south. In 1872 the Ottomans took Ṣanʿāʾ, a city that lay in ruins, without resistance.[74]

The wars and natural disasters of the nineteenth century led to the growth of a variety of religious movements. Many Jews and Muslims came to believe that they were living in apocalyptic times.[75] For the Jews this meant the rise of multiple messianic claimants. As Ḥabshūsh wrote:

> Our land conceives and bears messiahs at every moment; one falls, another rises. Those easily seduced give up their possessions to them, . . . satisfying

> the desires of the messiahs with their silver. . . . And why is this? Because of the hardships of exile, because of the paucity of income, because of the lack of education, because of the lack of rabbinical supervision. Thus, folly reigns and enlightenment stands far off.[76]

The most famous false messiah was Shukr Kuḥayl, a Ṣanʿānī Jew who was familiar with both traditional Jewish sources and the Qurʾān.[77] In 1859 Kuḥayl claimed to be the messiah and came to be accepted as such by many Jews and even by some Muslims. Even Jews who denied his messianic claims seem to have regarded him as sincere on account of his asceticism and humble demeanor. Nonetheless, concerned by the unrest he had caused, Islamic authorities executed Kuḥayl in 1863, displaying his head in Ṣanʿāʾ for three days.[78] Kuḥayl's gory death, however, was not the end of the matter. Five years later, a man proclaimed himself to be Kuḥayl resurrected. In contrast to the first Kuḥayl, the second was generally regarded as an impious and exploitative pretender. He was eventually captured by the Ottomans, but what happened to him afterward is not known. Ḥabshūsh was no bystander in these events. He tells us that he had made such enemies of these followers of the second Kuḥayl that he feared for his life.[79] At another point, Ḥabshūsh describes how he was waylaid when Halévy was incorrectly suspected of being the second Kuḥayl.[80]

Some Jews responded to social instability by turning not to messianic hope but to concepts of Ottoman and European modernity. During Ḥabshūsh's lifetime these ideas were transmitted to Yemeni Jews, not through European colonization (as with North African Jews) nor primarily through the Ottoman Tanẓīmāt (as with Iraqi Jews),[81] but through exposure to (mostly European) Hebrew literature and Jewish travelers.[82] As Daniel Schroeter, a historian of Morocco, has shown, European Jewish travelers in the Islamic world tended to view themselves as part of a "civilizing mission." "Eastern" Jews were "pre-emancipation versions of themselves" who, "through emancipation and modernization," could also become enlightened.[83] In Yemen the most important of these travelers were Halévy and Glaser. Halévy is sometimes credited by Yemeni Jews with initiating the Jewish Enlightenment movement of Yemen by offering a powerful Jewish critique of magical practices and of Kabbalah.[84] The movement began as a small circle led by three individuals—Yaḥyā Qāfiḥ, Saʿīd al-ʿArūsī, and Ḥabshūsh—who were close to Halévy and Glaser.[85] At its height, the movement, which came to be known as Dor Deʿah (Generation of Knowledge), ran its own educational system and synagogue.[86]

Although Halévy was involved in the development of the Dor Deʿah movement, he should not be regarded as its sole generator. Before his arrival, Yemeni Jews were already debating whether prayer should be according to the rite of the rationalist philosopher Moses Maimonides or according to a Sephardic rite that was influenced by Kabbalistic traditions.[87] The existence of this earlier debate gave a convenient foothold to the new debate on the status of Kabbalah and later to debates on the status of modern science.[88] During Ḥabshūsh's lifetime, debates between Dor Deʿah followers and the traditionalists were conducted with courtesy. Beginning in 1912, however, the debate grew sharper and was brought for judgment before the Muslim authorities, who imprisoned key members of Dor Deʿah.[89]

Ḥabshūsh and the Land of Yemen

A particularly thought-provoking feature of *A Vision of Yemen* is Ḥabshūsh's understanding of himself as a Yemeni. His sense of identity, and perhaps even nationality, contrasts sharply with many concepts of diasporic Jewish identity commonly articulated by both Zionist and anti-Zionist thinkers. That is, Ḥabshūsh acknowledges the horrors and regularity of persecution, but this acknowledgment does not impinge on his feelings of belonging in his land. Neither does Ḥabshūsh view himself as alone in these sentiments, which at one point he labels "love of homeland" (*ḥubb al-waṭan*), a term that was popularized by nineteenth-century Arab nationalists.[90] Ḥabshūsh sees Yemen as the land of his most ancient ancestors, and he feels the land connecting him to them. They had migrated to Yemen on the orders of King Solomon to accompany the Queen of Sheba back to her home and had loyally remained there for generations.[91] Ḥabshūsh's feelings of connection to these past generations is evident throughout the work and in his passion for writing history. Gravesites are a prime locus for expressing this connection. On his travels, Ḥabshūsh happens upon a Jewish graveyard, the 400-year-old remnants of a Yemeni Jewish community of which he had no knowledge. In the graveyard he begins to imagine what their lives must have been like, and he is overcome with a grief born of empathy. He then envisions the Devil tempting him to deny the familial tie that he senses binding him to them. "What are these people to you," whispers the Devil, "who have already passed away and been buried? What do you know of their lineage, ancestry, and beliefs that you pray, cry, and beseech your God for the good of their tombs?"[92] But the gravestones establish a connection that he believes it is a sin to deny. The land of Yemen thus plays a role for Ḥabshūsh that native lands played for other Romantic nationalists. The land creates and reinforces the tie between its living inhabitants and their ancestors.

What about the living non-Jewish inhabitants of Yemen and the graves of non-Jewish communities? Interestingly, Ḥabshūsh demonstrates a profound sense of connection to them too. His feelings of connectedness even extend to the ancient Arabs of his land whose fall from supremacy he mournfully describes in rhymed prose.[93] Ḥabshūsh does not see his status as a religious minority as making Yemen any less his home. He is aware of Muslims who use their religion to ill-treat Jews, but he does not regard this behavior as inevitable. Did not the Prophet, he remarks, have "a Jewish neighbor with whom he spoke amiably?"[94] He speaks of his own friendships with Muslims and of Muslims who are generous, of good character, devoted to "reason," and who go out of their way to protect Jews.[95] Ultimately, he believes that a propensity to commit evil is something that attaches to people regardless of their religion: "An evildoer is an evildoer, regardless of whether he is a tribesman or a Jew."[96] Under such circumstances, he says, Yemeni Jews know that they must treat the iniquities visited upon them by Muslims with forbearance.[97]

These sentiments do not, however, lead Ḥabshūsh to view the situation of either Yemen generally or of its Jews in particular as being tolerable, nor do they lead him to believe that there is no need for European-style modernization or for the heavy hand of imperial interference. On the contrary, Ḥabshūsh views Yemen as being in desperate need of interference. He grieves for "beautiful Yemen, which is now a land of killing and violence."[98] Yemen, Ḥabshūsh repeatedly tells his readers, is a terrifying place in which to live, with cycles of famine, disease, poverty, strife, and prosperity that span centuries, affecting everyone, Jews and Muslims alike.[99] As for the Jewish community specifically, Ḥabshūsh says it was on the brink of destruction when Halévy visited.[100] Nonetheless, he unwaveringly accepts the land as his home.

Differing from both Halévy and Glaser, as well as from the many Yemeni Jews who began to migrate to Palestine during his lifetime, Ḥabshūsh seems to reject the allure of the early Zionist movement. Although usually silent about such matters, he expresses amazement when he meets a Yemeni who yearns to immigrate to Palestine. The man, says an astonished Ḥabshūsh, is distressed about life in Yemen, even though he makes a good living. "How will you be able to live in the land of Canaan," he asks him, "when you are from an eastern land?"[101] Ḥabshūsh's rootedness in his land, at the very moment when such commitments were beginning to be forcefully challenged in his community and beyond, provides a sad witness to one of the world's most ancient Jewish communities that is now no more.

A NOTE ON THE TEXT AND TRANSLATION

Eduard Glaser read and valued *A Vision of Yemen*, even annotating his copy of Halévy's travelogue with references to it.[1] However, he never shared it with others as Ḥabshūsh hoped he would. Instead, the manuscript was consigned to the dusty anonymity of Glaser's voluminous papers. It was only in 1936, decades after Glaser's death, that *A Vision of Yemen* resurfaced. Browsing through a collection of manuscripts, Shlomo Dov Goitein, a German Jewish professor of Islamic studies at Hebrew University, came across fragmentary versions of the work. Curious to see whether a complete manuscript survived among Glaser's posthumous papers, he wrote to Nikolaus Rhodokanakis, a Greek scholar based in Vienna. Although the political climate in Europe worked against such a transaction, Rhodokanakis nonetheless found and sent a copy of the manuscript to Goitein. The favor was not performed easily. After nearly two years of wrangling, Rhodokanakis finally convinced the university authorities to let him send the manuscript to the Jewish-owned Schocken Publishing House in Berlin for a photostatic copy to be made and sent to Jerusalem.[2]

Glaser's copy of *A Vision of Yemen* is our best manuscript of the text, but Goitein discovered that it was flawed as a result of having been sent from Yemen with several pages missing. Hearing that the scribe of the manuscript, ʿAmram Qoraḥ, was still alive and had become chief rabbi of Ṣanʿāʾ, Goitein wrote to him asking whether he had access to another copy. The rabbi did not have one, but he did have some—although not all—of the missing pages that had inadvertently not been sent to Glaser. To fill additional lacunae, Goitein used the fragmentary manuscripts of *A Vision of Yemen* that had first alerted him to the existence of the work.[3] Nonetheless, lacunae still remain, and the reader is forewarned that the longest of these occur toward the end of the work, leaving some mystery as to how the journey of the two travelers concluded. Furthermore, *A Vision of Yemen* gives the impression of being hastily assembled and lightly edited. There are several instances of missing words or lines of text. In addition to these challenges, there is Ḥabshūsh's delight in literary experimentation. He plays with linguistic affectation, dialect, narrative digressions, stories within stories, internal monologues, and even occasionally a form of magical realism. The confluence of these factors renders *A Vision of Yemen* less polished and more rough than one might expect from a formal work of either history or literature.

My translation relies on Goitein's edition of *A Vision of Yemen*.[4] Goitein divided the work into chapters, and I have retained these divisions, although I have given them my own titles. Like Goitein, I have also added section headings to better guide the reader through the text. To read *A Vision of Yemen* is to be in the presence of a truly talented storyteller. Ḥabshūsh's narrative flow, however, is occasionally hampered because he lacked the convention of the footnote. To remedy this, I have sometimes moved Ḥabshūsh's parenthetical statements to the notes. The page numbers that I have placed in the margins of this translation refer to the pagination, also retained by Goitein, of Glaser's personal manuscript of *A Vision of Yemen*.[5]

Ḥabshūsh began writing his travelogue in Hebrew. For Yemeni Jewish writers Hebrew was the standard choice for any formal piece of writing. Arabic, the language of speech, was usually reserved for informal written communications. Ḥabshūsh's Hebrew, which bears the influence of the European Hebrew newspapers he read, is quite florid and is filled with literary allusions.[6] This style of writing ceases when, at the instigation of Glaser, Ḥabshūsh switches the language of his travelogue to Arabic.[7] The Arabic portion, which encompasses the majority of the work, is written in a straightforward, almost entirely unornamented style. Although the Hebrew portion of *A Vision of Yemen* demonstrates Ḥabshūsh's familiarity with the Jewish literary canon, the resulting prose displays an affectation. In contrast, the Arabic portion conveys a sense of immediacy and realism that is heightened by Ḥabshūsh's sporadic recourse to the registers of local dialect.

The form of Arabic that Ḥabshūsh uses is Judeo-Arabic, and it is worth discussing for the non-Arabic-speaking reader something of the nature of this dialect. Arabic is a diglossic language—a language in which the spoken vernacular often differs significantly from the written language. Whereas the written language is largely standard across the Arabic-speaking world, the vernacular varies considerably in both vocabulary and grammar. In the nineteenth century Muslims did not write extensively in the vernacular, and it is only in recent times that the vernacular heritage has begun to be celebrated. Jews, however, did frequently produce literature in the Arabic vernacular, but they wrote it using Hebrew characters. The practice of writing the languages they spoke in Hebrew characters was shared by most premodern Jews across the world, as the languages of Yiddish, Ladino, Judeo-Persian, and so on attest.[8] Because the Jews of the Arab world generally spoke a dialect of Arabic that was similar to that spoken in the places in which they lived, one of the joys of studying Judeo-Arabic texts is that they provide a window into the everyday language spoken by both Jews and Muslims alike.

Because of its close connection with spoken Arabic, Judeo-Arabic varies considerably by region. Other factors also cause written Judeo-Arabic to vary. One of the most important of these is the balance that the author strikes between literary and vernacular elements. Although this balance varies considerably from writer to writer, in Yemen Judeo-Arabic writers of literary works generally wrote in a register that was closer to literary than to colloquial Arabic.[9] Ḥabshūsh's Arabic is representative of this Yemeni tradition, although he does make use of select Ṣanʿānī Arabic words and occasionally a more colloquial register, especially when writing dialogue. A notable feature of Ḥabshūsh's Judeo-Arabic is that, like many other Yemeni Judeo-Arabic works of this period, it contains few Hebrew or Aramaic loan words. In other parts of the world Jews have often peppered their language with Hebrew and Aramaic terms and expressions, but the Yemeni Jews did so to a much lesser extent. The almost total absence of Hebrew from Ḥabshūsh's Arabic-language writings sometimes sounds strange, but it is attested to in works by other authors.[10] For example, Ḥabshūsh translates almost all Hebrew names into Arabic. The name Joseph is rendered Yazīd, where the usual Arabic equivalent is Yūsuf. He chooses Yazīd because it is a literal translation of the meaning of Joseph, which is "increase."[11] Similarly, Ḥabshūsh translates Moses, for which the usual Arabic equivalent is Mūsā, as Rifaʿat, from the verb meaning "to raise up." For reasons of clarity, I have avoided translating these linguistic games into English. Thus, for example, I always refer to Joseph Halévy as Joseph, never as Yazīd.

Since its publication, *A Vision of Yemen* has been a source of both delight and dismay to its readers. Often the dismay stems from the same elements as the delight. Its heroes are deeply flawed: They are clever, ambitious, and manipulative, motivated by desires for money and prestige, and filled with prejudices stemming from a lifetime of experiences of both privilege and victimhood. The text refuses to adhere to literary or disciplinary conventions of genre, though it winks at those genres. Like many medieval trickster tales and folk literature, it frequently digresses to stories within stories, but those stories are often not tales of wonder but accounts of everyday life: how fishermen caught their fish, what happened when some teenage boys accidentally drowned, how a community dealt with the aftermath of extramarital affairs, and how a poor hungry man eventually went insane. Some of these stories are horrifying, some are inspiring, and others are mundane. If they are meant to convey a lesson, those lessons are often subtle and ambiguous, as true stories often are. Many seem fanciful and inspire doubt, as the best stories often do.

Without question, the work is an eccentric composition by an eccentric author, but it is that very eccentricity that gives it a stamp of deep authenticity. Such are the pleasures offered by Ḥabshūsh's *A Vision of Yemen.*

PART II

A VISION OF YEMEN BY ḤAYYIM ḤABSHŪSH

Translated from the Original Hebrew and Judeo-Arabic

AUTHOR'S NOTE

In 1892,[1] in Holy Jerusalem, my letter appeared in the *Ha-Or* newspaper.[2] I had addressed it to my lord and master of great and exalted standing, who enlightened my mind and awakened me from my torpor; my teacher who lifted the veil of ignorance from my thought, the patron, his Excellency, the traveler, Yazīd li-Bayt ʿĀṭif (Joseph Halévy) the Frenchman.[3] It was he who filled the hearts of the inhabitants [of Yemen] with hope when he came to us in 1870,[4] when we were in dire straits and on the point of being annihilated. The people imagined that his arrival and research would bring them the relief from adversity enjoyed by the rest of their coreligionists. They thought that he would strive on their behalf by informing charitable people of their plight in his letters. They did not know that he had already denied them in his heart and that their hopes were in vain. Twenty years have passed since my teacher's visit, and still some of my companions do not cease to hope for the merciful charity of their brethren who live under Ottoman rule and elsewhere. It was for this reason that I first published the aforementioned letter, but it did not result in any news from him.

I showed the letter to his Excellency, our dear friend, revered for his knowledge and good character, a master explorer, painter, engineer, and astronomer, [Eduard] Glaser, the Austrian. He then asked me, since I was an experienced traveler, to write down exactly what we had discovered and what had transpired between me and my teacher Joseph. To oblige him, I expounded on what had happened and what we had come across, even though many things had already gone from my memory because a long time has passed since our journey. In addition, I also discuss various matters which I saw fit to include. I will now begin to write in Hebrew and say . . .

⦅ CHAPTER 1 ⦆
ARRIVAL IN YEMEN

Dear reader, I present you with a taste of how we lived when the sage and 1
traveler Rabbi Joseph Halévy, the Frenchman, may God preserve him, came to our holy encampment to discover the hidden secrets of the sand and the ancient Sheban language. Yet again, the kingdom of Yemen had precipitously deteriorated. Tyrannical rulers arose in every village, city, and region. Muḥsin al-Shahārī was a descendant of ʿAlī and a "Commander of the Faithful," that is imām and king—but in name only.[1] Usually based in the small village of Bayt Zabaṭān near Ṣanʿāʾ, he did whatever he wished, either on the authority of his own teaching or on the authority of the commentators' interpretations of his religion. Thus, if it happened that he lacked cattle or property, he would soon come to possess it, his hands defiled by the blood of those who opposed him. Indeed, to line his pockets, he beheaded Sar Shalom ha-Levi al-Shaykh and imprisoned his brothers in a pit until they paid blood money.[2]

To exploit the Jews, al-Shahārī appointed his comrade and kinsman Sayyid Muḥammad ibn Yaḥyā Ḥamīd al-Dīn[3] as his deputy in Ṣanʿāʾ. This
deputy, having a deep knowledge of their books, had discovered a hidden 2
quality that we Jews possess: The Jew is like a leek, which, whenever cut, grows back just as it was before. From this he concluded that a Jew must pay money to the king and his deputy at any time it is requested, the aim being that a Jew should never have more than 7 riyals, or about 112 Ottoman qirsh.[4] We found out about this great new discovery of his through harsh suffering and torment. Perhaps he had discovered the existence of this "quality" in the margins of one of their saints' books, or perhaps it had been deduced from a logic that is alien to all people of integrity, and to us in particular. Had he had time to realize his plan, perhaps he would have continued, with his great power of reasoning, to explain to us the other "qualities" that we possess. Instead, however, the government of kindness and mercy, our gov-

ernment, the Sublime Ottoman Empire, may its glory be exalted, came to Yemen.[5] It is this same [Sayyid Muḥammad ibn Yaḥyā Ḥamīd al-Dīn] who currently serves as the imām for almost all the Arabs; his sermons and deductions having taken root in the minds of his followers. The imamate too fell into his hands as an uncontested gift from the previous imām, Sharaf al-Dīn, who resided in Ṣaʿdah.[6] If the Lord were to again hand him over to the sublime rulers of the Ottoman Empire, they would teach this imām proper justice.

At that time, we lived in the depths of a sea of troubles, surrounded by innumerable misfortunes. We were living in a land of oblivion, an Arab
3 land in which Dumah, Mishma, and Massa had made us dwell.[7] A war had broken out among them, which seemed like *the valley of slaughter*,[8] and a great slumber and darkness fell upon us with no one to awaken, support, and spare us. Because of our enemies' anger and destruction, there was no prospect of rescue. Plague, famine, and violence left us but few survivors in the city of Ṣanʿāʾ. In 1860,[9] the plague gained strength, taking prisoner whomever it saw fit.[10] But famine, in its mercy, embraced them, bearing them away in its arms. Violence dispersed [the Jews] in every direction; their houses fell into ruin, and their villages were destroyed. And from where else were their oppressors going to get their daily bread if not from a remnant of a remnant?! . . . [11]

4 It was at that time that the sage, the aforementioned Rabbi Joseph, came to the destroyed city of Ṣanʿāʾ. Journeying there by way of the Ḥarāz mountains, he had stayed at Ṣaʿfān in the home of Yaḥyā ʿUmaysī, an honorable merchant of blessed memory.[12] There he left his baggage and personal effects on the recommendation of the honorable and beloved Moshe Ḥanokh ha-Levi of Aden.[13] It was this Moshe who had sent letters to his acquaintances in Yemen (the aforementioned merchant, Rabbi Sulaymān al-Qārah, the great leader of all Yemeni Jews and chief of the court, and
5 Rabbi Yaḥyā al-Qārah, his eminent brother), asking them to help and support the sage as much as they could.[14] The merchant undertook to bear his expenses, whether great or small, because the sage had not brought money

sufficient for his needs on account of the dangerous roads. Moreover, his belongings and personal effects had to remain in Ṣaʿfān until the fury of the imām, who was looting and plundering at the crossroads of Ḥarāz, had abated.

The chief of the court and his brother, Rabbi Yaḥyā, joyfully received the sage Joseph with the kindness befitting a man who had come to us from distant lands, and especially one who said, "I seek my brethren."* Rabbi Yaḥyā honored him by telling his son, the wise Me'ir, to serve him until the servant who had accompanied him through the Ḥarāz mountains returned. This servant had been charged by the sage to go to the towns of Shibām and Kawkabān but had not been seen since.

I was young and so, when I learned of his great wisdom, I sought to hear from his very mouth about the [sacred] names and their combinations, which I had studied in the books of the poet Rabbi Sālim al-Shabazī and his son Rabbi Shimʿon.[15] *I did not hide my sins but informed my master [Joseph] of my transgressions.*[16] [The result was that] my eyes saw and my
ears heard what I could not possibly have imagined: He immersed me in 6
the ritual bath of salvation born of enlightenment, cleansing my intellect of the demonic filth that had dwelled within me. I gave the evil servants who did my will by means of invocations as a gift to serve others who were worthier and better than me. From then on, I was bound to him by ties of wondrous love, like a servant who is satisfied only when fulfilling his master's desires. I understood that his wish and desire was exclusively that of collecting Yemen's stone inscriptions, which the commoners call "Persian writing." They also say that they are amulets and that written upon them are the names of the ancient demon emissaries and the servants of their servants.[17] And who in those days, myself included, could resist searching for wood and stones like these!

At that time, I had a few transcriptions from the stones of which I had still not made use, for I did not know their names or functions. I placed these in an old manuscript of Rabbi Yaḥyā al-Ḍāhirī's *Book of Belles-Lettres*, which I cunningly brought to [Joseph].[18] I praised and lauded the eloquence and wondrous rhymes of this Yemeni author. The sage, however, paid attention

* These are the biblical Joseph's words in Genesis 37:16.

neither to my words nor to the author's sweet language. He said that, as a result of the author's deficient knowledge of Hebrew, he had been forced to express himself in the language of the Mishnah and the Talmud [rather than
7 in pure biblical Hebrew].[19] He then asked if I wished to sell it to him for the purpose of bringing it to press and preventing it from, God forbid, being lost and forgotten. He also said that, in addition to the agreed-upon price, he would send me a printed copy as a replacement.

"At the moment, I cannot close the deal with you," I replied, "but if you wish, I can leave it with you until I confer with my brother, and tomorrow I will give you an answer." Without this ruse, I would not have been able to know what he was looking for.

The next day, I came to him about the *Book of Belles-Lettres* and to show him the parts that were missing, but, in my heart, I knew I had not come on account of the book. I had come to learn about the ancient stones and on account of the transcriptions that I had laid inside the book. But when I got there, I could no longer find them. They had gone—disappeared and vanished! So, I questioned him. "Sir, I placed some scraps of paper in this book upon which there were some lists and now I can't find them."

He looked for them in front of him and behind him, eventually managing to extract them from under the pillow upon which he was sitting. He asked me, "How did you get them, and what do you do with them?"

I was afraid to tell him of their hidden meaning, lest he mock me, but I told him where I had discovered the stones from which I had made the transcriptions.

After he had confirmed that I had spoken the truth, *Joseph was not able to restrain himself.** He told me that his will and desire was that I transcribe all the stones that were to be found in the city of Ṣanʿāʾ in their correct order, and
8 he said that he would pay me once I had given them to him. When I heard his words, I rejoiced in my task, although I greatly feared lest this business become known to the Gentiles, who might kill me. So, for the sake of the money and for his sake, I hurried and did not delay. I managed to transcribe them all without being noticed by the Gentiles, except for those in a place

* Genesis 45:1.

called Zuqāq (meaning a narrow alley), through which many people come and go. There, with a straw, I made notes on the skin of my hand, which I later transcribed with pencil and paper. The Gentiles asked, "Why are you coming and going so many times?"

"I am waiting for a certain official to pass by so that I can do his bidding," I replied.

After that, without any mishap, I succeeded in transcribing all the stones that were to be found in the city, not missing a single one, for I had already known their location before I had thought to become one who sees without being seen.

When I brought these transcriptions to [Joseph], he was silent until he had examined them, one by one. He also compared them with some transcriptions that his new servant, the wise Me'ir, Rabbi Yaḥyā's son, had brought him. He found that these were corrupt and incomplete. In fact, this was because Me'ir had not tried to go to the sites for fear of the Gentiles. [Joseph] asked me, "How is it that you were able to bring them so quickly within a single day? Who showed you their locations? Were you perhaps able to do this because you had already prepared them beforehand?"

"I swear by our new friendship," I answered him, "that I had no other prepared transcriptions. It is *the distress of poverty that has made me great*,[20] forcing me to explore all the houses and markets of the city, and it is the hope of acquiring money which gives me strength."

Who can know whether he was really and truly amazed at my zeal or 9
merely praised me to my face? Whatever it was, the money he gave me as payment seemed great to me—he agreed to pay a quarter of a riyal, that is 4 Ottoman qirsh, for each stone I transcribed.

After that, he revealed that the goal of his journey was to reach the ancient city of Mārib.[21] He wanted me to drop my household responsibilities and follow him by way of al-Sirr, Banī Jabr, and Ṣirwāḥ until, by a direct route, we reached Mārib. Once there, we would do what we had arranged, and I would earn a lot of money. After I had heard his words, I said to him, "I am ready and prepared for anything you command me."[22]

I was both afraid and excited. I feared the evening wolves[23] that dwell there but was excited that the time had come for me to meet our brethren who dwell in the east. Called the "sons of Dan" by our educated and common people alike, they were said to rule over their Gentile neighbors, their sword drawn against their enemies. Because this falsehood has spread throughout all the towns of Yemen, people sometimes say that they appear in various places bearing weapons of war and looking like the Arab heroes.[24] God willing, I will explain this matter elsewhere.

My entire congregation (even the learned head of the court and his brothers, Rabbi Yaḥyā and Rabbi Abraham, with whom [Joseph] had stayed) thought that the sole purpose of his formidable journey was to search for the ten [lost] tribes who dwelled in isolation in eastern Yemen. These tribes were famous among us on account of a tradition received from Rabbi Falsehood, who was appointed by the great judge, known as "Distress, Foolishness, and Disgrace," and who was dedicated to leading his servant [the Yemeni Jews] with pride and conceit, as I will explain later.

CHAPTER 2
EXCAVATIONS IN GHAYMĀN

Because his tools and baggage had not yet arrived from Ḥarāz, the sage was forced to delay his travels. He then fell ill, and Rabbi Yaḥyā, who was a Yemeni doctor, gave him Yemeni medicines, which greatly helped him.

The chief imām had challenged the Arḥab tribe to fight against his men in the mountain cities of al-Ḥaymah, which is on the road to Ḥarāz.[1] His men were to fight both for his sake and so that each might go to Paradise as a martyr. All those who fight in a war prescribed by religion are called martyrs and have a portion in the Garden of Eden, a place that no eye has ever seen. Because of the war, all roads were blocked and much blood was shed. Joseph did not have enough self-control to stay with us until the rage of the rebellion had passed. Instead, he became angry and indignant to no advantage, making himself even sicker. Since, among my acquaintances and associates, I am considered a doctor of the spirit, I said to him, "The town of Ghaymān is nearby, a short four-hour journey from Ṣanʿāʾ. I will go and see if it has any inscriptions. If it has none, I will return to search for a different medicine for you."

"Go and don't dawdle on the way," he replied in a whisper, for he clearly 11
did not believe me.[2]

I departed on foot, carrying a tiny bottle of snuff. I had to ask passersby which road led to the town of Ghaymān, for I knew the way only from hearsay. When I arrived there, I found three wretchedly poor Jews living in humble homes. The rest of the town's inhabitants were Arabs of the Banū Bahlūl tribe. Their houses were built from the remnants of the ancient ruin, which lay beneath them. Each stone in the wall screamed, "I am more than two thousand years old!"

In Ghaymān, I went in disguise. I changed my name and the name of my hometown and assumed those of the Jew with whom I was staying—I could do this because there was no one there who knew me. I asked this Jew to show me the houses and courtyards that had the inscriptions I sought, offering him whatever payment he wished. He decided to do it not for the money but for the sake of all Israel. He thought that, through my secret knowledge, the powers of impurity that the ancient enemy sorcerers had cast upon us by means of these stones could be nullified and broken. To this very day, according to the story taught by the rabbis of Ṣanʿāʾ, their power is great enough to subjugate and humiliate us before our Gentile neighbors.

Fearing that our activities would become known to the Gentiles, [the Jew devised a ruse]. He told his wife to go, as was her custom, to collect the dust that they needed for their work, which was that of extracting the salt needed to make gunpowder.[3] Wherever there was an inscription, she would drop the
straw basket balanced on her head and search for and collect dust. Follow- 12
ing her at a short distance, this was my signal, for she could not show me by pointing with her hand.

After three days, I had seen all the inscriptions except those in the great mosque. On the final day, I went alone to investigate them from the outside. Inside the courtyard, a schoolmaster was teaching some children. When he saw me coming and going, he came out in a great fury, brandishing his stick and shouting loudly, "Woe, an impure one! Woe, a Jew! Why do you sit in this fortress with nothing to do? It can only be to aid our enemies and foes."

"Don't think I'm at the mercy of those I meet," I shouted back. "Be careful when you speak to me, whether for good or for evil. My patrons have given me a letter of protection. Don't bring their wrath upon you, for you are only a schoolmaster!"

Continuing his quarrel with me, he said, "This is the third day that you're sitting idly, with not so much as an iron tool for boring stone mills or a needle for sewing leather clothes.[4] This means that you can only be a sorcerer."

"And what makes you so familiar with the ways of magic?" I shot back. "Didn't you ask me to perform a little magic for you yesterday? I don't know if it was for your wife or for some other woman who doesn't pay attention to you, but I told you that my business is snuff—and look, I've got some right here! Beware, or it will not be me with a complaint against you, but my patron."[5]

Upon hearing these slanderous words, he became even angrier and in-
13 quired the name of my patron. He and the children who were with him returned to the mosque, and the women who had gathered looked at me as they would upon someone who had been stabbed.[6] Fortunately for me, there wasn't a single man around, as they had all left the fortress to work in the field. But when the Jew with whom I had been staying returned from gathering wood in the field and heard about the argument, his heart died within him. He was afraid for his own life on account of his Gentile neighbors but was even more afraid for mine. I also thought that I should flee for my life and get out of there.

I turned over some ideas in my mind, but I was at a loss as to how to flee that same day. Soon, the Gentiles who had been in the field gathered for lunch, and the man with whom I had argued came to inform the chief of my iniquity. Two men were sent to arrest me. They found me in front of the Jew's house and brought me to the chief. When I came before him, even though he looked angry, I was sure in my heart of his integrity.

"Where are you from?" the chief questioned me.

"From the town of al-Rawḍah."

"Who is your patron?"

"So-and-so from the Ḥārithī tribe, so-and-so from the Hamdānī tribe, and so-and-so from the Sanḥānī tribe."

"What is your business?"

"I am a miracle worker."*

"What have you sought in this ancient city for the past three days?"

"This is not a city, but the palace of an ancient king, famous in Yemen
for his glory and magnificence. His name was As'ad al-Kāmil,[7] and he ruled 14
before the reign of the Ishmaelites. I read in my *Book of the Will* that this palace was built through the sorcery of Zahrā, the daughter of al-Azhar and the grandmother of As'ad. Hidden inside it are her charms and treasures, as well as those of her fathers, As'ad and the other Himyarite kings. These await the believers on the Day of Resurrection, but the people whom the Lord wishes to honor can still find treasures of silver, gold, precious stones, or *dharār*."

According to the Arabs, *dharār* is a fine-particled and rare material of great quality—the most valuable thing in the world. Place a grain of it into a few talents of copper, tin, lead, or even cow's milk, and it is transformed into gold or silver, according to how rich one wishes to become.

When the chief heard these prophetic words, his face ceased to be angry and instead assumed an expression of compassion and good will. Treating me with respect, he brought me to his home for lunch. After the meal, he produced a pitcher of coffee and a hookah. No speeches or declarations were to be heard, only the bubbling of the hookah and pleasant chatter about different matters. When the time came for their afternoon prayer, he left with his companions and I remained alone, my thoughts racing. After he had performed that which was commanded by his prophet, he returned
home alone and whispered to me, "*The secret of the Lord is with them that fear* 15
him.[8] Now tell me if you have already found the treasure and, if not, also tell me. Do not fear and do not hide anything, for I will take care of anything you need."

"Everything depends on the will of heaven," I replied. "*Do you not know? Have you not heard*[9] that the stone inscriptions are protective formulas for several different treasures? I must therefore transcribe and contemplate them. Perhaps God will favor us and we will dig, find them, and become rich. I am

* Ḥabshūsh uses the Arabic term *ṣāḥib kitāb* (possessor of a book), which he immediately translates into Hebrew as *ba'al ḥefets* (master of the will). My translation, "miracle worker," is an attempt to capture both of these terms. The *ṣāḥib al-kitāb* works his magic by sitting alone at night reading magical texts. If he is able to control the *jinn* who spring forth from them, they become his servants and he can use their power. Cynthia Myntti, "Notes on Mystical Healers in the Hugariyya," *Arabian Studies* 8 (1990), 171–72; and Erich Brauer, *Ethnologie der jemenitischen Juden* (Heidelberg: Carl Winter, 1934), 360–62.

a man who knows the law and regimen of the stars. I do not fear or dread the demons who guard the treasure, for their seven masters are my allies. And now, let us arise and go about the city to see if there are any inscriptions left in the houses that I have not yet transcribed."

To the chief, my words sounded like those of a prophet. Without delay, he led me inside the houses, into their rooms and to all the places that had been hidden from me. I transcribed the stone inscriptions, the final one by candlelight, without anyone *uttering so much as a peep of protest.*[10] We returned to his house in the darkness of night. After dinner, most of the locals arrived. For the next six hours, they lounged and chatted about whatever came to mind.

That night there was no sleep for my eyes nor slumber for my eyelids.[11] I placed my trust in the Forbearing One[12] and in the fact that the villagers[13]
16 are simpleminded and ignorant, a legacy that their forefathers bequeathed to their sons and students. Early in the morning, I told the chief that I needed seven workers to follow me, willing to do everything I asked without contradicting me. He immediately called two of his servants, who were two wild young brothers, and commanded them to do my will. They were charged with obtaining whichever workers I wanted and also with preparing a breakfast to my liking.

HOSPITALITY IN GHAYMĀN

The chief then hurried out on his way to make peace with a neighboring tribe, and his loyal servants gladly brought me to their home. They called to their virgin sister, Muḥṣunah (meaning "the pleasant one"),[14] ordering her to prepare a meal of wheat bread, cow butter, and sheep's milk and to host me until they returned from their mission. I sat amazed and astounded at a home entirely lacking in cleanliness and light. The stench of animal droppings, or whatever it was, rose up my nose, and my eyes watered from the smoke of the fire. Muḥṣunah was alone in the house with no one to help her. First she lit the oven; then she took some wheat, cleaning, grinding, kneading, and baking it. She then placed the butter urn on the edge of the oven, a little away from the coffee pot. At this point, when everything was ready, her brothers arrived, and I was invited to eat. After washing, the four of us sat down at an old straw table, weighed down from much use and falling apart.

The girl washed out some of the remaining dough from the pot in which she 17 had kneaded it, then, taking the bun from the oven, she placed it in the pot. One brother poured the butter into the pot while the second poured in the milk. And Muḥṣunah, with filthy hands that only I seemed to notice, folded in and mixed the contents, which at any moment seemed ready to become dough again. There was nothing for me to do but pronounce the benediction, *[Blessed art thou, O Lord our God, King of the universe,] who brings forth bread from* my hungry stomach through vomiting.* They began to dip into the pot, two fingers at a time. They licked the butter and milk floating on the surface of the buns with such gusto that the smacking of their tongues against their palates could be heard from afar. In Arabic this is called *madhāq*. Muḥṣunah sat opposite me, solid as a wall. Owing to her enormous frame, she was forced to use four cupped fingers to fill her broad, barrel-like belly. They ate their daily bread with the spoons with which nature had endowed them, cleaning and sucking them in their mouths. Only a horse or a donkey would know how to enjoy itself from such eating—this is what is called *madhāq*!

When Muḥṣunah felt droplets of sweat on her broad cheeks, she wiped them, not once or twice, but many times with her palm. She then wiped her palms upon her thighs, thus priming them to receive all manner of dirt and filth. Had Samson been in Yemen, he would have exchanged the jawbone of the ass for Muḥṣunah's cheek and would have been able to strike his enemies with double the force.[15] Her face had the likeness of a lioness, even if 18 it was a likeness sketched with the abundant soot that clung to the pots and jars. Her eyes burned like fire with passion for her food and from toil, even though dust and flour had turned her eyelids and forelocks a dull white. Her hair, continually smeared with ghee, was never washed, lest its oil be lost. Her old grubby head covering was like a bag open at its sides and tied at her cheeks with two cords, called *qarāqish*—young women dress like this rather than wearing the *ṣūna*.[16] As for her garment, which she wrapped around her hips each day, she only rarely exposed it to water and then only in order to kneel down for prayer. The garment, which covered her body down to her heels, was like a long straight bag, except that it had two sleeves, narrow in some parts and wide in others.

* Ḥabshūsh is parodying the standard benediction over bread, "Who brings forth bread from the earth."

After this sight, which made me forget all my own sorrows, I saw another which seemed strange and bizarre to a man like me. After what was a pleasant meal for them but a deathly poison for me, she removed the heavy table together with the pot and replaced it with a small, broken earthenware table. On it were three clay cups, some old, some new, with a coffee pot on the right. Muḥṣunah filled the cups, her eyes so unblinkingly fixed on me and her
19 older brother that she spilled the coffee. Only then did she remember that her brother had told her to serve [not spill] the refreshments—what had she been thinking about? Then suddenly, she got up and, while standing in front of me, loosened the belt of her tunic with her hand so that it fell to her heels. She then quickly took off her pants which were patched with all kinds of tattered rags. Patch upon tear, tear upon patch, and haphazardly adorned with mud, animal dung, sourdough, and I know not what—it was a unique work of the artist Poverty. When I saw this strange sight, I thought that perhaps she'd skipped her morning prayers and was performing a makeup prayer, but this was not her intention. She just wanted to treat herself to a clean and light garment. The pants, because of their heaviness, had fallen to the ground. Muḥṣunah removed them, took the pot—from which we'd eaten and in which she'd kneaded the dough—and put the pants inside it, throwing in a little water and leaving them to warm up a bit on the edge of the oven. She then sat down to drink, without a belt or anything else. I was still drinking my coffee, silently wondering what more would happen, when the workers who had been summoned on the chief's orders arrived with their spades.

EXCAVATIONS IN GHAYMĀN AND THE RETURN TO ṢANʿĀʾ

After drinking my fill of coffee and reciting the Blessing of the Guest upon the householders in general and upon Muḥṣunah, *the woman of valor*,[17] in par-
20 ticular, I led them outside to the gates of the fortress. There, I measured 20 cubits from the gate and ordered them to dig at an old ruin in which remnants of ancient buildings stood. Most of the locals had gathered there, bringing their wives and children. They came to see the golden treasure that I, *with great power, a strong hand, and an outstretched arm*,[18] would win for them from

the demons guarding it. By the sweat of their brows, they dug in good spirits and with sounds of celebration. When I, the masquerader and searcher, saw some change in the dust between the ancient granite stones buried there, I took a little to test in front of them. It was extremely fine and distinctive, like flour or ashes. I folded it in a small piece of paper and hid it in my breast as though it were a precious amulet. When they saw this, they were in wonder, and they said to each other with absolute faith, "This is *dharār*!"

While contemplating this fake *dharār* lying between the clods of earth in the excavation, I became aware that my lie would soon be discovered. I could not claim that there was treasure inside the mountain when the ruin rested on bare rock with no way in. So that they wouldn't find that their toil had been in vain and begin to panic, I ordered them to rest a little until I had considered the matter. I went down into the excavation and again
measured its length, depth, and height and also its distance from the gate 21
of the fortress. I noticed that the ruins were incomplete in the eastern part facing the river. With my staff, I traced a line along the incomplete space and sat by myself whispering incantations. They had worked so excitedly and vigorously with every tool they had that the eastern wall had speedily appeared in its original state—because of its strength, it has remained whole to this day. No one would believe it if they were told that a building like this could exist in the land of the Arabs, but in the valley of Sheba and the city of Mārib and environs, all the ruins are of this kind and are even more wonderful.

Amazed at the sight before me, I glanced at a hole I saw in the excavation between the legs of the diggers. In it was a thing burning like sparks of fire, sparkling and undulating before my eyes, and shooting forth and then returning back into the hole. I fastened my attention on it. There it was, just as they believed, one of the guardians of the threshold of the treasure. Since I was sitting at the opening of the hole, I feared for my life, lest it lunge at me with the sharp swords that lay on the tip of its tongue and pour forth its wrath. It certainly would not have heeded any whispered charms from me, even if I had been the wisest of magicians. So, leaping over the thing crawling about in the dust to stand at the edge of the pit, I cried out, with the rumbling voice used by magicians, to those standing there to follow me and topple down a

stone from the top of the wall. All of them gathered, trying to roll down the
22 great stone with iron bars, but they were unable to do so. When the guardian of the treasure saw that its power would fail against me and the great multitude of people, it turned into a viper. With great anger, it shot from its hiding place and hastened to the river to summon its demon friends to fight and drive us out of there. When the women saw it, they cried out and the children fled. When the men saw this, they were amazed and alarmed. They hurriedly fled, terror gripping them as it does a woman giving birth. I pursued it eastward, enraging it with the seven oaths invoked with the terrible name hidden between the letters *kaf* and *nun*, but it did not listen to me.[19] By the power of the seal of Solomon, son of King David,[20] I warned it to stop until I had questioned it about the gold or silver. It did not listen to me, perhaps because it was the length of eight men's arms. It raced ahead of me like a flying bird, not heeding the angels that I had provoked against it on that day, at that hour. Only those poor people, who were hoping to get rich, took heed of the names of the angels of rage which I spoke as I pursued it until it saved itself by vanishing into one of the gorges. With noise and clamor, the mountains echoing my cries, I leapt to a hilltop, then raced to a gorge, and from there to a mountain range, until I disappeared from the people and treasures of the fortress of Ghaymān. I had saved myself from that battlefield. After sunset, I reached the city of Ṣanʿāʾ, *by way of a rough road*.[21]

23 At the crack of dawn, I went to tell the sage Joseph and Rabbi Yaḥyā al-Qārah of my adventures.

"Why have you embroiled yourself in great dangers using such cunning, deception, and trickery?" Rabbi Yaḥyā asked me.

"How else could I fulfill the wishes of the sage Joseph and remedy my lack of money, which I need to live in this age of poverty?" I replied. "It is this that has compelled me to do all of these things. How much more so since these Arab tribes, they and their ancestors, can be dealt with only by resorting to their gullibility."

Not only did the sage Joseph have no mercy on me, but he also claimed that I had copied the transcriptions of a single stone twice in order to receive a double payment.[22] Because I did not know the script, this had not occurred to me. But, when I consulted the list of places from which I had copied inscriptions, I showed him that one was from inside the city, while the second was from a lintel at the entrance of a mosque outside the fortress.

"Now, as my recompense for healing you, I need you to bless me with the 'Blessing of the Redeemer who bestows good upon sinners'"* I said to him.

Not only did he fail to thank me for all my toil and trouble—the truth be told, because of that terrible event, my hair began to go white—he also reduced the payment we had agreed on by half. That is, for each stone I received an eighth of a riyal, which amounts to 2 Ottoman qirsh. Without protest, I rejoiced in my portion and in being saved from the fortress of Ghaymān.

However, that same week, on the morning before the holy Sabbath,
I heard a voice calling to me and a knocking at my door. Unthinkingly, 24
I answered, and behold, there were the chief's two servants whose prandial customs I had observed in the company of Muḥṣunah, their sister. Sulaymān Jizfān,[23] my Jewish neighbor, was with them. He had revealed my identity and the nature of my business, which I had not made known in Ghaymān. When I saw them, my heart stopped. With trembling lips, I returned their greeting, doubling and quadrupling it as was customary in their eastern lands, and ushered them in. My house was bare of food—I didn't even have a hookah or coffee to serve—so while we were still exchanging greetings, I sent one of my brothers to the market for what we needed, including some bee honey with which to win their hearts and soften their tongues. The gift of that meal convinced them to open their mouths to praise me rather than to fight and argue. This even though my neighbor, who had tattled on me behind my back, went on to belittle my ability to control demons, spirits, and harmful sprites. *Their throats were an open grave*,[24] swallowing everything before them. They listened attentively to my tale of great deeds and secrets, that is, of my battles with the demon guardians of the treasure which, as they themselves had seen in Ghaymān, had transformed into vipers.

"They have not yet vanquished me nor have I vanquished them, and I still continue to fight them in my house in the darkness of night. If God wills it, I shall vanquish them and will come to you, bringing forth silver, gold, or
dharār from the treasure houses of the Sheban kings. You need not persist in 25
entreating me because I am unable to do anything, whether great or small,

* The blessing said upon deliverance from great danger.

without the grace of God. It is this you should tell the chief who sent you. Do not think that I have already gained some benefit from the *dharār* that I took to test. Behold, you can see it in front of you. If you like, take it and return it to him."

They sincerely accepted the truth of my words and made the Blessing of the Guest for the host. They also prayed for success in the name of their prophet and his five pure and holy companions.[25] Before the arrival of the Sabbath, they went on their way. As for me, I went to the synagogue. With a tranquil heart I welcomed the Sabbath, wholeheartedly repenting for my deceit and reciting the Psalm *to the God of my Life*.[26]

And you, dear reader, if I have wearied you with my foolish words and vain thoughts, do not blame me! Believe me and you will see the character of my soul as I, with the spirit possessed by my countrymen, performed my mission for the sage Joseph. You can then judge whether I was *a faithful messenger to him who sent me*,[27] that is, to the sage Joseph who hardened his heart and was not afraid of the tyrants of Arabia.

When Rabbi Sulaymān al-Qārah and his brother, Rabbi Yaḥyā, were informed of what Sulaymān Jizfān the Jew had done to me, that is, identifying me and even bringing the chief's servants to my house, they were greatly
26 afraid. But they were not disheartened, for they were now indeed certain that I was a miracle worker!

⟨ CHAPTER 3 ⟩

JEWS, MUSLIMS, AND FOREIGNERS IN ṢANʿĀʾ

STATUS OF JEWISH MINORITIES IN YEMEN AND SOME NOTES ON ASHKENAZIC VISITORS

After these events, the sage Joseph asked to see and walk about in the roads and markets of Ṣanʿāʾ, but they did not let him because they feared the Gentiles. The sage said, "Bring me a man to show me the road and whatever happens to me happens."

The chief *parnas*[1] and his brother, Rabbi Yaḥyā, warned him not to show himself among the Gentiles, lest they make false accusations against him that might also endanger the Jewish community. The honorable and learned Joseph Badīḥī, may the Lord preserve him, told him the story of one Ashkenazic[2] sage who had come to Ṣan'ā' in the time of the exalted and revered Sar Shalom ben Aharon Ha-Cohen al-'Irāqī, of blessed memory.[3] The latter greatly rejoiced at the coming of the Ashkenazi, who stayed at his house and ate at his table. Out of fear for the Ashkenazi's life, he ordered him not to be seen outside, especially in the streets of the Gentiles. But the day came when the soul of this sage longed to see the king of Yemen, who was called al-Mahdī.[4] When Sar Shalom saw how ardent his desire was to see the king with his army, he became greatly worried and said, "You will not be able to endure their recklessness and evil character, but, if you bind yourself to these principles, perhaps you will be saved."

"Tell me and I will prove my strength," said the sage.

"When the people first see you, they will begin to shout, 'He's a Jew!
A Jerusalemite! He's a dog! He's a donkey, the son of a donkey!' They will 27
surround you, their eyes burning and enraged faces glaring at you. They will gnash their teeth, hurl curses at you, and degrade you with ridicule and humiliation. *Some of their sages, who study their books, who have upon their foreheads the mark caused by prostrations,*[5] *and who are called 'jurists,' will not turn back and cease their cursing until the phlegm from their nostrils spurts out of their mouths and they spit it in your face, and only then will they go on their way. After they go, the breath contained in their spittle contaminates him who has no desire to be purified.*[6] They will mock him, 'O contaminated one, O sweat of a dog! A dog's urine is purer than him! He contaminates the tail of a dog!' The children will mock and throw stones at him with no one telling them to stop. Their governors and a few of their notables will be silent, and woe to any who stand up against the crowd or reprimand them. They will then seize him and, while beating him, lead him to the governor to testify that he has cursed their God and king. And who when called to judgment has ever been acquitted?!"

After hearing these principles, the Ashkenazic sage said that he had the strength to bear such hardships and that he still wanted to go to the king's gate, regardless of what might happen. When Sar Shalom, *the high priest among his brethren,*[7] saw that he would not listen to his advice, he nonetheless did as he asked because he respected him.

28 On Friday, before the king was to go forth with his army to conduct the day's obligatory prayer, the Ashkenazi brought along another Jew to accompany him to the king's gate. They had gone a short way when the Gentiles, both young and old, gathered around to see this Jew so strange in dress, language, and appearance. They accompanied him as though he were a stealthy thief, cursing and abusing him until they arrived at the street in which the king's palace was located. The Jew then rented a small stall and put the Ashkenazi inside it so that he could see the king with his ministers and soldiers as they went to their prayers. The crowd beat at the walls and door of the stall. However, though they beat at the door with sticks to frighten him and threw stones at the wall to agitate him, the sage reluctantly resolved that he would be as forbearing as a Yemeni Jew, if not more so, and so he was.

Even after the king had returned from worship to the palace and most of his soldiers had gone on their way, the Ashkenazic sage remained in the stall with the Jew. They were accosted by a young Arab boy who could find no better means to enhance his reputation among his friends than with the stinking carcass of a cat that had been dumped there. Using the tip of a stick he had in his hand, he picked it up and threw it into the face of the Ashkenazi. The cat carcass did not wound or bruise the Ashkenazi, but the pus and slime spilled out, stuck to his face, and dripped down his beard. The Ashkenazi hurried to retrieve from his breast the document detailing the principles of forbearance of which Sar Shalom had informed him, but
29 he did not find a principle relating to this situation. The stench burst into his brain until he forgot that he was in Ṣanʿāʾ, in Yemen! This visitor then cast off the coat of forbearance of the Yemeni Jews and put on the coat of zeal of the Ashkenazim. He grabbed the cat carcass and forcefully struck the young showoff. Just one blow later, nothing remained in his hand except a shin and a thigh. The rest disintegrated into bits upon the Muslims who stood around him and whom he loudly cursed. Then and there, the Gentiles falsely charged him not only with rendering them impure with the blood of the carcass but also with practicing sorcery against them and cursing their God, king, and land. With thunderous fury, they struck his back with sticks and stones, beat his face with their fists, and, with cruel blows, they dragged him to the king's court. Soon, a rumor spread throughout the city that the Jerusalemite had been killed, and the heavens of the Jews were darkened.

In his mercy, the illustrious Sar Shalom, who was good both to his own people and to others, hurried to the king to intercede for that unfortunate whom he had previously warned and whom he had taught all the rules of forbearance required of Yemeni Jews. When the aforementioned minister came to the king's gate, he found the thoroughly beaten unfortunate lying unconscious in the outer courtyard. The ministers and servants of the king, and all who stood there, made way for Sar Shalom, the gentleman whose righteousness and honesty were known to all. He then approached the king to entreat on behalf of 30
the unfortunate visitor who had been persecuted with the blows of barbarous men. The king and the chief adviser of the kingdom, who was a judge, gave him permission to intercede on the Ashkenazi's behalf before the throne of judgment. This judge was then sent to bring the Ashkenazi before them.

When he came, they asked him, "Why have you made this scene?"

The Ashkenazi brought forth from his breast the document listing the principles that Sar Shalom had taught him. Having read the principles to them, he said, "Why didn't you tell me that no end of vermin, reptiles, and scorpions could be thrown on my head, face, beard, back, and garments? Fear God and judge!"

The king and the judge gave no further reply but hid their laughter from him. They ordered Sar Shalom to save him by hiding him in the Jewish quarter, lest the lawless mob swallow him up. They left the king, and the afflicted man regained his composure. When they reached the house of Sar Shalom, he again said, "Why did you not tell me all of this from the first?"

"Did we not tell you from the first," Sar Shalom responded, "that forbearance is the principal virtue that the Yemeni Jews must exercise with their Arab neighbors? The proof is from scripture: *Mishma, Dumah, and Massa.*[*] The Jews hear their libels against them but remain silent. *They give their cheek to those who smite them, are satisfied with disgrace,*[8] and are silent. They endure the heavy yoke of the exile without complaint."

Irate and brokenhearted, the Ashkenazi cried out, "I listened to and ac- 31
cepted all of the principles that you mentioned, but I was not able to bear

* Genesis 25:14, referring to the names of three of Ishmael's sons. Sar Shalom's prooftext relies on the Yemeni Jewish tradition of homiletically interpreting these names (according to their root meanings) as an injunction for Jews in times of persecution to "listen, be silent, and endure." See, for example, Moses Maimonides, "Epistle to Yemen," in Y. Shailat, ed., *Epistles of Maimonides* (Jerusalem: Ma'aliyot, 1987), 1: 160–61 (Hebrew).

that stench. No one mentioned a cat to me. There was no dead cat in your principles, no cat putrid and swollen like this. If you had told me, I would not have endangered my life, for I certainly would have known that I did not have the strength to bear such filth and stench. So now, return me to your neighborhood. If the Lord decides to keep me alive, I shall proclaim my experience of this cat, an experience I purchased with my heart's blood. Perhaps God, hearing this cry of Israel and Judah, will take pity on them wherever they are."

The cry of this wanderer came to the ears of the king, al-Mahdī, and he issued an order to all the people that they never again practice such foolishness. But who listens? Since then, this incident has become a Jewish proverb: "At least there was no cat! At least there was no cat!"

The author says: In our own days, many incidents like these happened in the city of Ṣanʿāʾ. The first such incident was that of the sage Baruch,[9] whom they killed suddenly without any charge. The second was that of Moshe Masʿūd, the alms collector from Safed.[10] He was with his son when one night he was robbed of all the money that he had collected as alms in Yemen, but their lives were saved. After him, this very year, they falsely claimed that the sage Ḥayyim had cursed their prophet, land, and religion and imprisoned him for two months. The Jews redeemed him and he left, but he died in the town of Raymat Waṣāb from the strain of his sufferings.[11]

JOSEPH HALÉVY'S CLOTHING

When the sage Joseph heard these words of advice and caution, he took courage and did not listen to them. When the city notables saw the greatness of his desire to see the streets and markets of Ṣanʿāʾ, they dressed him in Yemeni Jewish garb and appointed me to guide and protect him.[12]

These are the garments they gave him: A hat called a keffiyeh was placed on his head—I don't know whether it was borrowed or given to him as a gift.
32 It was as stiff as wood and measured a sixth of a *seʾah*.[13] It had been pasted with a tree resin called *ṣamgh* and patched with many rags until it was twice as thick as it was tall. Its top was sewn and pasted with white and black cotton.

As a gift, Rabbi Yaḥyā al-Qārah dressed him in a robe that he had previously worn on the Sabbath and festivals. Where it had been torn, the rabbi's wife had sewn it up as was necessary. Because the sage's height was less than that of the rabbi, the robe, which had reached the rabbi's shins, reached the sage's heels and completely covered his hands and feet, unlike those of the Yemenis, which leave hands and feet uncovered.

Blessed also is my dear friend, the Yemeni astronomer, Sa‘īd the son of the honorable Joseph ‘Arūsī,[14] who gave him a thick and heavy gray woolen shawl called a *shamlah*. It allowed him to cover his whole body so that he could hide that he was a European, for his face, eyes, and features bore witness that he was not a Yemeni.

I stretched the *shamlah* over his head and back like a tent and told him to grasp its edges with his hands and hold them against his heart (as is our custom during prayer). Because he had never tried to walk like this, he soon found it very heavy and said, "This *shamlah* is not suitable for human use; it is suitable as the pack saddle of a donkey." 33

"My friend gave your honor this heavy, fringed shawl," I replied, "so that you would be sheltered from the storm, the wind, and the rain. If it is heavier than others, remember that the sages have said, *You have come to the city, behave according to its customs!*"[15]

EXPLORING ṢAN‘Ā’

On the morning of that same day, fearing the Gentiles, I took my life in my hands and led him into the city. He was wrapped up so as to cover everything but his face, as is done by those who pray, or by sick people who cover themselves with the *shamlah* when they walk about with their canes in the roads and markets. As I walked through the city gate, which is called Bāb al-Sabaḥ, I prayed that we would leave unharmed. We passed through the Garden of the Sultan[16] and saw the southern part of the city near the house of Minister Muḥsin Mu‘īḍ.[17] No disaster befell us until we reached the road in which there is a school for their jurists called al-Jāmi‘ al-Kabīr (the Great Mosque). Because of the holiness of that road, they had built a market there for selling the rams that are sacrificed on the festival of ‘Arafāt . . . ,[18] and it was there 34
that some of the Gentile boys began to surround us. When they saw the sage covered in his *shamlah* as sick people are, its fringes dragging on the ground, 35
they said, "A Jew with a wrapped-up head! He must be a Jerusalemite!"

With raised voices, the Muslims, most of them youths, encircled us, *yea, they surrounded us*,[19] so it was with great difficulty that we passed through three

markets.[20] When we reached the grain market, we were almost unable to go any farther because of the many people who came to see this strange Jew in their land. How could they glorify themselves before him except with curses, insults, and invective? The boys boldly got in his way to intimidate him, threatening to make the very earth split with their chorus of voices, hammering on the pillars and doors of the market stalls with their sticks. Their noise brought their neighbors to the market, most of them standing at the entrances of their stalls, to see what the crowd was doing and find out what had happened. With great difficulty, we came to *the crowning city*[21] and found ourselves in the middle of the apothecaries' market. Most of the sellers were standing at the entrances to their stalls to see the hubbub. Among them stood an old man leaning on the chain that hung at the entrance of his stall. When he saw the sage and recognized me, he called out to me, "Hey, it's Ḥabshūsh! Hey Jew!" and so on and so forth. "Why have you brought us a Jerusalemite to laugh at? One of the people nearly attacked him, which would have been
36 inexcusable. You should go to prison for this!"

"This poor man came to us three months ago," I said, "and every day he grows sicker. Using charity money, he paid some people to go buy him some medicinal drugs that were known to him, but either they or the drug sellers took the money and gave him other drugs. Today he had another attack of illness, as you can see with your own eyes. He begged me to do him the kindness of bringing him to the apothecaries' market so that he himself could identify the medicine known to him and buy it with whatever money necessary. And now God, may He be praised, has presented you to us, you who are a wise old sage who understands medicinal drugs. He will pay you in full if you give him what he is looking for, and you will achieve merit before the God of heaven!"

The old man had a change of heart and, turning toward the mob, he cried out, "Muslims, you should be ashamed of yourselves! It is disgraceful for you to chase after a Jew. What interest can you have in a sick Jew who sojourns in this land? Remember God, pray on behalf of the Prophet, be honorable, and go on your way!"

When they heard his rebuke, many of them left. Some, however, still stood around us but kept silent.

To earn his money, the old druggist assumed the role of an expert physician. He sought to understand both the illness itself and the specific remedy

which we had asked of him. After having made a thorough search of his 37
merchandise, he brought out something the name and nature of which was known neither to him nor to us.

"This is the remedy that is required!" the sick sage said.

So I paid the druggist the number of coins that he decreed. He then commanded and warned us not to be seen again in the city, lest we be hurt by its ruffians, who are called *shayāṭīn* in Arabic.[22] So I said to him, "And what am I supposed to do when they surround us like bees?"

When he saw that we had no hope, he came out of his store, took the Frenchman by the hand, and walked him to the edge of the market of the Jewish silversmiths, which is called Sūq 'Aqīl. There they let him into the store of a Jew who was told to hide him until the sun had set and then to lead him to the Jewish neighborhood. And that is what happened.

CHAPTER 4

STRANGERS AMONG THE TRIBES

LEAVING ṢAN'Ā'

A few days later, the sage Joseph's sickness attacked again and he could no longer bear to stay at Rabbi Yaḥyā al-Qārah's house.[1] His belongings had still not arrived from Ḥarāz, because the aforementioned king, Muḥsin al-Shahārī, was still fighting for the cities of al-Ḥaymah. When I saw how eager he was to accomplish his mission, I advised him to go with me to al-Madīd, one of the villages of Nihm, which was a full day's journey from Ṣan'ā'. As a
child, I had heard that an Indian traveler had once gone there and found a 38
man who had a stone that was inscribed in the Himyaritic script. The traveler asked to buy the stone from the man, but he refused to give it to him until he had raised the price to his liking. After he had sold it, he asked the Indian to reveal the secret of the stone for which he had not hesitated to pay so dearly. After he had entreated him for some time, the Indian took a key and inserted it into a small hole in the stone. A door in the stone, the existence of which had not been known to the Nihmī, then opened like a chest. Inside it, there was a small gold box and inside that, a glittering sword that

was bent like a strap, and with it a ring with a precious stone embedded in it. There was also a small gold tablet inscribed with the most precious names of the angels who stand before God.

I heard all of this as a child from a Jewish Nihmī man from the town of al-Madīd. He said that he himself had seen this stone and that it had flown into the skies of their land. If a listener disbelieved him, this storyteller would jump up and swear to every aspect of the story, so as to make him believe this nonsense—this is the custom of our fools. I, the writer, granted the storyteller only the existence of the chest and the box. Because at that time I was
39 looking for stones with inscriptions, I advised the sage to travel there until the rebellion ended and his belongings arrived, saying, "Perhaps we will find what we are searching for there, and when, God willing, we return from Nihm, we will find everything ready. We can take what baggage we need and go eastward from Ṣanʿāʾ by a direct route to Mārib, which is in the land of the Sabaeans that you desire."

My advice pleased him, but it did not please Rabbi Yaḥyā, because he feared the Arab tribes.

I left my home on the second of February 1870.[2] Leaving behind my brother and my son, we departed from Ṣanʿāʾ and traveled toward the town of al-Rawḍah. Rabbi Yaḥyā al-Qārah accompanied us to the end of the Jewish quarter. When he parted from us, he lowered his eyes, which were like a river of tears. Struck dumb with crying, he prayed that God save us and return us in safety. The sage Joseph was also emotional, and, as for me, my knees quivered and my mind was disquieted by his great worry for us. However, after some moments, I collected my thoughts and said, "Why should I fear the town of al-Madīd, which is only a single day's journey away and in which 500 Jews live? It is not a place of grief and lamentation for Jews. Perhaps, God willing, we will return from there to Ṣanʿāʾ and wander no further. As for our terrible journey to Mārib, we will see what we will do, but for now, we have nothing to fear."

At that thought, my legs became steady, my mind calm, and we left on
40 our journey empty-handed with neither money nor provisions.

I strode in front of the sage with my staff, and he followed me in his Yemeni clothing, described earlier.[3] We passed the ancient Jewish cemetery, located inside the city near the Rūm Gate. When I saw the shattered tombstones, I became angry, but when I told him of my distress, he paid no attention.

Perhaps he thought that the tombstones belonged to Himyarites and not to Israelites. Even the Gentiles who live next to the cemetery know very well that these are Jewish graves and, in the deeds to their houses and the surrounding lands, they call the place "the graveyard of the Qarāmiṭah."[4] I searched in the chronicles of ancient Ṣanʿāʾ and in the dictionaries of their language for a connection between the word *Qarāmiṭah* and the Jewish graves, but they do not mention it. Thank God, a seal that I found in the grave of a 1,080-year-old man revealed the answer as clearly as the sun. Some ancient nails, some large, some small, and which weighed 200 *dirhams*, gave further evidence. However, these were not fit for use, as their metal had rusted away, as I will explain later.[5]

ARABIC: THE NEW LANGUAGE OF *A VISION OF YEMEN*

The one who travels along the frontiers of his land, Ḥayyim ibn Yaḥyā ibn 41
Sālim al-Futayḥī, known as Ḥabshūsh, said, "When the teacher and traveler, [Eduard] Glaser, saw and heard the first part of my account of what happened to my teacher Joseph and me, as well as some of my other descriptions of events in the Hebrew language, he was greatly amazed and said, 'Who taught and educated you, a Yemeni no less, in the eloquent Hebrew which you speak so well?!'"

"God be praised!" I replied. "We are the inheritors of books, and even though we gloss them with the help of the Arabic language, which is what we use in Yemen, do not think that we are devoid of knowledge of Hebrew.[6] Although sorrows have darkened our hearts and dulled our minds, we still have the ability to translate from one language to the other without a teacher."

"If your words are true," he said, "I would like you to compose the remainder of this book in the Arabic which is used by your Ṣanʿānī Jewish brethren. This will be of benefit to researchers. After you have composed it in Arabic, go back and translate it into Hebrew. Also, translate the first Hebrew section into Arabic so that your ideas can be explained in two languages—that way you [Yemenis] will also benefit."

I liked his proposal and accepted it without hesitation because I saw him as sincere—a man like him would not deceive his friend and be ungrateful.

I knew that our Yemeni forefathers were eloquent speakers of two languages. The proof of this is in the honorifics noted in their books. In our own day, everything has changed. Our language is completely different from that of our ancestors, and there is also a great difference between the dialects of the various regions of Yemen. We will now return to our subject.

MORE ON UNFORTUNATE VISITORS TO YEMEN

42 We immediately left the ancient graveyard by way of the Rūm Gate, then headed west of Shuʿūb for two hours until we came to al-Jirāf. There we saw tombs by the road that were different from those of the Bedouin in the shape and size of their headstones. When we asked the local tribesmen about them, they said that they were the tombs of the Qarāmiṭah, but they did not know what the word meant. After an hour, we arrived at al-Mazāʿiqah, a place to the west of Rawḍat ibn Ḥātim in which our Jewish brethren dwelled. Most of these Jews were refugees of the great calamities that occurred in Ṣanʿāʾ. One of them was Yūsuf ibn Yaḥyā al-ʿArūsī, who devoted most of his life to alchemy without achieving any result. Another was his son, my friend Saʿīd, who had given his *shamlah* to my teacher, Joseph Halévy, the Frenchman, to conceal himself in while he was a stranger among the tribesmen and Jews of Yemen. Because Yūsuf al-ʿArūsī very much liked to learn and teach, it was his custom, insofar as his means permitted, to invite every stranger to his house, especially if the stranger seemed knowledgeable. For that reason, he brought my teacher to his house and served him all the food he could afford. Yūsuf al-ʿArūsī warned me not
43 to let anyone know that my teacher was at his house. He worried that he would be harmed, as had recently happened to a foreign Jew by the name of Rifʿāt (Moshe) of Baghdad,[7] who had visited al-Rawḍah after Jacob Saphir.[8] (They had tried to seize Saphir and rob him of everything he had, but he fled and was rescued. The Jews were then imprisoned on account of his flight and were not released until they paid a fine. I too was one of those imprisoned at that time on account of Jacob Saphir.)[9] When the Baghdadi foreigner came to the market of al-Rawḍah, he asked where the Jewish neighborhood was. In the market, there was a *sayyid** who was a patron of the Jews of al-Mazāʿiqah. The people said to the *sayyid*, "Do us a favor, take this Jew with you to the Jewish neighborhood."

As they went on their way, the *sayyid* thought to himself that he also de-

* An individual who claims descent from Ḥasan or Ḥusayn, the grandsons of the Prophet Muḥammad. Isaac Hollander, *Jews and Muslims in Lower Yemen* (Leiden: Brill, 2005), 46–47.

served a favor. He was, after all, a *sayyid* in straitened circumstances, and what was this Jew if not a means of making a living sent to him straight from God?! So, when he arrived at the Jewish neighborhood, he drew his dagger and sought to kill him. The foreign Jew screamed and fled, and the *sayyid* took the Jew's donkey with everything that was on it and brought it into his fortress.

The Jewish youths of al-Mazāʿiqah then sought the help of their tribal patrons. The tribes of al-Rawḍah gathered at al-Mazāʿiqah, the Jewish neighborhood, to see what had happened. The *sayyid*, intent on a fight, locked his fortress and perched on the roof with his revolver. The Baghdadi shouted, "They took my donkey, my money, and my book!"—for he was a miracle worker.

The patrons confronted the *sayyid*: "What is this evil thing that you have 44
done in the middle of the Jewish neighborhood? If you had done it outside the neighborhood, we would not have reproached you at all, but doing this inside the neighborhood means great shame for us. So bring out what belongs to the Jew without a fight."

The *sayyid*, however, raised his rifle and said, "I want a fight! Let anyone who has a claim against me approach my gate. God has provided me with what I now possess. Who is there who will contest what He has provided me?"

After many words and after much effort had been expended, he returned the donkey to the Jew but kept everything that it had carried.

TREATMENT OF SNAKEBITES

That night, Yūsuf al-ʿArūsī went out to look for the foreign Jew so that he could host and comfort him. He was searching about to find him when a snake bit his toe. He let out a deathly scream, on account of the snake's venom, and the people accompanying him carried him back to his house. There, taking a blade, he cut open the bite and surrounding area until the blood flowed out. They then tied it from above and washed it in hot water. Then, he again cut it open to release the blood and washed it in hot water. After that, he dressed it with a poultice of garlic and *ubab* gum[10] until the Lord saved him and he was healed. There was thus no need to bring him to the house of al-Sirḥī, who has the precious stones that are used to treat snakebites. Other people who are bitten by snakes are brought to al-Sirḥī's house, even if it takes a full day of travel. Al-Sirḥī then treats them kindly, abandoning all his work and striving to heal the victim.

This is a description of his work. He places the precious stone on the
45 bite, leaving it until the poison is drawn toward it. He then removes it with tweezers and places it in milk. After repeating this process a number of times, the bite is healed within an hour. Those who are carried in to him return on their feet, and it is a well-known truth that many who are not brought to him die. The people who possess the stone accept no reward, save God's recompense. We know of no other such stone in Yemen except for this famous one.

People claim that precious stones have many occult healing properties. For example, there is one that prevents blood loss so long as it is worn on the body. There is one that prevents ejaculation, even in a man who has sex all night long. There is one that makes water dissipate and desiccates, and another that attracts water to the surface of the earth so that it becomes a stream. There is one that removes pus from the body when it is laid on a person, or it can remove a disease from the eye and heal it. There is one that brings wealth or increases beauty, rank, or prosperity. According to them, there are innumerable such occult remedies. The commoners believe that there are other occult remedies even more effective than precious stones—amulets, charms, and incantations—but despite all their excellence, they do not get any results.

Yūsuf al-ʿArūsī thought that my teacher Joseph knew something about these special properties, but we heard nothing from him about them.

HALÉVY TELLS OF HIS TRIP TO ABYSSINIA

46 Although my teacher did not generally woo audiences, as travelers do, with reports of the places he had visited and about what he had seen and heard, he did share some stories. One of the stories he told was of how he had traveled to Abyssinia and discovered the black Jews who live in that region.[11] One of the strangest things he said was that our black brethren did not believe that he was of Jewish descent because his color differed from theirs and because his body was so white. Because their settlements are cut off from the rest of their brethren, they think that all Jews are black and rest their claim on a passage in the Song of Songs: "I am black but comely."[12] My teacher

Joseph responded to them with the Bible verse "I am Joseph your brother" and with the verse "Look not upon me that I am swarthy, that the sun hath tanned me; the sons of my religious community[13] were incensed against me, they made me keeper of the vineyards; but mine own vineyard have I not kept."[14] After this response, they accepted and acknowledged him [as a Jew]. These stories of my teacher, "the traveler," were among the strangest that we had ever heard. We spent the rest of the night discussing various other matters. Yūsuf al-ʿArūsī said that, in his own lifetime, an Abyssinian Jew had
visited Ṣanʿāʾ, but that they had not learned anything from him. I asked him, 47
"How is it possible to learn nothing from such a well-traveled person?"

"You are correct," he answered, "but don't you see this even among our friends who dwell here in al-Mazāʿiqah, where you won't find anyone rich in either wealth or wisdom?"

This is because of the wretched way in which they make a living. Some are lime-plaster workers, others potters, others leather workers. These are the occupations of the Jews of al-Rawḍah. Poverty has destroyed their hearts, and they have no ability to do anything that requires either reason or money.

JOURNEY TO SHIRĀʿ

The following day, we traveled through the al-Aḥqarī plain on the road to the villages of Arḥab. While we were traveling, I noticed in the riverbed whose path we followed some shards of Himyarite limestone that the rains had swept down from the mountain crevices into the river. I was certain that in those places there had to be Himyarite inscriptions, so I said to my teacher, "Do you deny Jacob Saphir's claim, stated at the beginning of his book, that the people of Yemen have sharp eyesight because of their custom of applying kohl and that they see things in the distance better than those who do not apply it? So now, I ask you, what do you see in those far-off hills that surround us?"

My teacher raised his eyes but could not discern a thing. "I see nothing except the clouds on the edge of the horizon," he said.

"Praise God," I replied, "as Jacob Saphir witnessed, our eyesight is 48
sharper than others. That haze you see on the edge of the horizon is a range of mountains. On them I see Himyarite buildings, which no doubt bear the inscriptions for which we are searching."

He, however, denied my words, and what I had theorized based on my knowledge did not even occur to him.

A short while later, I entered one of the villages where I found three or four inscribed stones. I transcribed them, although they were broken. These were the first inscriptions of our journey. That evening, we came to al-Ṣubayrah, a village in Arḥab. Our Jewish brethren welcomed us insofar as their means permitted them. That evening, I asked them whether they would do us the favor of working with us and procuring a riding animal for the sage. A boy from Ṣanʿāʾ who had a donkey put himself at our service, trusting the others to pay his wages—and, to this day, he is still trying to collect the money because they didn't pay him anything. The boy brought us to Shirāʿ, another village in Arḥab, and took us to the synagogue, as is the custom among the Yemeni people: Jewish strangers enter the synagogue, Muslim strangers enter the mosque. Many rich and charitable Yemenis open special rooms of their houses to all poor and wretched wayfarers. The master of the house himself honors the stranger, providing him with everything he needs, including coffee, a hookah, and food. May God give them a good reward!

THE STORY OF A JEW KIDNAPPED BY THE TRIBES OF ARḤAB

49 In the village of Shirāʿ, we were greatly afraid of the Arḥabī bandits. Although some tribes are more treacherous than others, the reputation of the Arḥabī tribes for [banditry] is well known among the people of Yemen. At that time, it happened that one of their chiefs ambushed a Jew from Ḥarāz. He was one of those who had emigrated from Ṣanʿāʾ and had settled in the Ḥarāzī mountains in the town of Manākhah under the protection of the governor of Ḥarāz, al-Dāʿī al-Makramī.[15] This Jew had traveled to Ṣanʿāʾ for business, as was his custom. As he was leaving Ṣanʿāʾ through the gate of the Jewish quarter, the chief, who had been lying in ambush for him, grabbed him and brought him, all tied up, to the land of Arḥab, where he imprisoned him in his house. The sheikhs of Ṣanʿāʾ had no means to release him because he had been captured outside the city gate; the sheikhs of the Ḥārith tribe who controlled the road would not intervene, and the governor of Ḥarāz*

* That is, the Jew's own patron.

could not liberate him because of the distance involved. The Jew therefore languished in the custody of the tribal chief for a month, suffering all manner of tortures. Each day, the chief threatened him, demanding that he send to his family for money for his release. Were it not for the chief's mother and wives who had mercy on him, he would have died from the violence of the tortures. He was saved by fleeing from his prison in the middle of the night, after having already paid the chief a lot of money.

HALÉVY IS IMPRISONED

As for ourselves, what we dreaded befell us. One of the sons of al-Zubayrī,
who was in charge of Shirāʿ, came to the synagogue to threaten us in the 50
hope of extorting money. My answer to him was, "Take what you want from
us, for we are strangers who seek alms from you and from others."

Because he could not find any charge to pin on us, he claimed that my teacher Joseph was the Jew who called himself Shukr Kuḥayl,[16] the one who, claiming that he was the emissary of the awaited Messiah, had been stirring up the people. Muslims, and most Jews, cannot fathom the intention of the scholars who placed in their books this doctrine, which gives solace to hearts stricken with grief from suffering. Because of this doctrine, many throughout Yemen uprooted themselves to follow this fool who called himself Kuḥayl. He named himself after the first fool whom they killed on Mount al-Ṭiyāl, which is in the territory of the Banū Jabr, and assured his poor, foolish followers that, a few days after he had been killed, his head, which had been hung on the Yemen Gate in Ṣanʿāʾ, had been returned to him as good as new, and his body had become upright and no longer disemboweled. This was what his followers believed, and who can contradict fools and imbeciles for whom everything that is impossible becomes real by virtue of the strength of their devotion to it?! Their imaginations abound with tales of miracles, but there is no need to trouble ourselves with these empty matters.

Let us return to our business. The Arḥabī chief, that is, al-Zubayrī's son,
imprisoned my teacher Joseph in the synagogue. He gave orders to the Jews
of Shirāʿ to bring us back to Ṣanʿāʾ as prisoners for the imām Muḥsin al- 51
Shahārī, who would already know about our troublemaking.[17] Some Jews,
fearing for us, pleaded with him to release us, but he would not agree.

While we were delayed, I asked a Jewish woman to show me the places [with the inscriptions] that we sought. She placed her basket on her head and went, as was her custom, to gather firewood. After she had searched around the tribesmen's homes, she led me to an empty valley near the village. I found a few inscriptions on the mountainsides, and among them was the name *msḥqm*.[18] On the mountainside opposite it, at a height of ten paces, was a cave excavated by human hands. Upon climbing up to it, I found on the entranceway some lines of inscrutable writing that had been effaced with the passing of time. However, it was clear to me that this cave was a tomb for someone called Ḍumqāl. Hanging from the entranceway, I transcribed the inscriptions. Above the cave, there was a high mountain atop of which was an ancient abandoned fortress about which the locals tell stories.

After I returned to my teacher, it became evident to him that there were
clearly many inscriptions in the crevices of this mountain. However, on
account of fear of the tribesmen, who would dare search for them? After
al-Zubayrī freed us—which was on the very same day that he had impris-
52 oned us—I hired a Jew who was more courageous than his coreligionists
to lead me to the ancient ruin that they call old Ṣanʿāʾ. There I found the
name *Sana*ʿī, written in Himyaritic script, as well as a few inscriptions. We
also searched the slopes of the aforementioned mountain near where the
tribesmen dwell.

⟬ CHAPTER 5 ⟭
CLIENTS AND PATRONS

RETURNING TO SHIRĀʿ
TO SEARCH FOR INSCRIPTIONS

The next day, we set out for the Land of Nihm. As an act of charity, our brethren in Shirāʿ gathered some barley for us. Because they were so poor, they gathered [only] 8 *uqqah*s, the equivalent of half a *qadaḥ*.[1] We used part of this to pay the wages of the Jew who had brought the wagon for my teacher. This man accompanied us to al-Madīd, where we gave him the rest of the barley. Once there, he brought us to one of their four synagogues.

Once my teacher Joseph had overcome his fear of the Arḥabī tribesmen, it occurred to him that I should return to Shirāʿ in the hope of finding further inscriptions. The next day, I headed back to Shirāʿ alone, intentionally returning by a different route. I was so busy gathering inscriptions at the aforementioned mountain next to Nihm that the sun set while I was still out in the field. I wandered back to Shirāʿ in the darkness of night, arriving when everyone was asleep. I knocked on the door of one of the Jews whom I knew. In great fear, he said, "Who is this who bangs on my door in the middle of the night, even though I am safe in the protection of God and in the protection of my tribal patron?" 53

"Don't fear, open up," I replied.

"I don't open the door for anyone at night," he said. "Anyone who has a demand or claim against me can come in the morning to bring the matter before my tribal patrons."

"I take refuge in God from the accursed Satan," I replied. "Why do you need to be worried and concerned when I am your friend Ḥayyim Ḥabshūsh, the companion of the sage. It's not right that I should hear such words from you, I who request your shelter and ask for your help on this one night because of our recent friendship."

When he realized that it was me, he hurried with fear and trembling, but also with shame, to get up from his bed. He opened the door and let me in, saying, "What brings you here again after we had happily delivered you safe and sound? Don't you know that today the tribesmen searched for you, questioning and threatening us because of you? They claimed that, after you climbed the mountain, you set it alight with your witchcraft with the result that, last night, fire flowed from every side of it.[2] This is what the tribesmen swore to today after you left us. And, if we'd known this about you, we would not have saved you from their malice. So return the way you came, and don't let anyone see you. Be very careful not to let anyone notice that you came to my house, lest they make trouble for me on your account."

I felt even more afraid than before and said to myself, "Even spending the 54
night in the field with scorpions as my bed and snakes as my pillow would be easier than this, and I'd even be able to protect myself from harm. In these circumstances, however, the only escape is by fleeing in the night."

"My brother," I replied, "your news has driven all thought out of my mind. My wits are confounded, and my nerves are in shock. Nevertheless, I do still want to stay with you for an hour or two until I can gather myself and find a way out of my predicament."

In great fear and with much reproach, he gave me a place to stay. This place, which lay beneath his house, was more revolting than a prison for those condemned to eternal confinement. Leaving me there, he went to sleep in his room with his children. However, after a short time, he returned, intent on turning me out of his house. Sensing his wish, I said, "May you be well rewarded for what you have done this night. I am ready to go, but please accompany me to the edge of the village." However, he was too afraid to go out, so I left alone and he immediately went inside, closing the door behind him.

Placing my trust in God, I returned to my teacher in the land of Nihm. After giving him the inscriptions, I told him what had happened. However, because he was a man of courage, he was not one of those people who feel for and validate others. On the contrary, he was one of those who are dismissive and unresponsive toward them.

THE JEWS OF THE TOWN OF AL-MADĪD IN THE LAND OF NIHM

55 When staying among our brethren in al-Madīd, we did not feel the great fear of their tribesmen that we had felt of the tribesmen of Arḥab. This is because the character of the Nihmī tribesman is not like that of the Arḥabī tribesman. For this reason, the Nihmī Jews are a little bolder and more courageous than other Jews, even to the extent that their voices are louder and their houses are higher. But the [Nihmī] tribesmen do not gripe that "the houses of the Jews are higher than those of the Muslims."[3] This is because there is peace between them and the Jews.[4] It is possible that this is due to their fear that the Jews might seek refuge from them among other tribes, a matter that would cause trouble and strife, as is the way of the tribes.

Tribal mores stipulate, "The client is in the image of his patron." This means that the respect that a client (whether Jew or Gentile) receives in the tribal markets and villages is a measure of the power, strength, and integrity of the tribesman who has taken him into his protection. Also, a weak person or someone who has made an unsuccessful demand or claim against tribesmen arising, for example, from a case of murder, debt, or another such offense, must take a cow or sheep and slaughter it at the village gate or in the market of the tribesmen from whom he seeks help and protection. These tribesmen will then handle the matter according to what the Ṭāghūt (tribal law) requires.[5] The Ṭāghūt, and not the Islamic Sharīʿah, is the law of the tribes. God willing, I will explain this law later in this work.[6]

A SCANDAL IN AL-MADĪD

We now return to our subject. It happened that there was a wedding in the 56
house next to the synagogue in which we were staying.[7] Through a hole in the wall shared with the groom's house, snatches of their revelry reached us. On the day that the bride was introduced to the groom, through the hole I heard the raised voice of a woman. I knew the voice but could not put a face to it and was perplexed. I recognized her hollering but did not know who she was. Was it possible, by God, that I had a friend in this foreign place? I had also seen another girl in the street dressed in Ṣanʿānī clothes, but I did not recognize her because she bashfully hid her face, and I never saw her again, nor did I again hear that voice. Who were they, and where did they come from? I was too embarrassed to ask.

When I returned to al-Madīd five months later, I was told who they were. They were from Ṣanʿāʾ, where it had become known that, to make a living, they were offering themselves to any Arabs who wanted them. This continued until the elders of Ṣanʿāʾ drove them out of the city. Concealing their disgrace, they came to al-Madīd. There, the people were deceived by them and married them according to law and custom. While my teacher and I were visiting al-Madīd, one of them was getting married in the house next to the synagogue in which we were staying. The people of that house served
us *harīsh* porridge[8] and ghee, as is the custom among the tribes. Further, even 57
though we had never met them before, they invited us to the feast. Then, [on my second visit] they told me what it was that had first alerted them to what was going on between the Ṣanʿānī women and their lovers. It occurred on the Day of the Morning, which is the day on which the bride enters the house of the groom.[9] On that day, the bride secluded herself with one of the young men, and, when the people found them, he was sporting with her.

"Why are you naked with this young man?" they asked her.

She said that she had a pain in her bowels and that, for medical reasons, she had withdrawn with the man for a massage so that she would not meet her groom with such pains. That was her excuse. As for her sister, after we left, the *marī** took her for a wife—he was also one of those who were deceived. The women continued in their previous ways until they so angered the locals, both Jews and Gentiles, that they sought to kill them. Their lovers, after having tried in vain to protect them, helped them to flee. Under cover of night, they stuffed the women into sacks, lashed them to the backs of camels, and traveled away with them as though they were merchandise. That is what became of the decency of these village people, and I, after this story, will tell no more of such vulgar events.

NIHMĪ TRIBAL LAW AND THE JEWS: A WAR IS DECLARED TO RECTIFY AN INJUSTICE AGAINST A JEW

Dear reader, if you wish to be taught about the character of the Nihmī
58 tribesmen, their concern for their laws, and how they strive to guarantee the rights of their protected peoples to the full extent of the Ṭāghūt, I would have to stray from the purpose of this work. Nonetheless, pay attention and consider the following story.

A Jew from al-Madīd, who was a protégé of Ibn Miʿṣār, set out from Ṣanʿāʾ with his merchandise. On his way, he was accosted by a band of robbers. "Don't rob me," the Jew told them, "for Ibn Miʿṣār is my patron, and he will not allow you to rob and humiliate me."

But they did not listen to him and continued to beat him, taking his donkey and everything he had. He went to al-Madīd, and the people gathered around at his cry: "I have been robbed and beaten. My patron has beaten and humiliated me."

He did this until his patron arrived with some bystanders and inquired, "What happened to you, oh Jew?"

* *Marī*, meaning "my master," was a title used by scholars and teachers. Sometimes, as in this instance, Ḥabshūsh uses it as the equivalent of "rabbi," a title that was not used in nineteenth-century Yemen; sometimes he uses it merely as a term of respect. On account of this ambiguity, I have left the term untranslated. J. Tobi, *Yalkut Teman: Leksikon* (Tel Aviv: ʿAmutat eʿeleh be-Tamar, 2000), s.v., *marī*; and Yehuda Nini, *The Jews of Yemen, 1800–1914* (New York: Harwood Academic, 1991), 106–7.

"Oh my patron," he said, "al-Jarādī attacked, robbed, and beat me. I put my faith in God's protection and in yours."

"Do not fear," the tribal chief replied. "I will give you everything that was taken from you."

That very day, he gathered 500 men from his tribe and prepared to make a night raid on al-Jarādī, who had attacked his Jewish client. During the assault on al-Jarādī's fortress, two of Ibn Miʿṣār's men were killed. After the assault, al-Jarādī fled with his men to the land of Khawlān and sought the protection of the Banū Jabr tribe. Ibn Miʿṣār entered the fortress, retrieved the Jew's property, and then pillaged and destroyed it. He then returned to 59
al-Madīd and gave the Jew his property.

As for al-Jarādī, he kept raiding Nihm from the land of the Banū Jabr and caused them much trouble. Ibn Miʿṣār therefore took a cow and a few of his men and traveled to the land of the Banū Jabr. When they reached the grave of Jabr ibn ʿAlwān, the forefather of the tribe, they slaughtered the cow at his grave. The chiefs of the Banū Jabr approached and said to him, "You are safe, you are safe. Whatever you request, you are the chief."

"My request is for al-Jarādī, who has committed a crime against us," he said. "Let us place our rifles in your hands, as is the custom, and let us be judged by you regarding what he did to the Jew who is our client. If he is the guilty party, take from him what he owes us, or expel him to his land and we will pursue our claim on our own."

When the Banū Jabr chiefs learned that al-Jarādī, whom they had been protecting, was the guilty party, they forced him to return to his land so that the two parties could achieve justice among themselves. After his return, they remained at war and the raids continued until Ibn Miʿṣār had avenged the deaths of all his men and had killed al-Jarādī and his brother.

This whole affair was carried out for the sake of the Jew, Sālim Mask al-Aqḍaʿ. Later, I will explain why this Jew fled from Ṣanʿāʾ and moved to al-Madīd. For indeed, this story is an alarming one.[10]

CHANGES IN JEWISH-TRIBAL RELATIONS AS A RESULT OF OTTOMAN RULE

From the time the banner of the sublime Ottoman government was unfurled
60 and the imperial armies spread throughout Yemen, the people put aside their disputes and their customs of tribal protection. Our brethren [in Nihm], with the aid of the Ottoman Empire and their tribal patrons, lived in greater safety and peace than others, with the result that, because of their ambition and tenacity, they managed to acquire jewelry and fine clothes. But the tribes came to envy them because of this. In October 1893,[11] their patron, Chief Ibn Miʿṣār, sought mastery over them, calling upon them to pay him the *jizyah*,* which they used to pay to him before the Ottoman Empire annexed Yemen. In addition, they were not excused from paying the *jizyah* owed for the past twenty-two years. If they did not pay this, they had to pay him and his companions the bloodwite for the four men who were killed on their account in his time and in the time of his father and grandfather. At that time, the bloodwite was paid only by Ibn Miʿṣār and the tribes, and the Jews, according to tribal law, were not obligated to pay it. For that reason, Ibn Miʿṣār claimed their *jizyah*, which amounted to 2 Ottoman piasters per person per year, or 1½ liras for all of his clients per year.

There were eighty Jewish men in al-Madīd who were required to pay the *jizyah*. When Ibn Miʿṣār called on them to pay him after they had already paid the *jizyah* to the Ottoman empire,[12] it was difficult for them and they
61 did not pay him anything. He therefore summoned them to judgment before Muḥammad ibn Yaḥyā Ḥamīd al-Dīn,[13] whom the people of Ṣaʿdah had appointed as imām. Ibn Miʿṣār did so because he knew that this *sayyid* would compel them to pay the Islamic *jizyah* and would not take into account their payment of it to the Ottomans.

The Jews were not able to seek protection against this summons from another tribesman, who would have been termed "a Patron of Sin." This term refers to a situation in which a patron sins against his client, and then a second patron (the Patron of Sin) judges the matter one way or the other. Most of the time, this leads to a bloodbath in addition to the original monetary damages imposed. This, however, is the law of the Yemeni tribes.

* According to Islamic law, Jews are required to pay the *jizyah* (poll tax) in exchange for religious toleration.

As for the Jews of al-Madīd, they were advised to take a head of cattle and slaughter it at Ibn Miʿṣār's gate to soften his heart and make him rescind his claim against them. However, they had already heard his answer to Chief Ibn Abū Luḥūm, the sheikh of Milḥ, who had petitioned him on their behalf: "How can I relinquish the *jizyah* on their account when they are richer than our tribesmen? Don't you see that all a tribesman has is a revolver worth 1 riyal and a dagger worth a quarter of a riyal? The Jewish woman, on the other hand, wears silver jewelry worth 50 riyals."

This answer shows Ibn Miʿṣār's great compassion for his tribesmen, for their poverty had increased since they had ceased their raids out of fear of the Ottoman Empire.

As a result of their predicament, some of the Jews said, "Let us go to
Ṣanʿāʾ and bring our complaint before the Ottoman Empire to which we 62
paid our *jizyah*. They will give judgment against Ibn Miʿṣār and persuade him to cease troubling us." Others said, "If we complain about him to the Turkish government, we will bring upon ourselves many misfortunes. Ibn Miʿṣār will set his men against us, attacking us from all sides, and we do not have the power to guard ourselves against them. Only God can guide them toward justice so that they do not wrong us."

In the end, the Jews placed the matter in the hands of Ibn Miʿṣār's paternal cousin, who said to them, "Do not fear! Go on your way and I will speak with him."

So, he visited his cousin and said, "Look favorably upon what I request of you if you are truly a brother and a friend to me."

"I welcome you and your visit," Ibn Miʿṣār replied. "And, by God, I look favorably upon anything you request, except for that concerning the Jews."

"Far be it from you to say such a thing, for I came here only for the sake of this matter," his cousin answered. "You know that the Jews have always been our clients, and we need them for everything. How can we afflict them while both we and they are now under the Ottoman yoke? If they were to flee from us, we would be a laughingstock before all the tribes, and their flight would cause us great loss."

"It's all right, my cousin. Your words are true," Ibn Miʿṣār said, "but I have already sworn an oath regarding them. How can I go back on my words when they are wealthier than our tribesmen?"

63 "If they are richer," replied his cousin, "that is to our advantage and to the glory of our tribe. Don't you know that Chief Nājī ibn Abū Luḥūm used to tell the Jews whom he protected that they should not come to his house for a claim or for anything else without first putting kohl on their eyes, anointing themselves with oil, decorating their heads with flowers, and wearing Sabbath finery? He told them not to come before him looking beleaguered, lest it reflect badly on him. If, on the other hand, they were dignified, he too would possess dignity in the eyes of the tribes. But as for you, my brother, since you have already made an oath, we will take 7 riyals from them to absolve you of it."

And that is exactly what happened.

INTERLUDE: A CONVERSATION WITH A 140-YEAR-OLD MAN

We now return to our subject, that is, to the land of Nihm to which we had traveled from Ṣanʿāʾ without finding any Himyarite remains. Because the people had told us that there were great ruins nearby, I set off for one located to the north. However, I found nothing there, save for a broken potsherd. The potsherd looked odd to me, so I took it to my teacher as proof that there were Himyarite remains. He was as amazed as I was at its ancient craftsmanship and kept it.

After that, I asked our brethren about places with inscriptions, and they informed us that they were to be found on the mountain road to the village of Milḥ and in the nearby village of al-Sūdah. They also said that a
64 140-year-old man named Marī Saʿīd al-Bāridah lived there, who had not lost his strength.[14] On my teacher's orders, I went there and found the old man whom they had mentioned teaching children to read. In truth, however, he was lacking in learning. Despite his age, most of his beard was black and he still had his teeth. He had not lost his sight, but his eyes were weak and slow in moving, and he was hard of hearing. He was still fat—his body had not yet become emaciated—and his height was almost that of King Saul. After I had greeted him as they do in eastern Yemen, that is, with long-winded greeting and praise, I asked him to tell me about the wondrous happenings and great events of his time.

"I don't have any such stories," he said. "What can you mean by 'wondrous happenings and great events'?"

"For example," I replied, "tell me what you know about the imāms who ruled during your youth and of the jihad of your Nihmī tribal patrons, either on behalf of the imāms or against them, so that I can tell your age from that. Also, tell me of your experiences of wars and strife, of years of hardship and prosperity, so that I may profit from your instruction."

"Yes," the old man began, "I knew Chief So-and-So, the ancestor of
the Such-and-Such tribe, who today are in their fifth generation. He had a
broad face, a short neck, fat legs, and slender fingers. Now Chief Taʿzān was
jealous of him and contested his right to the chiefdom, so, after his death,
Chief Taʿzān forced the latter's sons from the chiefdom. In those days, there 65
was war between the tribes, which led to the killing of Chief Taʿzān. Chief
What's-His-Name took his place and after him came Chief Taʿzūz. But
today, they are all gone. There are no So-and-So's and What's-His-Names,
no Taʿzān and no Taʿzūz, only people whom I don't know and whose fathers
I don't know. As for your talk of years of hardship and years of prosperity,
poverty has clung to me from my youth until this very day and, in times of
famine, my tribal patrons, may God preserve them, fed me and my family."

"My dear sir," I said to him, "I have no need of such stories. Since you have neither knowledge of the dynasty of Ṣanʿāʾ nor of world affairs, tell me about the way of life of the Jews among your tribal patrons, of what befell them in bygone ages, of what your forebears told you, of what you read in their books, or of what you yourself have experienced."

"Yes," he replied, "I'll tell you what happened to me when I took a wife for my son ʿAyḍah from the land of Khawlān."

"Don't tell me about ʿAyḍah or about his wife Shūdhiyyah," I interrupted him, "but tell me about your laws of marriage so that I can learn your customs."

THE MARRIAGE CUSTOMS OF THE JEWS OF NIHM

"Know," the old man said, "that the Jews of the countryside have different laws and customs from those who live in towns. When they seek the hand of a young woman in marriage, they bring a sheep for the meal on the night of the betrothal. After having dined, they commence discussion of the marriage and establish conditions, each according to the customs of his village, regarding the sum of money and the clothing that the groom must provide

for the girl. Most people in this region stipulate that three items of clothing
66 must be given to the bride, namely, leggings, a robe, and a head scarf, and a shawl for the bride's mother. They also agree on the number of men who will accompany the bridegroom on the day on which the marriage contract is concluded. If there are ten men accompanying the groom, twenty men must accompany the bride, that is, the number of men accompanying the bride must be double those of the groom. When these men arrive with the groom, the people at the house in which the ceremony is held greet and welcome them, giving them ghee or oil. The man of the house anoints the legs of the guests from above the knee to the sole of the foot, one by one, until he finishes all of them. Then he gives them a kohl container so that they can make up their eyes with Isfahani kohl.

"When they are finished with this, he gives them coffee and hookahs. He then brings them food—either porridge and ghee or bread and ghee—all in great quantity. If one of these things was omitted or forgotten, there is a claim against him and they bring him to judgment before the sheikh, who requires that the guilty party give satisfaction to the injured party by slaughtering a bull or sheep in his honor.[15] This is the case whatever the error, including errors committed in the process of anointing, the application of kohl, the portion of meat, or even the coffee, if it is made with too few coffee grinds. In each case, the matter is brought for judgment, and the guilty party must make restitution for each error according to its seriousness, the restitution being set at one, two, three, or four sheep. If someone offends his companion with words—by insulting him or such like—each word has a cost, set at one or two bulls or a sheep. Instead of one bull, two sheep can
67 be substituted. If he threatened or raised a hand against his companion, for example, if he struck him, the cost of the blow is a bull and 1 riyal, but if he struck him two or more times, the injured party receives only one extra sheep. If they exchanged blows, the number of blows is assessed and the one who inflicted more blows pays for the excess. If they are equal, insult for insult, blow for blow, the two of them must pay restitution to the place, that is, to the hosts, the amount being dependent on the seriousness of the offense. When the guests are seated, each is seated in a specific place, which must not be changed so long as he is a guest. If someone enters and sits in his place, this is an error and he must pay an indemnity according to the law. While

they are seated, the guests have priority in leading songs and hymns, taking turns one after another, and no one has the right to interrupt the turn of his companion to remind him of the tune, or anything else. If he does interrupt him, he must make restitution with a bull or a sheep.

"After the engagement ceremony, they dine, beat drums, and dance. Then they take the trousseau and select four witnesses to assess its value: two to represent the bride's family and two to represent the groom's. The kohl container, even if it is made of a reed flute, is valued at an eighth of a riyal; the kohl applicator, even if it is made from wood, is valued at an eighth of a riyal; the comb, which is used for the bride's hair, is valued at an eighth of a riyal; and everything else is valued at double its value. Objects made of either
real or fake silver are valued at 1 riyal per ounce. The beads on her neck, 68
whatever they are worth, are calculated at 1 riyal per hundred. The earrings, even if they are iron chains, are valued at a high price, that is, a quarter or half a riyal. They add the total, from which they subtract 1½ riyals, a sum called 'the groom's present,' which is used for his clothing. This subtraction of 1½ riyals from the total is the tradition in all areas of Yemen. Once this is done, they draw up a document setting out the groom's obligation to the bride with respect to all that she has brought into his house.

"After all this, they bring the bride to the groom, both of their heads adorned with flowers. When all the family of the bride and groom arrive, they are warmly welcomed, and a sheep or bull is slaughtered at the entrance of the house. This is the proper manner of welcoming. Then they enter with drums or tambourines and song, and each takes his place. They are again anointed and make up their eyes with kohl, for it is the tradition that when a guest arrives at the house of his host, one of the women of the house comes and anoints him, rubbing oil from above his knee to the sole of his foot. Then, according to tradition, coffee, hookahs, porridge or bread and oil are served. For the second course, they eat pancakes and soup or porridge and soup. At the end of the meal, a person gets up and divides the meat among everyone, placing a piece beside each person's hand. This is called 'the portion,' and if one person's portion is too small or if the server forgets one of the guests, this is an error. After the meal, the server is called to judgment and must give satisfaction to the one whom he forgot in the amount of half
a sheep or a whole sheep. At night, while they beat drums and sing, all the 69

guests give the groom gifts of money, wheat, or whatever else they wish to give. This is obligatory for anyone who comes to celebrate, even if he is a tribesman. This is the way of the Jews who live among the tribes."

Dear reader, this is the way matters are to this very day. What more can I add regarding the principle of error, the witnesses, the rulings according to tribal law, and the justice of the Ṭāghūt?

THE VILLAGE OF DARB AL-ḤANSHĀT

After all this, I returned to asking the old man my original question: "What do you know about the stories of the ancients and the events recorded in their books?"

"I don't know anything," he responded, "but my grandfather used to tell me that his family once lived in the village of Darb al-Ḥanshāt.[16] They lived a peaceful life and were very rich because they had many fields, which they used to sow and cultivate, as is witnessed by the old deeds to their fields that have now been transferred to the tribesmen. In addition to their work in the fields, they manufactured farm instruments from iron and jewelry from silver and copper, and they worked alongside their tribal patrons in leatherwork and woodwork. Mostly, however, they made pottery, the charred remains of which you can find to this very day around the ruins of Darb al-Ḥanshāt, piled high as a mountain. Only a few of them were involved in buying and selling. Their renown is indicated by the fact that most of their gravestones bear inscriptions."*

"What caused their village to be destroyed?" I asked.

"It is said," he replied, "that when they took the Jews from the various
70 regions of Yemen and drove them to Mawzaʿ in the Tihāmah, most of them died, either on the way or in the Tihāmah itself. Those who managed to return from the Tihāmah could no longer live in their villages. Instead, the tribesmen gave, sold, or rented land to them so that they could set up shacks."

Indeed, I had grown up hearing such reports, and I was already familiar with some corroborating evidence of the expulsion and exile of the Jews in 1679.[17] It was at that time that the village of Darb al-Ḥanshāt was de-

* Yemeni Jews did not usually inscribe their gravestones. See Joseph Halévy, "Voyage au Nedjran," *Bulletin de la Société de Géographie de Paris* 6 (1873), 262; and Erich Brauer, *Ethnologie der jemenitischen Juden* (Heidelberg: Carl Winter, 1934), 228–30.

stroyed, remaining so until our own day. I then asked him about the location of the village, and he said, "It is near us. Let me send one of the boys to guide you to it."

So I visited the ruined village and found its cemetery on the mountainside. As he had told me, there were indeed many inscribed Jewish tombstones. But as for Himyarite inscriptions, I found none. When I returned to my teacher in al-Madīd, I told him what I had seen. My story surprised and amazed him.

"Go back immediately and transcribe the inscriptions for me in the exact form of script in which they appear on the tombstones," he said. "Do not change it according to your own style of script. Go now so that you will be back by evening."[18]

When I saw how enthusiastic he was, my fatigue left me and I agreed to go back without any objection. I ran as fast as I could but, because I had left my teacher only after the afternoon prayer, it was already close to sunset when I reached the ruin. I transcribed what I could and then returned to the Frenchman in the darkness of night and gave him the transcriptions. I thought that he might give me some recompense in addition to what had 71
been arranged for me to receive upon my return to the land of Arḥab. I don't know why he didn't put me down for some recompense or reward—perhaps because he lacked ink or paper. Other than these Hebrew inscriptions, we found nothing else in al-Madīd.

Our brethren, may their memory be inscribed for a blessing, provided us with food in sufficient measure, neither too much nor too little, for their lot was easier than that of the Jews of Shirāʿ, because of the help of the tribes. In contrast, the Jews of Shirāʿ had no work except burning and crushing limestone, which they, their wives, and children did, and producing leatherwork for the tribesmen. For this reason, poverty was clearly visible among them and among our brethren in the land of Arḥab in general. Because of their great poverty, their tribal patrons took pity on them and, during this time, paid their *jizyah* to the Ottoman Empire out of their own pockets.

THE OCCUPATIONS OF THE JEWS OF AL-MADĪD

As for our brethren in al-Madīd, some of them are laborers, some are carpenters, blacksmiths, silversmiths, or tailors. Some of them are merchants, some seeking their livelihood by traveling to places that grow coffee; and a small

number work the land. They have a valley in which only the *ḥawṣ* tree grows. The tree is a kind of palm, which they cut, break into pieces, and transport
72 on camels to Ṣanʿā' to be used as brooms. Their women produce wickerwork with a kind of grass that they call *ḥindīd*. It has no leaves, only a thin stem about three paces long. They make wicker covers, mats on which food is served, jewelry chests, and other such utensils as are used by Yemeni people.

FISHING

In the winter the Jews of al-Madīd travel to fish in the Khārid River, which flows from the land of Arḥab and from which the people of the Jawf draw water. These fishermen buy *ḍafar* seeds from Ṣanʿā'.[19] The seeds are brought there from the land of Ānis and are more expensive than wheat. *Ḍafar* is a grain that resembles the indigo grain. They grind it, blend it with a little barley flour, and then mix it in a skin. A swimmer then dives into the water and pours the flour mixture into an eddy. The swimmer's companions wait for the fish to appear at a distance of eleven paces or more from where the *ḍafar* was poured. The moment the fish smell or eat the *ḍafar*, they become intoxicated or stupefied, looking as though they are dead. The water drags them deep into the eddy and, after that, carries them quite a distance away. The companions of the swimmer who poured the *ḍafar* watch the surface of the water carefully for the stupefied fish. When they see them appear, floating on their bellies, they jump into the water and retrieve them. The big fish have
73 a severe reaction to the *ḍafar*. Some are immobilized by it, whereas others flee from the fishermen. They call the male fish *awshāj*, and the weight of a big one is 3 or 4 *uqqah*s. After gutting them, they bring them to Ṣanʿā', traveling all day and all night, lest the fish begin to stink. Before the Turks came, they sold them only to Jews. Sometimes, the Bedouin would fall upon them near the Khārid River and rob them of their fish. There are three rivers that are famous for fish: the Khārid, which flows from the land of Arḥab; the Surdud, which flows from the land of Ḥaymah; and the Nabʿah, which flows from the land of Ḥadā'. But the fish of the Khārid are the best and tastiest in the world, and only the fish of the Khārid are generally brought to Ṣanʿā'.[20]

Because our brethren in the land of al-Madīd had little money, they collected 4 *qadaḥ*s of sorghum, sold them for 4 riyals, and donated the money to us to help with the expenses of our journey.

A DISPUTE ABOUT THE KABBALAH

The Jews of al-Madīd and Milḥ are well-read connoisseurs of books known to them and no one else. Some of them have powers of memory unmatched by other Yemeni Jews, to such an extent that we found some who were able to recite the weekly Torah portion by heart—without a book! This is also the case with their other books, of which they know chapters, sections, or portions by heart—to say nothing of the prayers. They study these books in the villages of their tribal patrons when they are free from work. According to most people, their scholars are more expert in the principles of the law and its particulars[21] than the scholars of Khawlān, Arḥab, and elsewhere. However, 74
if they have a legal problem or difficulty or if there is a conflict between them, they send their questions to Ṣanʿāʾ and abide by the rulings of its scholars.

Among the rigorists of al-Madīd are those who follow the books of the Kabbalah, which are books of secret signs and enigmas. They brought their case against their brethren, the scriptural literalists,[22] to my teacher Joseph for judgment. It concerned whether women should be barred from letting locks of hair hang exposed on their faces, as is the style of tribal women. The rigorists claimed that such adornment is forbidden, because exposing hair is a great sin. Their proof is from the *Holy Zohar*, which they claimed is a book of the ancients and which they attribute to the great elder of Mishnaic times, the revered Shimʿon Bar Yohai, may God be pleased with him. The scriptural literalists responded, "The custom of our fathers is holy law. We will not change anything we have inherited from our ancestors."

There had previously been a great argument regarding this matter, which had been brought for judgment before the chiefs of their tribal patrons. The chiefs, as was their custom with their clients, took both sides to 75
Ṣanʿāʾ so that its Jewish scholars could judge between them. These scholars ruled that, because the matter did not endanger the foundations of religion, those following their ancestors' custom were not forbidden such adornments and those who had sworn off such things for themselves were not permitted such adornments. This prohibition was similar to one imposed by one of the imāms in 1848.[23] Imām al-Nāṣir[24] was an ascetic who prohibited the people, both Jews and Muslims, from singing songs, whether on occasions of celebration or lament. After he was killed, people came before the imām who replaced him to ask what was to become of the prohibition against singing.

His answer was, "There are those for whom singing is forbidden, but one who sings shall sing."

My teacher Joseph was amazed at their argument over this matter and said to them, "I see no prohibition or objection to this form of adornment since the Mishnah says, 'A woman may go about with a Gentile hairstyle.'"*

His answer was hard on the rigorists, and they disputed it. This dispute spread among our brethren throughout eastern Yemen. There were those who forbade this adornment, and there were those who continued their earlier customs. There were those who hid their hair but replaced it with strips of sheep's leather to resemble it or who allowed two tufts to be exposed along the sides of their faces so that they would not appear ugly. This matter was especially important to those women who did not have any jewelry and had to make do with the adornment of locks of hair. This then is a partial description
76 of the current situation of the Jews of Yemen. I will further expand on it later.

QALT AL-YAHŪD AND A DIRGE

We have already mentioned that we did not find anything that we were searching for in al-Madīd. However, our hearts were satisfied with what we had found in the land of Arḥab and with what they had told us about the lands that lay to the east. For that reason, we set off eastward, and our Jewish brethren took it upon themselves to accompany us to Milḥ by way of the highlands of Shayḥān, which is a mountainous, uneven route. In the highlands of Shayḥān we found what we found: a page worth of inscriptions in Arabic and a few in Hebrew.[25] In contrast, in Qalt al-Yahūd, we found nothing.[26] *Qalt* in Arabic means a detested, low, and empty place that lies between mountains. While it was still dark, we emerged from there through the ravine of Shayḥān, and by the time we arrived at the village of Milḥ, the sun was high in the sky. But, as time passed, its mountains became red, its hills darkened, and a fog covered it, such that it seemed to me that I was in one of the regions of hell.[27]

I have seen the abode of the wretched:

* Mishnah, *Shabbat* 6:5. The Hebrew term *pe'ah nokhrit* is usually understood to refer to artificial locks of hair. However, the literal meaning of the phrase is "foreign (or Gentile) locks." Halévy buttresses the case of those who wish to continue the custom of sporting a Gentile hairstyle by interpreting this Mishnaic phrase literally rather than idiomatically.

hills, plateaus, and barren land.
They snatch at sustenance fleetingly,
famine clings to the earth.
When the rains cease,
all are mired in poverty.
The tribes flee their land,
bringing their tents and beasts to wander on 77
to the western lands of Yemen,
there to be branded "nomads."
When rain falls in abundance,
they return and are called "men of affluence."
They plow and pasture like the rich men of the villages,
but soon they are poor again.
Their lives pass in hardship
and constant search for sustenance.
Indeed, they live far from a source of water.
The vapors cannot reach them,
and the land becomes empty and desolate.
Nearby is the wadi of Sheba, which occupies the heights.
The descendants of Ḥām established themselves there with vigor.
The children of Qaḥṭān (Yoktan)[28] erected a fortress.
Inside it they built cities and castles,
and the tribes there were victorious.
They dammed up the streams and gorges,
reinforcing the barriers with boulders
and extracting metals from the mountainsides.
Cattle was their currency, and also silver from the cities.
Their cities were like gardens with rivers,
their abundance like trees scattering their fruit,
but the splendor of those days ended.
When the Persians came, they extinguished its light.
In this they were preceded by Abraha the Najāshī,[29]
who ravaged, harassed, and slaughtered the people like animals.
Abraha the Najāshī was the very Abyssinian
who built an edifice resembling the Temple in Ṣanʿāʾ.

78 He adorned it with colored stones,
diamonds, rubies, and emeralds,
but the Sanḥānī (Kinānī) filled it with filth thereafter.
Soon the situation of the church changed.
No longer can one find a civilized man
in the fortress of Kutb, fortress of Nihm.
May God send his bounty to this land,
which saddens those who pass by
and makes them burn with grief,
for He is the Merciful and Compassionate One
who takes pity on those who now dwell in this land.
Amen.

This is a sketch of the land of Nihm and its surroundings as I saw it after leaving Qalt al-Yahūd.

HOSPITALITY IN MILḤ

When [our Jewish brethren from al-Madīd] brought us to Milḥ, they led us through a courtyard to the lowest level of the Jewish teacher's house. After they closed the door, we felt around in a darkness as thick as night until we came to the kitchen. There, although it was the middle of the day, we could see only by the light of the fire on which lunch was cooking. The fire's smoke agitated my nostrils and made my eyes water.

"How can people live in a place like this?" I said to myself. "And what did I do to deserve such punishment? But, be patient my soul, for *God loves the patient.*"[30]

As I was wiping the sweat, tears, and whatnot from my face, the *parnas* and master of the house, Yaḥyā ibn Saʿīd the teacher, arrived. The moment this sage saw my teacher, he treated us with great honor, saluting and
79 embracing us, as is the custom in eastern Yemen. He then told his wife to open the hatch in the kitchen ceiling so as to reduce the smoke, as we desired. While we were still exchanging greetings, he climbed the ladder that passed through the hatch and invited us to follow him. Fearing the smoke and the heat of the sun, I did not want to sit on the kitchen roof. A stranger, however, cannot contradict the words of one who welcomes him, so we fol-

lowed him up. Welcoming us to his rooftop room, he took down a carpet
from a peg and spread it out for us. He brought a hookah and coffee and
we relaxed. He then hurried to slaughter a sheep for our refreshment. We
then told him of our quest and he told us about the places that he knew of.
The next day, after provisioning us with ghee and *harīsh* porridge, he hired
a Jew to accompany me to some of the places he had mentioned. I found a
place in the Barrān valley in which there were a few inscriptions on a mountainside written in red paint—the tribesmen baselessly claim it to be virgin's
blood. In Barrān, I also saw an underground place in which people dwelled
that was built from great Himyarite stones that were sculpted like soap.[31] I
then went to nearby Musawwarah and arrived at a very great Arab ruin. On
my return, I saw some lines written on a piece of plaster on a ruined dam
between the mountains. I returned to my teacher Joseph and informed him 80
of what I had seen. He told me that the underground place that I had seen
was an ancient graveyard.

THE INSCRIPTIONS OF MILḤ

The traveler said: Because of the passing of time, I no longer remember
everything that I obtained in Milḥ except for what I collected when climbing
the mountain, by way of the ruin of Shayḥān, to the Fortress of Kutb. The
latter was a high fortress in Nihm that is now a ruin with no inhabitants. Our
brethren said that the road was strewn with stones upon which there were
both Hebrew and "Persian"[32] inscriptions. I found some of them, but they
were merely stones cut for building purposes. This is evidence of the great
number of people who traveled through and built there. The place lies between two villages, both called Ṣirwāḥ: the Ṣirwāḥ of the Banū Jabr tribe and
the Ṣirwāḥ of the land of Arḥab. On the side of the fortress facing al-Madīd,
I came upon a picture of a man together with an inscription. The man was
laden with weapons: a bow on his shoulder and a long dagger attached to
his waist, as is the custom of the Arabs. The same style of dress can be seen
among the tribal Bedouin of Yām. I copied this image, at great risk to myself,
for it was on the peak of the mountain overlooking a terrifying precipice. It
was so high up that I was almost unable to see the people in the valley below,
who looked like flies. Suspended between the earth and sky, I moved like a
snake, my hands gripping the ledges of the rock and my feet digging into the 81

cavities of the mountain—all this to make a mental note of the image of the inscription so that I could transcribe it in ink when I got back. I continued like that until, with great fatigue, I completed the task. Would that my teacher had taught me the Himyaritic script, for I could then have read and transcribed it without all these tribulations. Instead, he had promised me before leaving Ṣanʿāʾ that he would teach me only after our return and after we had finished our work. I was therefore filled with excitement and applied myself enthusiastically to the task despite the difficult circumstances—for the sake of science and for the sake of the wages.

At the end of the day, I returned to my teacher, gave him the transcriptions, and informed him of what I had found. He, as was his custom, noted everything down on slips of paper, not in a notebook.[33] We found no more inscriptions in that place.

My teacher questioned the Jews on their knowledge of the mountains, valleys, rivers, and ruins and also about the villages and their inhabitants, to gain knowledge of their particulars. And they, as was their way, added a valley here and left out a mountain there. They are not to be faulted for this, for they knew no geography until they were informed and enlightened by his words. According to them, there was treasure in all these places, and especially in the ruins, and they thought that he was only making inquiries on account of it.

The common folk believe that the *jinn* sometimes bring out their buried treasure to dry in the sun, to barter with, or for some other reason that only
82 they know. Because the *jinn* prize this treasure so greatly, it is rare for someone to find even a handful of it, and never more than that. These are the words of those who want to become rich. The word *jinn* in the language of Yemen is possibly taken from the word *jīnā* (ugliness).[34] This is because the people imagine these creatures to be ugly, and so they call them *jinn*.

TRIBAL HIERARCHIES

My teacher said that he wanted to go out of the house to see how the people lived. So we went out and met a Qarawī[35] man who spoke with such friendliness that my teacher agreed to write a couple of words in Arabic letters for him. The Qarawī was greatly amazed.

"How is it that a Jerusalemite Jew can write the script of Islam?" he said, and he praised him greatly.

After this, word went around that this was not a Jerusalemite but an angel from heaven. Because his physique and skin color were different from theirs, they said, "This is an angel!" This Qarawī was one of the people called the Qarār. The name is perhaps derived from the word *maqrawī* (a peddler who frequents villages). They are a well-known tribe in eastern Yemen who do not have a lineage like the rest of the tribes. The Jews call them Ham, meaning that they are tribes descended from Ham, the son of Noah. Even though they are Muslims, they are looked down on by their tribal patrons, who do not intermarry with them, attend their meetings, or enter into their wars. Like the Jews, their permission to dwell in the land is dependent on their
becoming the clients of a tribe. They are treated like slaves, and the tribes 83
honor the Jews more than them. The Qarār stand in contrast to the people called the Hujar.[36] The latter have a distinguished and honored status in the eyes of the tribes, who use them as judges for arbitration and also intermarry with them. They have the right to enter tribal territory, dwell there, and acquire it. Moreover, they do not have to participate in tribal affairs if they do not wish to, whether for war, raids, or the payment of tribal indemnities.[37] It is always forbidden to injure them, and, if someone sins against them, whether by theft, murder, or the like, all of the tribes come to take their part, just as a patron would take the part of his client.

A TRIBAL CONFLICT BETWEEN ḤAḌŪR AND NIHM

The following story illustrates what I have said about these times. It happened that a Nihmī tribesman and his wife, who was herself from a Hujar family, went to dwell in the land of Ḥaḍūr, which lies a half-day's journey west of Ṣanʿāʾ. The man was killed, and no one knew who killed him. The woman returned to her land, and a rumor spread that she had been unfaithful to her Nihmī husband and had helped a Ḥaḍūrī man to kill him. When the news reached the Nihmī tribes, they gathered together at the Sunday market to decide how they would deal with the matter of their dead comrade. The
tribesmen formed a circle, as was their custom, with their leaders in the cen- 84
ter. One of their chiefs began, saying, "Hear ye, the good comes from God."

"The good!" they responded.

He then recited words of admonition and poetry to rouse their spirits from their torpor and their hearts from their languor. After this, he said, "Know, oh tribesmen of Nihm, that men who have no lineage, no renown, and no capacity for anything have derided, scorned, and behaved haughtily toward our tribe. But, thank God, we are not ones to be derided or scorned, for we have the capacity, with the help of God, to uproot mountains and more. Not satisfied with all that they have already done, the people of Ḥaḍūr brazenly disgraced us by killing one of our own. We have been disgraced without cause. There was never an indictment or claim made either against the slain man or against us. Oh tribesmen, know also that in these times all women, except my mother and sister, are debauched, all guns are broken except my gun, and I do not know what is true or false."

[In making this last statement,] the chief was referring to the claim of those who suspected the wife of the slain man. After he had finished his speech, another chief, who was a member of the woman's family, answered, "May God exalt you and your kin. Your words are correct, but let us get the slain man's wife and ascertain the truth from her. If she was the cause of his death, let us kill her and take the reparations from her Hujrī family, as is required by law. We must also collect our damages from the people of Ḥaḍūr who wronged our brother, when he was a poor wretch living in exile among
85 them. If, on the other hand, the wife is proven innocent, then we shall give her what the law says is due to her: the bloodwite for the slaying of her husband.

After hearing his words, the tribesmen all acknowledged that he was correct. They therefore sent two chiefs to summon the woman and persuade her not to flee or refuse to present herself before the people. They tricked her into accompanying them so, when she got to the meeting place, she asked, "What's with all these people here at this big assembly?"

"Do not fear," they replied. "It must be on account of your slain husband."

When they saw that these words had changed her demeanor, they counseled her to escape and seek the protection of the Banū Samḥ tribe, because they are stronger than the other tribes. She listened and did not protest. She then leaped into a gathering of Banū Samḥ tribesmen and, throwing herself at their feet, said, "May God and you tribesmen pity me and, through God's protection and your own, save me from death. I suckled where you suckled. My family is of the Hujar of the tribes of Nihm."[38]

"Be strong, be strong, oh woman, for you are safe," they replied. "Even if you are guilty of murder, debt, or whatever else, you have already been saved."

Immediately, they hurried to stand up, for they had been sitting, and, lusting for a fight, they lit the match cords of their rifles. At that moment, their leader bellowed at the top of his voice, "Listen all of you, for it is the Banū Samḥ tribe that speaks. We came to this meeting on account of another
claim against our neighbor, the Banū Jabr, regarding the war between us; 86
but now we find that we have fallen into the matter of this woman and have abandoned that claim. We are now defending her and sacrificing our own lives and money to fight against anyone who disputes with or makes a claim against her, and we are demanding that the slain man's family provide her with what tradition requires!"

When the leaders saw that a fight was going to break out, one of them, raising his voice, spoke up: "Listen all of you, I wish to inform you of our decision. Our companions have conferred their protection upon this woman, according to the tribal law. This is right, irrespective of whether her cause is right or wrong. Her people live among us, I myself am related to her, and who can violate this law? However, payment of the bloodwite is due from the woman's father [to the relatives of the slain Nihmī man], so that she herself may be indemnified from all claims against her. Moreover, we have a claim to blood vengeance against the Ḥaḍūr tribe, as well as to bloodwite, because they wronged us, killing one of our companions while he was dwelling in their land. This is my solution. What do you think, oh tribesmen?"

"You speak truly!" they answered.

After they had accepted this judgment, he said, "Payment of the bloodwite is to be made after twenty days."

Then, in front of all the men, he put down his revolver and powder horn as a contribution to the woman's father who was obligated to pay the bloodwite to the heirs of the slain man. He also gave his ornamented dagger and his horse and saddle, adding, "I have in my house such-and-such an amount
of wheat, such-and-such measures of ghee, such-and-such cattle, and so 87
many dirhams."

When all the tribesmen had left the ceremony, he brought what he had collected from his friends and the friends of his friends, from his acquaintances and from the acquaintances of his acquaintances, to the Hujrī woman's father's house to help him pay the bloodwite. The collection, which was designated as a portion of the bloodwite, included dirhams, wheat, animals, weapons, and much else. On the appointed day, some of their leaders came to the market for the payment of the bloodwite and witnesses came to testify to the value of the goods. The custom of the tribes when paying the bloodwite is to exaggerate the value of an item worth 1 riyal to 4 or 8 riyals. Even if the item is only a wooden staff not even fit to be a weapon, they count it as worth 1 riyal. For this reason, people have a proverb when they are bargaining: "Appraise it for me, not for a bloodwite."

To this day, [the tribesmen of Nihm] and their enemies, the people of Ḥaḍūr, still attack one another. Even though [the Nihmīs] took the bloodwite from them, the claim of the slain man still remains.[39]

The bloodwite in Yemen amounts to 770 riyals, but, according to tribal law, the bloodwite of a Jew is quadruple that, that is, 3,080 riyals.[40] According to tribal law, injuring a Jew, even so much as a hair of his side-locks, incurs a severe punishment, whereas similar judgments are not issued for Gentiles. The reason for this is probably that, in ancient times, the Jews were
88 the leaders and chiefs of Yemen, and therefore anyone who dared to kill one of them was compelled to pay quadruple the bloodwite. And anyone who injured a Jew, even only slightly, was given a severe punishment because their rank was that of the rulers of Yemen. Even after they became weak with the passing of time, the legal tradition remained. Alternatively, it is possible that these laws were simply agreed on by the Jews and tribesmen of Yemen and remain in effect to this day.[41]

TRIBAL JUSTICE FOR A MURDERED JEW

Now let me tell you about a terrible event that happened in these times. A Jew from Milḥ by the name of Joseph Shukr was a client of the Abū Luḥūm tribe (the most powerful tribe of Nihm). One day this Jew, as was his custom, went to do some leather repair work for his customers, who were Marhabah tribesmen. He was at the door of his friend, a tribesman, when another tribesman, who was out of his mind, came upon him unawares and hit him on the head with a block of wood, knocking his brains out and instantly killing him. The killer claimed that he had killed the Jew because the latter had bewitched him. Immediately, a great cry of "for shame, for shame" was

heard from the tribespeople—women, children, and men—who passed by. The custom, at times of conflict and murder, was for a clamor to be raised to gather the people. This distressing sound spread throughout all the villages and in all the lands of Nihm until, on that day, 2,000 men from the house of 89
Ibn Abū Luḥūm, the Jew's patron, gathered bearing weapons. A like number gathered before Ibn Miʿṣār, the patron of the killer who belonged to the Marhabah tribe. The tribes were on the point of battle when their Hujrī judges came forward to intervene and extinguish the flame of war.

"If everyone submits to arbitration," said Ibn Abū Luḥūm, "we will willingly lay down our guns according to the law. If not, we will not quit the body of our client until the flame of war has been kindled, even if we are all destroyed by it."

They then handed their guns to the judges and agreed on a time to be judged. Ibn Miʿṣār claimed that the murderer was insane and that, because he was insane, he would pay [only] the bloodwite of the Jew [and would make no other payments of compensation].

"I will accept only the judgment of the tribal chiefs of Bakīl, Ḥāshid, Arḥab, and Khawlān," Ibn Abū Luḥūm replied.[42]

Accordingly, a second meeting was arranged to which these chiefs would come. The judgment from this meeting was that Ibn Miʿṣār had to pay the sum of four bloodwites, which equaled 3,080 riyals, and also had to pay compensation for all the expenses, which were very great indeed. If the murderer had not been insane, they would have given a judgment calling for both blood vengeance[43] and bloodwite on behalf of the Jew who had been killed. After Ibn Abū Luḥūm took the quadruple bloodwite, he paid half of it to the murdered man's heirs and kept half for himself. This is what happened in the village of Milḥ, may God safeguard their prosperity and preserve their souls. Amen.

DIGRESSION: A HISTORY OF RECENT POLITICAL TURMOIL IN ṢANʿĀʾ

In Milḥ, I met Shukr al-Maswarī, an old man who was originally from Ṣanʿāʾ. 90
I asked him why he lived in Milḥ, and he told me that he had fled from Ṣanʿāʾ in the days of Imām Muḥammad ibn Yaḥyā.[44] The reason: One of the imām's officials had decreed that he be jailed after his brother, Sulaymān

al-Maswarī, had taken his wife's razor and killed himself with it! That was his answer. And you, dear reader, if you ardently desire to contemplate the events of the past, for that is my intention, I will explain some of the events that happened in Ṣanʿāʾ. If not, leave this market, for you have no need of it, and you may go to any other market you like!

This is the story of Sulaymān al-Maswarī, the aforementioned Jew who killed himself.[45] In 1836,[46] Imām ʿAlī ibn al-Mahdī ʿAbdallāh's own troops plotted to attack him by surprise in his home, tie him up, and loot whatever they could find in the palace and in his treasury.[47] This they achieved because of the imām's naïveté and decadence. The Yemeni government was
91 largely undermined. Ruffians scorned its decrees until it no longer had control over taxes or the treasury. The upshot was that the government became weak and the tribes became mighty. Because of their poverty, the governing family allowed one of their children, the aforementioned Muḥammad ibn Yaḥyā, to be raised by others. When he became an adult, people began to talk about him [as a potential heir to the throne]. [Under such circumstances,] it generally happens that a member of the governing family sees himself in a dream as the imām with all the people as his servants. This young man, however, prophesied in a dream that he would not be able to achieve the imamate without first traveling to Egypt and seeking the help of its government. And so that's what he did. With a little money provided to him by some Egyptian pashas, he returned to Yemen and, while traveling through the town of Raymat Waṣāb, he claimed the imamate. He did this with the help of Sharīf Ḥamūd, the ruler of Tihāmah, and also of Yaḥyā ibn al-Muntaṣir, the sheikh of Raymah. When he finally entered Ṣanʿāʾ, ʿAlī ibn al-Mahdī, who was the imām, acknowledged him as ruler and swore an oath of allegiance, thus causing him to realize his prophetic vision. In this way, he achieved the glory of kings that he had ardently desired and assumed the throne of Yemen in 1845.[48]

Wishing to ameliorate the condition of his subjects and rid them of injustice, this imām ordered a wooden pavilion to be erected in the square beneath his residence so that he could be close to the oppressed. He called it "al-Tūmah." The people rejoiced, saying, "We have never had so kind and good
92 a man as imām." However, there was no longer any revenue from alms, the tithe, or anything else that the people used to pay to the Yemeni government.

This was because the tribes had become mighty and had annexed most of the land that used to provide government revenue. Also, the treasury had become depleted and no longer had the treasure of previous kings—except for the treasure of death, that is to say, the treasure of gunpowder and sulfur. So the imām took this and divided it among the Jews, forcing them to pay him its full price. Because Jews do not engage in battle and had no need of it, they sold it at a great loss. Further, to fund the government, the imām appointed two men from Egypt who were experts in leveling charges against people in order to seize money from them. The name of the one was Muḥāfiḍ and the name of the other was Abū Zayd. Their first order was to go and make claims against the rich of Ṣanʿāʾ, including Muslims and merchants. When the people of Ṣanʿāʾ learned about this, they agreed that they would attack and kill these agents, so they gathered everyone from their houses and the markets and staged an uprising. However there was one man who, loving peace, succeeded in reconciling the parties on condition that the agents neither make claims against nor take anything from them—and so it was. In this way, it happened that there remained no one from whom to expropriate money except the Jews.

A CONSPIRACY AGAINST THE JEWS OF THE ROYAL MINT

The matter began with Ibrāhīm al-ʿImrānī, a Jew who had a copper jar filled
with riyals that he had hidden and buried. It would have remained hidden 93
had not another Jew, who was his servant, stolen it. When the two of them brought their dispute before the government agent, he immediately arrested them, both the plaintiff and the defendant. After imprisoning them, he seized three times as much as was in the jar as dues for the treasury. Afterward, he said to himself, "All Jews have money by the barrel, not by the jar, and this jar is proof of it." From then on, he did not cease to make claims against Jews, taking everything they had.

In previous Yemeni kingdoms, the business of minting the coins of the country was given to Jews, and many people made a living from it, not just the moneychangers. Through this work, they acquired much property and
jewelry . . .[49] 94

At that time, the commissioner appointed to the imām's mint was a Jew by the name of Yūsuf al-Shaykh Levi, an insolent man who sought to

increase his wealth by stealing silver alloy from the mint.[50] His fraud, however, became known to the aforementioned official Muḥāfiḍ and to Imām Muḥammad ibn Yaḥyā. He was imprisoned and shackled, and severe charges were laid against him. Fearing for his life, he visited the disaster upon others. He claimed that he was innocent, having given the right amount of silver to the mint under the terms prescribed, and that it must have been the Jewish
95 silversmiths who had debased it.

In Yemen, we do not have pure silver ore, only silver alloy. At that time and before that, the silver alloys of Yemen had two-thirds of the silver content of 7 dirhams, and a copper content of 3⅓ dirhams. This was the measure of the alloys made by the Jewish silversmiths. The mint's commissioner, Yūsuf al-Shaykh, had claimed that the silver had been overly mixed with copper. The official and the imām were happy that he made this claim, because it enabled them to take a bounty from both sides: from the commissioner, Yūsuf al-Shaykh, and from the Jews. They immediately gathered all the Jewish moneychangers and imprisoned and laid charges against them, claiming that that they had cheated the Muslims. In addition, they alleged that, according to the tradition of the Prophet, their wives were forbidden to them and their children were illegitimate because they had paid the bridal price for their wives with adulterated silver [and had thus invalidated their marriages].

Because the government had urgent need of money to maintain itself, it imposed a 2,200 riyal fine upon the silversmiths. However, in those days of intense poverty, a fine of even a single riyal was a great punishment, especially for common people. And when the collectors, iniquitous as they were, levied the fine and tripled its amount, the people's cry went up to the very heavens, for they had nothing with which to pay it. But no one would listen to them. Some therefore fled their homes, but it did not help them, for the fine was collected from their houses. Some sold or mortgaged the titles
96 of their houses and were thus able to pay. Some sold their tools, and some were imprisoned until they were able to pay. Among these was Sulaymān al-Maswarī, the very Jew whose brother I had met at that time in the village of Milḥ. Sulaymān saw the charges and the punishments with which his companions were afflicted in prison. Knowing that he had nothing to mortgage, sell, or loan, he thought of another way to save himself. Telling them that he agreed to pay the sum he owed, he asked them to set him free from prison

so that he could go to his house to get the money. They released him into the custody of two guards on condition that he pay the amount in full, which was 42 riyals. When he reached his house, he took his wife's shaving razor and, while the guards and his family weren't looking, he killed himself with it. By the time they noticed, his blood had already drained and his death rattle was like that of a bull being slaughtered. When his wife saw this, she screamed at the top of her voice, "My husband is slaughtered! My husband is slain!" The children screamed, "Our father! Oh daddy! You have orphaned us! You have deprived us of our father!" As for the guards, when they saw this, they fled. Immediately, people came and sewed his windpipe and neck together with a silk thread, smeared it with a paste of wheat flour and ghee, and tied his head to his chest with rope so that it wouldn't move about. The wailing of his family and children had so alarmed the people, who were themselves
reeling from the harsh decrees, that most of them, both men and women, 97
stupefied with fear, stood on the rooftops all night praying to God in loud and terrifying voices that reached the palace. However, because they still had to pay what they owed, there was no pay for the men who came on the night of the funeral to accompany the body to the burial grounds.

Once they had paid their fine, the silversmiths, to ensure that such perfidy would not happen again, had no choice but to adopt the practice of putting their work in the crucible to check how much silver and copper there was in it. They no longer sold silver items in the markets without first passing them through the fire of the crucible and having them stamped with the name of the imām and inscribed with the name of the silversmith. Because the use of the crucible was not yet well known, they had until then made do with a touchstone, which is a test of silver made by grinding it with the tip of a black stone. In those days, there were very few articles made of silver, and no one used to ask for them except the royal house and the great men of the kingdom. Instead, the tribesmen and the commoners made do with iron, copper, lead, and glass beads. This was because money had not yet come into the hands of the people. But in our time, God, may He be praised, has made silver articles more plentiful than copper and iron articles were in the past.
This is on account of the rise of the Ottoman Empire, may God preserve its 98
glory. No doubt the time will come when the people will be asking for gold instead of silver.

FAMINES IN ṢAN‘Ā’
BEFORE AND AFTER THE OTTOMANS

Some fools complain that, [prior to the Ottoman annexation of Yemen,] there was great prosperity and that everything was so cheap that one could have 4 *qadaḥ*s of wheat or 10 *qadaḥ*s of millet for a single riyal; and 14 to 18 *roṭl*s of ghee and oil for 1 riyal; whereas today 1 *qadaḥ* of wheat costs 2 riyals, 1 *qadaḥ* of millet costs 1 riyal, 2 *roṭl*s of ghee cost 1 riyal, and everything has become expensive. They, in their ignorance, do not know that the reason for those cheap prices was the lack of demand for these commodities. Then, the light of the Ottoman Empire shone upon the city of Ṣan‘ā’, and it became illuminated such that all its activities flourished. Even a potter who used to earn 2½ buqshahs per day now earns 20. Also, a dog's yard, which could then be purchased at the price of a dog, is today worth 20 buqshahs, which is very cheap because the people now possess buqshahs.

Those wretches [who believe that Yemen was wealthier before its annexation by the Ottomans] do not think, understand, or remember what befell them then, especially during the days of the famine of 1816.[51] During the reign of Imām al-Mahdī ‘Abdallāh, the Bakīl tribes besieged Ṣan‘ā’ with the result that 1 *qadaḥ* of wheat reached the price of 10 riyals.[52] Even after the people had sold their utensils and beds for a pittance to buy food, after they
99 had sold pure silver valued at 12 to 15 dirhams for a single riyal, and after dismantling their own houses, destroying them in order to sell their beams and joists, the famine still did not spare them. Neither did the famine fear their corpses. Rather, it led men, women, and children to the infernal pit, not sating itself until it had destroyed streets of houses and entire villages. Had the rain not returned, falling on account of the Sublime Lord, all of the country and its inhabitants would have been destroyed. The famine returned again in 1826,[53] exceeding the previous one in its severity. It disappeared for a little while and then returned in 1836,[54] as though regretting that it had previously allowed some to escape and was now determined to collect double the debt, as it were, whether big or small. In 1858,[55] it returned, treating some gently and others roughly. Not wanting to be overhasty, it left a sufficient number of people alive so that it could return later to collect its debts, as has been its custom from time immemorial. This famine would not have been thwarted had the Ottoman Empire not annexed these lands. It opened

rivers of sustenance and planted trees of livelihood, guarding them from
the envious so that we, the people, could enjoy the very best of their fruits.
The fearsome and inveterate enemy, which is famine, is now not permitted
to enter the country because of the power of the "army," by which I mean
money. In the year 1885,[56] this enemy [famine] sent its "scouts," that is, the
sun, the winds, and the blight, to Ṣanʿāʾ, but the people defended themselves
against them with money and with the help of the Ottoman Empire. Even 100
flour and rice, which previous generations had never known, were imported
from the port cities. Had an event like this happened before the coming of
the Ottomans, with the harshness of that time and the lack of money, may
God hide from us what would have happened.

When the aforementioned Imām Muḥammad ibn Yaḥyā saw how the
people's circumstances had changed, he departed for Ḥudaydah, where he
sold the kingship of Ṣanʿāʾ to Tawfīq Pasha. Then, for a price, he escorted the
pasha and 5,000 of his soldiers to Ṣanʿāʾ.[57] But the people harbored resentment against the Turks, and so, on the day after their arrival, they attacked
them unawares, laying siege to the fortress of Ṣanʿāʾ and killing those Turks
whom they found in the streets and markets. Because of the civil strife, the
Turks detained the Jews in the fortress's mint, where they had been striking
coins in the name of the imām. Because the Jews did not have any food, they
cried out and were released. The siege lasted for a month until the two parties were reconciled on condition that the Turks, when set free, would return
to Ḥudaydah. The people then restored the imamate to the aforementioned
ʿAlī ibn al-Mahdī.[58] Assuming the throne, he ordered the imprisonment of
Muḥammad ibn Yaḥyā, who had escorted the Turks, and, after a short time,
they beheaded him in prison. The tribesmen then became strong, deposing 101
one imām and appointing another. They attacked Bīr al-ʿAzab, the Jewish
neighborhood, twice looting and destroying it, until the people abandoned
it and it became empty. Poverty reigned over everyone. But in our time,
God, may He be exalted, in his kindness, benevolence, and mercy gave us
this great empire, its magnificent pashas, and its victorious army. May God
lengthen its days and exalt its triumph. Amen.

ANCIENT BOOKS IN MILḤ

Said the expert in the art of travel: I digressed to tell of these dreadful events, but I will now return to where we were in our travels. When we had finished our work in Milḥ, I began to search for what I could discover of the vestiges of its early Jews. In the synagogue of the Banū Qāmis, I found a *tāj* of the Torah of Moses[*] that was about 400 years old, and in it there was an ancient sheet that was 900 years old. The sheet was an introduction to another *tāj*. Its script was green, red, black, yellow, blue, and gray, with curling calligraphy and ornamentation. This sheet was attached to the beginning of the *tāj* and on it was written "Persian Version." I also saw three other books. Two of
102 them were books of the Psalms written on parchment. One of them was 700 years old with lines arranged side by side like the poem in *Ha'azinu*.[59] The second book was about 500 years old. I brought the third book to my teacher Joseph. It was the second part of [Maimonides'] *Guide for the Perplexed*. But there is no guide for the perplexed except our Lord.

❨ CHAPTER 6 ❩
DEATH AND RUINS

PREPARATIONS FOR THE JOURNEY TO MILḤ

When we decided to travel to the Jawf, Yaḥyā ibn Saʿīd,[1] the teacher at whose home we were staying, contacted [Sālim], a Bedouin from Majzar, to guide us to our Jewish brethren who lived in the Jawf.[2] He told him that he was not to let anyone attack us and was also to let my teacher Joseph ride on his camel. That Wednesday, we left the transcriptions that we had made with Yaḥyā ibn Saʿīd. We also left our clothes, namely, my caftan, keffiyeh, and *shamlah*; and my teacher's watch, *zannah*,[3] and pants. He therefore made do with the caftan that Yaḥyā al-Qārah had given him in Ṣanʿā', even though it was torn and patched. As for his keffiyeh and the thick *shamlah* that my friend Saʿīd al-ʿArūsī had lent him, he was not willing to take them off.[4]

We left our clothes in Milḥ so that they would not become worn out and

* A *tāj* is a Yemeni Bible codex that contains both an Aramaic and an Arabic translation.

filthy like the clothes of our brethren who live in those regions. Because of their great poverty, their children, both big and small, go about completely naked. Even most virgin girls wear nothing on their bodies but a course *sham-* 103
lah, which is sewn like a sack with openings for the head and arms. This is by order of Fear and Poverty, the governors of those places.

Saʿīd al-Raḥbī very charitably gave me his son's prayer shawl to cover me during prayers, sleep, and so on, and although it was [as perforated with holes] as a sieve, I was nonetheless pleased with it. Yaḥyā ibn Saʿīd, after having already greatly honored us, gathered alms for us from his friends and from his own pocket, alms more generous than what they had gathered for us in al-Madīd. This is because, although their poverty was great, their hearts and hands were generous. In addition, they gave us provisions for the road to the Jawf. After I had paid Sālim the Bedouin his fee, they enjoined him before witnesses to be responsible for our safety until we reached our brethren, the Jews of al-Ghayl. In addition, a Jew from Ṣanʿā' traveled with us. He was a poor wretch by the name of Yūsuf al-ʿUzayrī.

SLEEPING UNDER THE STARS

That day at noon, the aforementioned Bedouin was to undertake his commitment. We traveled together and arrived at a house near Barrān, where we spent the evening. During the night, the Bedouin saddled his camel for my teacher to ride, and we traveled along the mountain slope, not on the plains, until we descended from the mountains. At the close of the day, we arrived at the end of Wādī Majzar. Here Sālim let his camel kneel down to rest, and we spent the evening out in the open. Sālim warned us not to raise our voices during the night, for he feared that, if the Bedouin noticed us, they would rob and kill us, and who knows what else.[5] It was our first night outdoors. We were 104
uneasy and could not sleep, and I wondered how our night would pass. While I was contemplating the radiance of Jupiter and the darkness of Saturn, I suddenly felt something touch me, moving from one of my limbs to the other. I knew with certainty that it was a snake, but I did not know what it was searching for around me. I greatly feared that my voice would be heard if I cried out or that I would move and the snake would bite me, having no mercy on me. In a low voice, I called to my travel companion, Yūsuf al-ʿUzayrī. Awakened from his sleep, he grumbled, "What do you want of me? Let me sleep."

"I can feel a snake on me," I murmured.

"Curse your father!" he snapped at me. "No one here is afraid, now let us sleep."

So I trusted in heaven, and this was not in vain, for I no longer felt the snake. I rolled my naked body in the donated sheet I had been given in Milḥ, my terrifying imaginings ceased, and I returned to my meditations on the constellation of Leo and the tail of Scorpio. While my mind was immersed in this sea of contemplation, the unfortunate Yūsuf al-ʿUzayrī awoke from his sleep, screamed, then fled in fear from the snake that had slithered into his coat.

"Yūsuf," I said, "go back to sleep, no one here is screaming like you."

But he continued his screaming, quarreling, and cursing until the Bedouin and his companion got up.

105 "We're all in great danger from the Bedouin ruffians who live around here," he scolded him.

During all of this, we heard not so much as a peep from my teacher Joseph.

We spent the rest of that night traveling, reaching Majzar on the morning of the next day. Sālim brought us to his home, a tent made of skin, and served us lunch. Their tribal chief came and welcomed us with kind words, then left after cautioning us not to say futile words in their land.

After we had rested for a while, he brought us by camel to the village of al-Ghayl. We passed by a place built from unhewn stones. Its rounded houses, which were both large and small, were arranged in two lines as though it were a market.

"What is this?" we asked Sālim the Bedouin.

"These are the *durūm* of the unbelievers," he replied.

"What are these *durūm*?" we asked.

But we heard no explanation of this name either from him or from others.[6] In the end, we discovered that they were ancient graves, as I will later discuss.[7]

When we left Wādī Majzar, the heat of the sun was overwhelming. We
were thirsty but could find nothing to quench our burning thirst. We were
still traveling when a young girl pasturing her flock appeared in the distance.
106 The Bedouin said to me, "You lead the camel while I approach that girl. She
will give us water from her waterskin or some milk."

So I led the camel on which my teacher rode, and the Bedouin went off until I could no longer see him or the girl. I was in torment with thirst and fear. He did return, but the next time we drank water was in al-Ghayl.

SABBATH WITH THE JEWS OF AL-GHAYL

On Friday, a half-hour before sunset, we came to al-Ghayl and the Bedouin brought us to the Jewish neighborhood. The moment I saw the first of the Jewish houses, I leaped toward it and entered. Because of my fear of the tribes, I did not wait for permission from its owner. When one of the women of the house heard me come in, she raised her voice, snorting and scolding, "Who's there at the door? Don't come in!"

But I did not listen to her and went ahead and entered. When I saw that she was combing her hair and washing in honor of the Sabbath, I was greatly embarrassed and stood where I was. When the woman saw me, she covered her hair with her kerchief and eagerly got up to greet and welcome me as if I were a dear friend.

"Oh *marī*," she said, "please forgive my shouting and snorting. I thought you were a Gentile, and we fear the Gentiles, for they come to destroy what we need for the Sabbath."

Grasping my hand in greeting, she led me into the guestroom and served me coffee. After her husband and brothers arrived, who also warmly welcomed me, she even gave me a few pancakes. I then asked for water to wash 107
my hands, feet, and face so that I could pray the Sabbath evening prayer in their synagogue. According to their custom, they gave me kohl and ghee to anoint my face and side-locks, after already having anointed my feet with ghee upon my arrival. As for my teacher Joseph, Sālim the Bedouin had already brought him to the chief of the Jews of al-Ghayl, the teacher Yaḥyā al-Ṣaʿdī. He was glad to meet my teacher and welcomed him with great respect. After the synagogue prayer, which was in Chief Yaḥyā al-Ṣaʿdī's house, people wanted to host me, but Sālim al-Ṣaʿdī and his brother Harūn, to whose house I had first arrived, said to their companions, "It would be disgraceful for us on this night to abandon our guest who arrived at our house."[8]

So they took me with them and I greatly enjoyed myself, even though they were very poor. For the Sabbath evening meal, they served nothing but three pancakes and half a chicken for all of us. As for the coffee, it was that which I had previously been offered when I arrived. I spent a wonderful night listening to their anecdotes and stories. At the end of the night, we went to the synagogue and found that the oil lamp that they had lit on Friday had already burned out.

Although both are from eastern Yemen, there is a great difference between the prayer melodies [of the Jews of al-Ghayl] and those of the Jews of
108 Radāʿ. After the prayer before the Torah reading, Chief Yaḥyā al-Ṣaʿdī invited us for breakfast, serving us milk and ghee, may God reward him well in the afterlife. In the synagogue, while they read the Torah with raised voices in a manner that seemed strange to me, they gave us coffee with ginger, cinnamon, and sugar. Their Sabbath clothes are not displeasing. Although, made of white cotton, they never see soap and know no washing until they are entirely worn out—but they are never worn out! They wear a coat that is open at the neck and reaches their knees. Below this, there is a separate piece covering the thighs that is tied above the waist with a leather girdle and onto the upper edge of the waist wrapper below the navel. They wrap anything they need inside it and call this [pocket] the *ḥazzah.* On this day, in honor of the Sabbath, they had filled them with toasted barley, some to enjoy in the synagogue, some to eat outside with toasted sesame seeds. Unlike other Jews, when they pray, they wear a small cotton tunic, edged with the legally required fringes, not a *shamlah.* These Jews are not like their brethren of lower Yemen either in their character or in their clothing. They do not wear a coat that is open at the neck called a caftan. Rather, they cover themselves with a piece of cloth, edged with the traditional fringes and split in the center so as to let the head through. They call this a *tallit qaṭan,*[9] and, underneath it, they wear the waist wrapper. On the Sabbath, during prayer, and on other occa-
109 sions, they go about with their entire body wrapped in a large cloth. This is similar to the custom of their neighbors from the Sudan, the inhabitants of Barbarah, who entirely wrap their bodies in a large piece of cloth.

Most women of eastern Yemen wear cotton dyed with indigo. They take their linen garment or *shamlah*, sew it up like a pocket with an opening for their hands and a slit for their head, and tie it around their bellies with a wool, leather, or linen rope. With these same kinds of ropes, they also bind their pack animals on their travels.

There is a great difference between the manners, character, and livelihoods of the Jews of lower Yemen and those of eastern Yemen. God willing, I will explain this to you elsewhere.

After we left the synagogue, a man invited me to his house. Their Sabbath custom is to gather together and chew grains of barley, called *ṭarūsh*, and sesame seeds. Unlike their brethren in the cities, they have no fruit. Most of them read Torah to their children and teach them to read it until lunch is served. Lunch consists of two loaves, no more, of wheat flour bread. This is a substitution for the wine or raisin juice required for the sanctification of the Sabbath (Kiddush), which they do not possess. This is the situation in many regions of Yemen. Because wheat is very rare, their meals on the Sabbath, festivals, and so on are made of millet. They call wheat bread *himūṣ* after the blessing ha-Motzi.[10] Most of their meals consist of *harīsh*, made of wheat 110
grains cooked with ghee or broth, and a sorghum porridge (*ʿaṣīd*) cooked the same way. My teacher Joseph was accustomed to eating millet and other such foods, but in Ṣanʿāʾ none of our dishes, such as cake (*kaʿk*) and white bread, seemed to agree with him.

After lunch, some slept, others returned to religious study, and still others chewed barley seeds or cleaned their clothes, while the women dried their hair in the sun.[11] Those who spend the Sabbath with the tribesmen and have not prepared food the previous day will be provided with what they need by the tribesmen. The tribesmen, however, will not sit down and talk with them as they usually do on other days of the week. This is because they believe that [Jewish] tradition requires Jews to seclude themselves on the Sabbath day and that it is forbidden for them to talk to anyone. For this reason, they do not interfere with the Jews on the Sabbath wherever they may be.

A JEW IS PUNISHED BY THE TRIBES FOR VIOLATING THE SABBATH

One of the most amazing examples of the [respect of these tribesmen for the Sabbath] concerns a Jew from the Ṣanʿāʾ region who did not take the commandments sufficiently seriously. One day, during a drought, locusts appeared that entirely covered the face of the sun and made the air throb with the beating of their wings. The people were very eager to eat them, and, as was the custom, they were ordered to come from every town and village to

catch them.* Some of them traveled for as much as half a day or even a full day to do so. On the Sabbath eve, this Jew went with them to gather locusts for himself. Some of his friends had forbidden him from doing so, but he did not listen to them. When the tribesmen saw him working, gathering locusts
111 and collecting them in his container, they asked him, "Is tonight not the night of the Sabbath? You are working by gathering locusts and are thus not keeping your Sabbath. Because you desecrate the Sabbath, you must be killed."[12]

So they beat him, stole his container, tied him up, and brought him before one of their judges, who sentenced him to imprisonment. He remained confined for some months until they made amends for his Sabbath desecration by confiscating his house and property and driving him from the land.[13]

INSCRIPTIONS IN BANĀT ʿĀD

My teacher Joseph paid no attention to these stories. As was his custom, he did not leave the house of the aforementioned elder, Yaḥyā al-Ṣaʿdī. However, because he was interested in the tribes of the Jawf and in the ruins and ancient buildings, he traveled once to al-Ḥazm in Hamdān with two Jews from al-Ghayl.[14] There, he celebrated Passover in the house of Sālim ibn Saʿīd, who is famous among both the Jews and the tribesmen for his good character and friendliness.** I celebrated the festival with our brethren in al-Ghayl, may God bless their children. I then followed my teacher to al-Ḥazm. When I arrived, I found him transcribing inscriptions at [the ruins of] Banāt ʿĀd from the upright posts that they call "stelae." These are located below the ruins of Haram, which today they call the ruin of al-Farʿ.[15] So
112 that I could earn my fee, I immediately took out my pencil and hurried to transcribe the inscriptions that he had begun but had not yet completed. However, he would not pay for them. After we finished transcribing them, we returned to Sālim ibn Saʿīd's house. Our Jewish brethren said that when the sage, my teacher, reached Banāt ʿĀd and saw the inscriptions on the stelae,

* Unlike most Jews, Yemeni Jews considered some varieties of locusts to be kosher. Yosef Qāfiḥ, *Halikhot Teman* (Jerusalem: Makhon Ben-Zvi, 1987), 218.

** This detail is corroborated by Halévy, who mentions spending Passover with one Sālim al-Ṣaʿdī, whom he thanks for helping him to collect inscriptions. He adds that in 1872 he received a letter informing him that Sālim had prematurely died after the tribesmen had persecuted him for failing to give them the riches that they alleged he and Halévy had discovered. In response, Halévy says that he sent money to Sālim's family to prevent further persecution. Halévy, "Voyage au Nedjran," 586–87.

he was ecstatic, clapping his hands, shrieking with delight, and joyfully dancing about. They were astonished at his behavior, for they did not know what he was thinking.

And now, dear reader, I have already told you what our Jewish brethren believe regarding these ancient ruins, but, if you wish, I will also inform you about this place and its circumstances, of ancient wonders and extraordinary things. As for my teacher, he never transcribed anything from the stones with his own hand save for here.

A DESCRIPTION OF AL-SAWDĀʾ

Because the Jews had filled our heads with stories about the ruins of Wādī Sheba and the Jawf, my teacher Joseph said to me, "Take the riyal we received as charity and do your work."

I returned to al-Ghayl in the company of my good friend Sālim al-Ṣaʿdī, at whose house I had previously arrived. I gave him the riyal so that he could pay for what I needed, such as paper and the like, and could hire people to 113
show me the area and the ruins. Since they do not have buqshah coins and do not even recognize them on account of living a Bedouin life far from Yemeni towns, they trade and barter only with wheat, ghee, barley, and riyals. Their custom is that "wheat" is usually half wheat and half straw and dust. Accordingly, Sālim took a riyal's worth of wheat and then added dust and straw to it until it became one-third pure wheat and two-thirds dust and such like. From this, I gave him his payment for coming with me to the ruin of al-Sawdāʾ.

This is a description of al-Sawdāʾ. Do not rely on me, dear reader, to describe the place with great accuracy because, with the passage of time, it has gone from my mind and I am also not a geographer. Nonetheless, listen to what I myself have witnessed. Beside the ruin of al-Sawdāʾ is a great forest with each tree pressed against the next because of their great number. On one side of it are the remains of a building, which resembles a market. It has a large raised room with marble stones spread out inside it—there is no doubt that it was a market for marble work.

Near the front of the ruin are many large clay jars arranged alongside one another. They are buried and today only their tops can be seen above the ground. There are also large furnaces, the largest as big as a room. . . .[16]

114 At one entrance to the ruin of al-Sawdāʾ, the dust of the city, which has been accumulating since ancient times, forms a mountain-like pile. At the entrance to the ruins, there is a stone platform and at its base is a wooden beam that the passing of time has not destroyed. On the platform is a large carved marble stone that was prepared as an altar or for some other use. Unlike those we had seen elsewhere, it had no inscriptions. I also found a place outside the ruin made of stones, baked bricks, and plaster. Until then, I had never seen ancient buildings made of plaster and mortar among the Sheban ruins. There was no doubt that this was a mosque, but it was not like those I had seen in Banāt ʿĀd and other such places. As for inscriptions, we found very few of them—and I have visited this ruin on other occasions.[17]

When Sālim al-Ṣaʿdī and I left the ruin, we came upon some human hair, four hand spans long, which the wind had swept away from its place. I approached and dusted the sand from it. I saw then that it was the lock of hair of a young Bedouin woman whom they had killed and buried, but whose body had not rotted and decayed. We returned her body to its place in the sand.

AL-FARʿ

I returned to my teacher Joseph and gave him what I had transcribed. For fear of the tribesmen, he was no longer able to go to al-Farʿ (located above
115 Banāt ʿĀd), even though it was close to Sālim ibn Saʿīd's house, where he had previously stayed. So I instead went to al-Farʿ, in which there were three Jewish homes. One of the amazing things that I saw there was a stone sculpted like soap that had once had engravings and a few inscriptions on it. However, with the passing of time, it had been destroyed and had become a heap of stones and gravel. That year, before we arrived there, the tribesmen had wanted to line the well of the al-Farʿ mosque with stones. While digging by the ruins to extract stones, they found a large copper cauldron that resembled a basin. It was as thick as a finger and inside it were copper statues and tablets. The tribesmen fell upon it, breaking it to pieces with stones. Sālim ibn Saʿīd bought it and carried it to Ṣanʿāʾ to sell. I learned about it in Ṣanʿāʾ and bought 50 *roṭls* of it from him. In it were fragments of statues and two tablets that I had found among them. I melted the fragments of the cauldron itself for my own work and, for reasons I do not understand, a thick sulfurous smoke arose from them. As for the tablets, I showed them to Joseph Arūjas,

who had come from Syria, but he would not pay their price.[18] In the end, I sold them to a merchant who had arrived from Aden at the price at which I had bought the 50 *roṭls* of copper. But now here I was, brought by my teacher, the Frenchman, to this place, which I had not ever imagined reach- 116
ing, for it is at the easternmost boundary of beautiful Yemen, which is now a land of killing and violence.

At the beginning of my book, I said that my greatest desire in my travels was to contact the Jewish tribes who do not live under the domination of others. My teacher had also accepted this made-up story because of all the nonsense people had said about it on our travels. However, our Jewish brethren of the Jawf had never discovered any Jews other than themselves from the eastern edge of Yemen up to the Persian Gulf. I will explain more about this later.

TWO CASES OF MISTAKEN IDENTITY AT MAʿĪN

After I had given my teacher the inscriptions from al-Farʿ, I decided to go with a Jewish guide to Maʿīn. I discovered many inscriptions there, as well as in a place east of it that is similar to Banāt ʿĀd. I will later explain the extraordinary things I found. One of the strange things that happened to me at Maʿīn occurred on a day when, because of the sun's heat, I fled to seek shade in a cellar in the middle of the ruin. The building (its roof made of hewn stone resting on pillars of planed stone, not wood) was as still as it had been of old. After having settled down there and fallen asleep, I heard a terrible cry. I awoke, opened my eyes, and, behold, there was a man as big as the ruin leaning over me. His mouth was open, he stammered, his arms were outstretched, his eyes were glaring, and his body shook. When I saw him and 117
realized that this was not a dream, I was seized with terrible fear. "The demons have come," I said to myself. In terror, I got up from my resting place, drew my dagger, and grabbed my stick. Gathering my strength for a fight and preparing to die, I shouted at the top of my voice, "Curse your father whether you are human or demon!"

Filled with fear, his strength left him and he fell to the ground, saying in a low, thin voice, "I am one of the best of men. I am not a demon."

I knew then that he was afraid, and so, treating him gently until his spirit returned, I asked, "What was it that upset you, making you so afraid that you fell down?"

"When I saw the thick hair on your body," he replied, "it seemed to me that you were a devil because devils have thick hair and live in ruins."

"What brought you to this place of devils?" I asked.

"I came here to search for treasure, may God grant me success," he answered.

"Like you, I too am here to search and so," I suggested, "you can now be my companion."

"And you mine," he replied.

We exchanged pleasantries and spoke a bit. After the sun's heat had decreased, we left the cellar. We walked, bent over, eyes on the ground, to see what God would provide us with from the ancient remains. We found silver buttons, which had been damaged with the passing of time. God had already
118 provided the Bedouin with a piece of gold worth one and a half dirhams. However, the jeweler to whom the Bedouin wanted to sell it was not satisfied with this God-given gift and gave him a piece of yellow copper in exchange. I was amazed by the chiseled part of it. Even though hundreds of years had passed, it had not darkened like the rest of it but continued to shine as though it had just been chiseled.

Another incident occurred in the ruin of Maʿīn. One day, the water in my waterskin was exhausted and, because of the sun's heat, I burned with thirst. Seeing a young girl pasturing a flock a short distance away, I headed toward her to ask for water or milk. But because she had seen me leaving the ruin, she fled whenever I drew near to her. This continued until the ruin, and even the flock, were far behind me. I became angry and shouted at her, "Oh girl, what is it that makes you so afraid that you run away from me?"

"Don't come near me," she said. "You are one of the demons!"

"God forbid and don't fear," I replied. "I am one of the best of people."

"If you were a person," she challenged, "there wouldn't be so much hair on your body."

"I ask God who created me thus for forgiveness," I answered. "I am neither a *jinn* nor a demon. Thank God, I am one of the best of the Arabs."

"What do you want from me and why are you following me?" she asked.

"I am thirsty and I want water or milk, nothing else," I said.

“My waterskin is over where you were standing with the flock,” she said. 119
“Go drink and take from it what you need.”

So I turned back and, from a distance, she directed me to the place and I drank and replenished my waterskin.

DISTRUST AND VINDICATION

After checking the remaining walls [of the ruin] that still stood on their original foundations, their upper parts and their bases, and especially the city walls, I noticed something surprising. Under the foundations of this mighty building, there were huge unfired mud bricks similar to those used today for building. I informed my teacher of this, but he denied it until, when I was elsewhere and without my knowing, he took a Jew from al-Ḥazm to accompany him to Maʿīn.

The Jew went with him, following the tracks left by my feet, but they did not find any inscriptions except those that I had already discovered and transcribed. Moreover, he confirmed [my description of] the surrounding walls, wonderous in the strength of their construction, in their still-enduring length and height, and in the size of their stones that were sculpted like soap. All of this with a foundation of unfired mud bricks! This is what I had described to him, no more, no less. After the Jew had guided him using my footprints in the dust, after he had seen with his own eyes what I had correctly described to him, and after he had informed me of his investigation of me and his conclusions, I said to myself, “It would be right for me to receive additional wages.” 120

If you ask, dear reader, how the Jew had discovered all the places upon which I had trod in the Maʿīn ruin, let it be known that in the Jawf, people, both men and women, can recognize a wayfarer by his footprints. They say, “Someone passed here,” when no one saw or heard him but they saw his footprints in the sand, whether he wore sandals or went barefoot—and most of them go about barefoot because the land is very sandy. Their sandals are a section of leather attached to the sole and connected by only two strips tied under the foot. Because the Bedouin have the ability to recognize footprints, they leave their tents unguarded and go about their affairs without fear of thieves. If something is stolen from them, they follow the tracks until they discover the thief. Even if he has fled a day or two earlier, they manage to catch up to him. I have checked this with an old Jewish woman and established it to be true. God willing, I will set this subject out in full elsewhere.

After my teacher Joseph's investigation of me, he placed his trust in me and no longer accused me of making omissions or errors—this was because he followed me to that place and did not find even a single extra or missing letter!

POVERTY AND CHARITY

121 I hired Harūn al-Ṣaʿdī to accompany me to the ruin of al-Bayḍāʾ. The house to which I had arrived when I first came to al-Ghayl belonged to him and his brother Sālim. At al-Bayḍāʾ, I transcribed the little I found there.[19] We then returned to the ruin of al-Sawdāʾ to search for what more we could find. At the end of the day, we headed back to al-Ghayl, hungry, tired, faint, and thirsty. When we approached the village, we saw alfalfa sown for animal fodder. My travel companion said, "Let's rest here and take refreshment on this greenery."

"How can we take refreshment when there is no food here?" I asked.

"Sit down and don't fear," he said.

I sat on the edge of the field while he went in among the alfalfa and, with his knife, cut two bunches suitable for feeding a horse or a donkey. He sprawled down next to me like a bull over its fodder and honored me by offering me the largest bunch.

"Pray, help yourself," he said.

I was amazed and said to myself, "He knows that I have no camel, donkey, horse, or bull to give this gift to."

Night had fallen. While I was still wondering what he intended to do with this alfalfa, the bunch still in my hands, he had already eaten the bunch in his hand and had gotten up to get another.

"Satisfy your heart by eating this excellent alfalfa," he said. "Why do you deprive yourself of this great greenery?"

"There's no doubt that he wants me to enjoy this fodder," I said to myself.
122 So, I broke off two stems, tasted them, and, because my soul was a human soul and not an animal one like his, I found them disgusting. I tried to persuade myself that the alfalfa would satisfy my hunger, but it wouldn't go down my throat.

"My brother," I said to him, "I'm not accustomed to eating this fodder. Let's hurry and return to al-Ghayl before it gets dark."

So we arrived at his house, and they offered us butter [for anointing our feet]. I awaited in expectation of dinner but did not know that, because of his great poverty, the alfalfa had been his meal for the night. Once I realized how poor he was, I told him that I had important business with their chief, Yaḥyā al-Ṣaʿdī, and that I had to go to him immediately. He said, "It's already nighttime and he has certainly gone to sleep, but I'll go with you."

"Stay where you are. I will go alone," I replied.

So I went to Chief Yaḥyā al-Ṣaʿdī's house—and they were indeed already sleeping—but he got up, welcomed me, and asked about where I had gone that day. I told him what had happened, and he immediately gave me dinner.

"Don't you know," he told me, "that when I gathered alms for you from my friends, that wretched man, Harūn al-Ṣaʿdī, who considered you persons of great honor, wished to contribute alms to you. Because he was poor and had nothing, he took the two silver rings from his wife's hand, her most beautiful jewelry that she would wear when going out in public."

"How could you permit collecting alms for us from these poor people who have nothing?" I asked him. "My teacher and I, thank God, are not seeking alms for sustenance but only for our travel needs." 123

"The law of our land is that we generously provide the guest with whatever he needs," he replied. "This is an obligation for both the great and the lowly among us, and we strive to fulfill it whether the guest is rich or poor. Had we not accepted Harūn al-Ṣaʿdī's wife's rings, it would have brought disgrace on us. He would certainly have brought us to judgment before our tribal patrons, and a fine would have been imposed on us, as is required by our laws governing honor."

I, however, had compassion for Harūn al-Ṣaʿdī and returned his wife's two rings to him, even though they were only worth a single qirsh. I also paid him, without receiving my teacher's permission, for coming with me to the ruins of al-Bayḍāʾ and al-Sawdāʾ.

When I gave my teacher the inscriptions that I had found, he said to me, "Why is it that all the lines that you transcribed from al-Bayḍāʾ are identical?"

"You are correct," I replied. "Nonetheless, this is what I found on the walls of the ruin."

And I was amazed at the stupidity of the ancients who built them.

SEARCHING FOR WATER ON THE ROAD TO BARĀQĪSH

After that, I returned to al-Ghayl and asked Sālim al-Ṣaʿdī, Harūn's brother,
to accompany me to the ruin of Barāqīsh.[20] I asked him because the Bedouin around there were his customers and we would therefore have nothing
to fear. I arrived and found many inscriptions, especially on the walls. The
contract between my teacher and me stipulated one-quarter of a qirsh for
every transcribed line. When I saw how many long lines ran the length of the
124 wall, I divided the lines to increase their number. I did this in this place only
and in no other.[21]

While we were in the ruin that day, our water ran out, so we went out to ask the local Bedouin for some. Seeing a tower house (*qaṣbah*) with people inside, I banged on the door, "Oh family of the house, give us water."

A woman began to answer me, but, when she saw me, she closed the door and would not answer. When I banged on the door and called to the family a second time, a woman's voice from the top of the tower said, "ʿĀ'ishah, who is at the door?"

"Someone whose name should not be mentioned."

When I heard what she said, I forgot my thirst and fled from that place.[22]

Later, we came upon an old woman from Majzar who lived in a small house. When we asked her for water, she answered, "Wait until my son returns from the field to give water to the cows at the well. He will draw water for all of us."

After sunset, her son returned, took some water containers, and left. The old woman then served us jujube fruit. Although we waited half the night there, the Bedouin did not reappear.

"You are making fun of us," I said to the old woman.

"I am worried about my son," she replied, "and I am now going to look for him because the well is not far from here."

She left, only returning some eight hours later, by which time I was de-
125 stroyed by thirst. The Bedouin grumbled that the reason for the confusion
was that the cows had fled and that he had had to spend all night chasing
them. This is what happened to us at the edge of Wādī Majzar, near the ruin
of Barāqīsh. The next day, we returned to my teacher, provided him with a

description of the ruin, and gave him the transcriptions. He retranscribed them in his own hand, as was his custom.

I returned to al-Ghayl and then headed to the vicinity of the village of al-Maṭammah in the upper Jawf. On the slope of Mount Silyām, I found a few inscriptions.[23] When we descended to the narrow valley to search for further remains, I found only the droppings of wild animals, as though the place was a beast's lair. The place gave me the shivers, and I fled.

I also went to the village of al-Ẓāhir, where I saw a large abandoned mosque. Jews used to live there, but now there are none.[24]

THE KHĀRID RIVER

Late in the day, when I was in a deserted place, I met a Bedouin woman carrying a clay pot filled with fish guts on her head. Thinking there was water in it, I asked her for some.

"Don't ask," she said, "because the Khārid River is right ahead of you. Go drink your fill!"

As she passed me, I saw that there were ten fish on her shoulders, each of
which was a cubit long. After I had seen their size, I greatly longed for fish. 126
I asked her for some, adding that I would pay her, but she again responded,
"The Khārid River is right ahead of you. Go and eat as much fish as you
wish!"

So I set off to search for that Khārid River that she had mentioned. By the time the sun had set, I still did not know where it was and had found neither water, fish, nor anyone to ask. However, through God's kindness, I happened upon Sālim al-Ṣaʿdī, who was returning from his Bedouin customers, and I complained to him about what had happened to me.

"Don't worry," he said, "because tonight I have enough fish with me for you."

He took me for dinner to some Bedouin, who were stoking a fire and grilling fish. Sālim brought out the fish from his pack, grilled them, and we ate. Although the fish were tasty, we were not sated and so the Bedouin offered us some of theirs. In this way, we sat for most of the night, grilling and eating. I asked them how they got the fish. They said that, because of the war among the tribes, the course of the Khārid River had been diverted upstream with the consequence that the water had stopped and the fish had been trapped. When I told my teacher about this, he said to me, "If you had brought me a little fish, I would have been grateful. Now go back to Barāqīsh and do not waste our time in good-for-nothing places like these."[25]

A JEWISH GRAVEYARD IN THE RUINS OF BARĀQĪSH

I returned to Barāqīsh and, while searching there, came upon an Arab graveyard. Over time, the winds and rain had pulled the sand from the graves so
127 that the bones of the dead lay exposed on the ground. I thought to myself,
"Can the bones of the master be distinguished from those of the slave, the
king from the servant, or even the worshipper of God from one who does not
worship him?" And I did not know.

Beside this graveyard, close to the ruin, was a Jewish graveyard. Most of
its tombstones were still standing and had Aramaic inscriptions in Hebrew
script. One read, "Bewailed and sighed for is the Master and Rabbi Meʿoded
Bayrab Yeshaʿ, etc." Most of the tombstones were inscribed, even those of
women. Among their names were "Mistress Nogah" (Brilliance) and "Mistress Yonah" (Dove). The stones were about 400 years old. As I wandered
among the rows of graves, I sank into deep reflection: "What was it that
had brought me to this desolate place? How did our brethren or fathers live
among their patrons? How did they make a living? What were their religious practices? And, were they related to the Jews of Ṣanʿāʾ and environs?"
I greatly wept for the dispersion of the Jews among the tribes and for their
scattering in every land and country in which their presence was permitted.
Grief, sorrow, and regret overcame me on account of the predicament of the
whole community. While I was sunk in this sea of melancholy and weeping,
128 sobbing and moaning among the graves, I imagined the Devil saying to me,
"What are these people to you who have already passed away and been buried? What do you know of their lineage, ancestry, and beliefs that you pray,
cry, and beseech your God for the good of their tombs?"

When this devil's wind struck the clouds of my imagination, the raindrops of my eyes dried up and the clouds above the burial ground dispersed. I went from there, and the light of the sun conquered me. Years later, while buying old books for Moshe ben Natanel Shapira[26] (who deluded us into selling them), I learned with certainty from the dates that were on some of them that I was descended from the people who were buried in that place and that my ancestors had lived in Barāqīsh.

DESCRIPTION OF THE RUINS OF BARĀQĪSH

After I had examined the ruin, I discovered that it had been rebuilt and inhabited three times after it was first built. I knew this because one side of the wall, which shared a foundation with the nearby houses in the ruin, was torn down and destroyed, and through it I could see ancient and magnificently constructed buildings. I cannot begin to describe their grandeur and splendor, the size of their stones, and their craftsmanship and architecture. It was as though each stone was laid so close to a matching one that a hair
could not fit between them. Once the first building had been destroyed and 129
covered in earth, they had built another above it with bricks and also with some stones from the earlier building. Then, the second building had been destroyed and covered, and they had built above it a third, and when that had been destroyed and covered, they had built a fourth time. There was no plaster or mortar in the first building.

The entranceways of their cities, houses, and rooms, as well as their windows, are a little smaller than those found today in Ṣanʿāʾ and elsewhere. This is a proof against those who argue that these great palaces were built by the sons of Shaddād ibn ʿĀd, the uncle of King Og of Bashan, who peopled the earth when there was still Paradise.[27] For how, I'd like to know, would they enter these palaces and houses if, as they allege, they were such giants that a single one could uproot a mountain, carry it for two or three days, and turn it into a palace, city, or village as he wished? No doubt, after all this exertion, they would squeeze in through holes in the walls—to this day I do not understand the source of this delusion. Another proof of this is what I saw at al-Farʿ, that is, Banāt ʿĀd. One of the extraordinary things there is that the outer door is so small that a person cannot enter unless he bends his head. The next door, which is the middle one, is a little wider and better shaped than the first, and the third, which is the door to the room that the tribesmen
call "the Makrab of Banāt ʿĀd," is the biggest of them all. This is its descrip- 130
tion. The wall to the right of the door is made of a single stone. The right and left door jambs are so skillfully made, polished, and engraved that they dazzle the mind. They also bear a few inscriptions. I saw some magnificent

walls that bent toward the ground and had holes along them so smooth that they appeared to be made of wood. The tribesmen say that the walls were nailed to each other. As for the main room, it was not walled but had great stelae arranged in rows on the left and right as one enters from the aforementioned door. It was when I arrived at this place that I found my teacher transcribing inscriptions. The stelae, having endured until our own time, the year [AH] 1311 [1893], are now as weak, cracked, and decrepit as old men. The Hamdānī tribesmen of the Jawf say, "These stelae have no reason to remain because they bring upon us the decrepitude of the unbelievers." Today they break them, burn them, and turn them into mortar. Had my teacher Joseph not promised to send me a saw to saw apart the stelae of Banāt ʿĀd in
131 order to send the sawn slabs to him, I would not have mentioned them here.

While searching for what I could find in the ruin of Barāqīsh, I found a hole in one room and through it was darkness. I threw a stone in to hear how deep it was and realized that it was shallow. After throwing down more stones and dirt to serve as steps to go up and down, I descended, crawled around, and realized that it was a cellar bigger than the one I had seen in the ruin at Maʿīn. It had upright marble pillars and was filled with fine sand into which a person could sink and die. While crawling about, searching for what I could find, I was amazed when my hand touched the door of the hall.

"How is it that this has stood until our own day and was not destroyed with the passage of time?" I wondered.

I struck it with the iron of my staff, which was my weapon, and behold, its sound was not that of wood but of metal. I rejoiced, saying to myself, "Today my Lord has provided me with a door of copper or silver."

I left the cellar to determine the location of the door from the outside in order to dig it out. After much effort, I recognized which corner it was on. I dug through the dirt, which was burnt ash, not clay, until the door was uncovered. [But it was not made of metal!] Although it had been ornamented and engraved like metal, not wooden, objects, it was made of a single stone. After I left the room, I discovered an inscription that was in the [unusual] form of a monogram.[28]

AN ENCOUNTER WITH TWO BEDOUINS

The next day, I searched the surroundings of the ruin without finding anything. When the sun became hot, I fled and found shelter in a hole in the demolished walls of Barāqīsh. I was sitting inside it, contemplating the aforementioned graveyard that faced me, when I saw in the distance two Bedouins passing on their way. I told myself that they had not seen me, but, because of their acute sight, their cautiousness, and their fear of raids and ambushes, they did see me, changed their course, and approached. 132

"Who are you?" they challenged.

I was so afraid that I could not answer. They lit the match cords of their rifles and drew a little closer, ready to shoot. As they came nearer, I abandoned my waterskin, bag of flour, provisions, shawl, and head cloth and left the hole. I then headed to the wall behind it to enter the ruin from the second side so that, if they followed me, I could escape through the other side. I fled into the ruin so as to get above the hole in which I had been sitting, and they too fled back along the route by which they came. Two days later, I happened
to spend the night with the Bedouin. When I asked, as was my custom, about 133
the ruins and ancient remains, they said that two people had seen a demon at midday in the ruin of Barāqīsh.

"What happened?" I asked.

They called one of them, saying, "Tell this guest about the demon that you saw in the middle of the day."

"I was passing by with someone," he said, "and behold, there was a hunched-over figure sitting along the walls of the ruin. We lit the match cords of our rifles and approached, ready to fight. When we shouted to him, he didn't respond, so we drew nearer and found that his face, hands, feet, belly, and back were hairy. Realizing then that he was a demon, we fled. Our Lord dealt kindly with us, and he did us no harm."

When I heard this, I thanked God who had made me look like a jinn to them and had robbed them of reason so that I could fulfill the commission of my teacher Joseph. After I had finished transcribing what I had found in Barāqīsh, I returned to al-Ḥazm and gave him what I had obtained.

THE MURDER OF IBN QAMLĀ AND A TRIBAL WAR

The next day, I climbed the ruin of Haram (al-Farʿ). I had no work there other than to transcribe the two or three remaining inscriptions that were on the side of the well of the mosque. I was determined to transcribe them, but they could be seen only through the window of the mosque. So that there would be no one there, I arrived around lunchtime. I was still absorbed
134 in my work when Ibn Qamlā, one of the rulers of the Jawf, came to pray the noon prayer accompanied by five soldiers. The ruler wore a sword, and the soldiers were armed with rifles. He entered the mosque as I left it and, after praying, left with his companions. Waiting for him outside was a black slave who belonged to one of his enemies. When the ruler saw him, he said, "Curse your father! Why is the match cord of your rifle lit?"

"I wanted to shoot a crow," the slave answered.

The ruler and his companions turned to leave, but the slave shot his rounds into him and fled. The ruler drew his sword, made four steps to kill the slave, but fell on his face and died. Some of his soldiers chased the slave but could not catch up with him. Immediately, the cry of misfortune spread and their peace was shattered. Beginning that evening and continuing for three days, the people gathered for war. There was the wailing and crying of men, women, and children, and the heavens closed in on the earth. This was all, however, to no avail. The slave fled to a fortress outside the village of al-Ḥazm, which he was able to reach because of the defensive gunfire of his masters, who shot at any of the ruler's people who approached. The hue and cry they raised and their many threats—and even a brave man would have been afraid of their menacing screams—were to no advantage. It only ended when the Shawwāf
135 tribe[29] came down from Mount Khabb and extinguished the fire of civil strife, making peace between them. How they did this we do not know.

THE TRIBAL LAWS OF WAR

As for the slave assassin, he had nothing at all to fear. According to the tribal law of the Dhū Ḥusayn, the Hamdān, and the *sharīfs*[*] of the Jawf, if a slave, woman, child, Qarārī, or Jew kills someone, retaliation is not visited upon

[*] A *sharīf* is an individual who claims descent from Ḥasan or Ḥusayn, the grandsons of the Prophet Muḥammad. Isaac Hollander, *Jews and Muslims in Lower Yemen: A Study in Protection and Restraint, 1918–1949* (Leiden: Brill, 2004), 46–47.

them but rather upon their family or patrons, [depending on the circumstances]. This is because [the slave, woman, child, Qarārī, or Jew] has no value. However, if a tribesman kills one of these people, his offense is very great. For this reason, if one side in a war is weak, they send their women and children ahead of them to fight. Because it is not possible for their opponents to fight them, they accept defeat. It is a matter of great disgrace for them to kill such people, regardless of whether or not they are deserving of death. The killing of tribesmen, however, is a point of pride. I have even seen and heard a Bedouin woman teaching her son, "May God make you one of the slain rather than dying the death of beasts." If one of them dies a natural death, his mother laments his lot and bewails him, "Would that he were bathed in his own blood rather than deprived of honor like this." I have also seen that most of their men have wounds from swords, sticks, daggers, or bullets, because of their wars and raids against one another. That being said, they have the blessing of many children, because each marries, over the course of his life, no less than forty to fifty women. The Jews of the Jawf, over the course of their lives, marry eight to ten women, and you will find that 136
some have three or four rival wives at a time. But the climate is bad for them on account of the sun's heat and the earth's dry vapor. It is for this reason that I have not found anyone there in our own day whom I knew when I visited with my teacher.

A STORY OF DEATH BY DROWNING

It recently happened that four young Jews from al-Ghayl went to Ṣanʿāʾ to make some purchases. On their way back, they came with their donkeys to Mount Rākiḍ, the mountain by which they would descend to the Jawf. As was the custom of travelers in these regions, they spent the night in the open. After unloading their beasts, two of them set off at night to draw water from a nearby eddy. After waiting for their friends to return, the other two went to look for them. The next day, when the Bedouin came to that place to draw water, they saw the Jews murdered in the water by the road to Rākiḍ. Immediately, a cry went forth from place to place: "What a disgraceful thing! Jews murdered in the water by the road to Rākiḍ." Those who heard it repeated it: "Woe, what a disgraceful thing, Jews murdered in the water by the road to Rākiḍ." In this way, the cry spread from place to place until it reached the

Jews of al-Ghayl and al-Ḥazm, which was a day's journey away. The Jews gathered to check who was absent and concluded that the dead were none
137 other than the four young men who had gone to Ṣanʿāʾ. Immediately, six people departed for Rākiḍ, taking three camels from their patrons. There they found their four countrymen dead in the waters of the eddy. They removed them, placed them on camels, and brought them to their families in al-Ghayl, who buried them in order that it not be said that they were murdered. Their donkeys then carried back their goods, which were presented to their families, and the Jews and some of the tribesmen mourned this loss of life. There is no doubt, however, that the true cause of what happened was the foolhardiness and lack of reflection of these four young men, qualities that they held in common with their tribal patrons. The first to draw water probably slipped into the eddy and did not know how to swim. The second, not wanting to see his friend drown, even if it meant losing his own life, grabbed him to pull him out, but the first seized hold of him and dragged him in with him. And the same thing happened to the others.

THE FAMILIES OF THE JEWS OF THE JAWF

The Jews of the Jawf number less than 150 people. There are eight families: (1) the Sharārah family and (2) the house of al-Asad, both of which came to the Jawf from Nihm; (3) Yahūdā al-Bāsil's family, who fled from Ṣanʿāʾ when Imām al-Manṣūr[30] sought to convert Jewish orphans to Islam, as I will
138 explain later;[31] (4) the Ṣuʿūd family from Ṣaʿdah; (5) the Jullākh family from Khawlān; (6) the Arḥabī family from Arḥab; (7) the Ḥijāzī family from the Ḥijāz;[32] and (8) the family of Sulaymān al-Jawfī. To the best of my knowledge, all of these families had migrated to the Jawf except al-Jawfī, whose son was one of those drowned at Rākiḍ. Migration is common among Yemeni Jews in general, but for these even more so. Among these families, only one is related to the families whose graves I visited in the Barāqīsh cemetery. Time confuses family relations, as is its way, until their traces are destroyed. This is even more the case in the Jawf and the village of Milḥ, for it has destroyed them utterly, not leaving so much as a trace. However, so great is the Jews' love of their homeland[33] that they are not willing to migrate from the place of their affliction. Instead, they say, "This land is the best that there can be in the world." May God have mercy upon them and upon us. Amen.

THE MURDER OF IBN QAMLĀ (CONTINUED)

This is the story of a cunning rascal. Shortly after the murder of the ruler Ibn Qamlā, a Qarārī[34] man hosted me at his house. He chatted with me in a friendly way until he realized that he had won my confidence and then said, "I have a secret for you, oh Jew, and only God knows this secret."

"What's your secret?" I asked. "Speak and do not fear, for I know how to keep a secret."

"I will not speak," he replied, "until you have sworn a solemn oath to
God. Swear upon the dust from which you were formed and unto which you 139
will return that you will not reveal the secret, lest I lose my livelihood or lest the tribesmen kill me on account of you."

I consented to his request because I believed his words. He then said, "Know that I am the gravedigger of al-Ḥazm. Once, while I was digging graves by the ruin of Banāt ʿĀd, I came upon bronze plates with inscriptions and drawings. I hid them where they were, afraid lest the tribesmen discover and take them, while I would reap no benefit. I want to show you the place where you will be able to find many of them. You can dig there at night and remove them; then give me my bounty and take your share. Come to me tomorrow and I will point you to the gravesite, but know that there are now divine oaths between us that forbid you from ever telling anyone of this matter."

As I left him, my head spun at the thought of this bounty that lay among the graves, but I still did not quite believe him.

"How about you show me something, even if it is only a hint of what lies there." I said.

"All I had I sold earlier to a man for a very low price," he replied, "and now I don't dare deal with the stuff at all."

When I returned to my teacher, I was in torment.

"Why do you look so distracted today?" asked Sālim ibn Saʿīd, at whose home we were staying. "I have already told you that I am your friend. With the help of God and my patron, I will save you from whatever has befallen
you. What is it that you fear? You and your teacher are as dear to me as my 140
own father."

"Praise God," I replied, "I have only one fear: an oath sworn to God between me and a certain Qarārī."

When he heard the name of this Qarārī, he said, "This gravedigger does nothing but deceive people, so beware lest he deceive you. Do not believe his words and oaths, for he is a liar like no other."

So I broke my oath and told him the Qarārī's secret. Now even more amazed, he exclaimed, "Praise God Who has made our intellects like a mirror so that I can explain to you the meaning of what you have told me; and praise God Who has created intimacy, affection, and compassion among the Jews as well as among strangers. This Qarārī, however, who is from the tribe of Ham, son of Noah, like his ancestor Ham, knows neither honor nor compassion. The truth is that he wants to steal the head of the murdered ruler, Ibn Qamlā, from his grave. He would then give it to his murderers, in exchange for a good reward, so that they could ridicule and disdain the murdered man's family. He would bring you by cover of night to the place in which he intends to kill you, that is, to Ibn Qamlā's grave. While you were digging, he'd go to the ruler's family and sons, saying, 'Come and see who it was who stole the head of your ruler. He is still digging for his body and limbs so that he can give them to your enemies for them to ridicule you with.'
141 They would come upon you stealthily and shoot you with a shower of bullets without ever asking you to explain yourself."

When I heard my brother Sālim ibn Saʿīd's explanation, my hair stood on end with fear.

"Let's go to the ruler's sons so that I can tell them of the Qarārī's deceit," I said.

But he stopped me from doing so.

"If you have anything more to do with the Qarārī," he warned me, "you will never be safe from his murderous affairs. Furthermore, you are a foreigner. Don't you know that in our lands all foreigners are ignored? Had you not pretended to be part of the Sharārah family, they would have taken you as a slave or would have killed you without cause."

I then remembered what had happened to me before this. One day, I left al-Farʿ to wander around al-Ḥazm. There I met a Jawfī youth who asked me who I was and which land I was from. My friends in Milḥ had already taught me that, when the tribesmen asked where I was from, I should say that I am from Nihm and am part of the Sharārah or Yahūdā family, for these Jews have long been clients of the Jawf tribes and are well known in the land. So I said to the youth, "I am from the Sharārah family."

"No," he replied, "you are a gift that God has sent me."

And he grabbed my hand and wanted to lead me away like a donkey.

"Young man," I cried out, "get away from me and shame on you."

We were still arguing when a Bedouin passed by.

"Sir," I called out to him, "separate me from this young ruffian. He is 142
blocking my way and holding me without claim and for no fault."

"Curse your father," the Bedouin rebuked him. "Young man, why do you interfere with this man who is from the Sharārah family. Let him go!"

"I won't let him go," the youth answered. "God has given me a good gift in accordance with the tradition of our law. Who is there who will interfere with me or snatch from me someone given to me by God?"

The Bedouin to whom I had appealed did not dare to deal with the youth but left us to our quarreling and went away. As for me, had I been a little further from al-Ḥazm and alone in the desert with this youth, I would have killed him. Afterward, another Bedouin passed by who recognized me from Sālim ibn Saʿīd's house.

"You have no right to this man, and he is not your gift from God," he scolded the youth, "because I recognize him from Sālim ibn Saʿīd's house and he is part of the Sharārah family."

Even though the youth had been defeated by his friend's words, he was unable to leave emptyhanded. Because I had nothing but some worn fabric to cover my nakedness, a tattered tunic over the skin of my belly and back (which had been given to me as charity), and a head covering lowered over my eyes, his eyes fell upon the remains of my shabby sandals, which I would not have deigned to go out with in my land. He swore, saying he would have to take them even if it cost him his life. I wanted him to take them, knowing that our brethren would provide me with better ones in place of them, so I
left them with him. But I did not get others while I was in the Jawf because I 143
did not dare to tell anyone of this incident. Only when we came to the land of Khabb did they give me new ones as charity.

Later, I hired a Jew to accompany me to Ḥazmat Abū Thawr, which is in the upper Jawf near the Khārid River. The river's source is in the land of Arḥab, from which it descends to the upper Jawf and ends at Maʿīn. Along much of the right and left riverbanks are the remains of impressive houses with irrigation channels. The buildings stand one beside another, but they are not arranged like a town or village. I cannot remember, as I usually do, either what inscriptions I collected or my impressions of the places in that region.

On our return journey, my Jewish companion went to visit his Bedouin customers. While I sat at the camel-hair door of the tent, I glimpsed a Bedouin woman sitting in a corner. She resembled—in height, youthful age, and figure—the slain woman whom I had pulled by the hair from the sand at the ruin of al-Sawdāʾ—but the first was dead and this one was living.[35] She was chewing raw meat like a hyena, the blood of the meat on her face and hands. I greeted her, and she, staying where she was, spoke to me, her teeth
144 chomping all the while on flesh and bones. As she spoke, I was amazed, for I thought that if she rose up and ate me, I would occupy only a corner of her belly.[36] Still occupied by these thoughts, my eyes fixed on her; I rested my back against a stone by the door and put my feet up, one over the other. It was then that I suddenly felt the sting of a scorpion, or something like it, in my foot. It felt like a flame burning from my foot to the center of my heart. The moment I felt the bite, I vigorously hit my foot with my hand, cut around the wound and, taking a clove of garlic and a lump of salt from my pocket, rubbed it with them. I put pressure on the bite several times to drain its poison and was healed within the hour. It is also possible that I was immediately healed because I had killed that which had bitten me. The Bedouin woman hospitably wanted to serve me raw meat, but I had no desire either for her meat or for her dripping face, so I returned to my teacher.

Sālim ibn Saʿīd had already arranged for a Bedouin from Khabb to take us to Mount Khabb so, in the meantime, I went to the ruins of Bakbakah. I had even wanted to go to Mount Lawdh but did not manage to do so. A Bedouin told me that in Bakbakah they had found a marble coffin containing the bones of a woman. No doubt they called this place Bakbakah, I said to myself, because of the tears wept (*bukāʾ*) for her. As for my teacher Joseph, he was so afraid during our sojourn in the Jawf that he did not venture out of Sālim ibn Saʿīd's home except to go to Maʿīn and Banāt ʿĀd—and it was in the Jawf that we stayed the longest.

⟪ CHAPTER 7 ⟫
JEWS BEARING ARMS

THE WEAPON-BEARING JEWS OF KHABB

One day, I no longer remember the date, the tribesman with whom we were 145
to travel to Khabb came and committed himself to convey us to the Jews there—and so he did. We left al-Ḥazm that night and must, no doubt, have spent the next night in the tribesman's home. After that, he brought us to the home of the late Saʿīd ibn Yaḥyā Ḥuwwah, who warmly welcomed us as though we were lost brothers, even slaughtering a sheep for our dinner. He also announced our arrival to the rest of the Jews in the surrounding villages, with the result that the sun had not yet set when eight men arrived. All bore weapons that were heavily ornamented but that were smaller than the tribesmen's daggers.[1] Their resolute expressions bore witness to the beneficence of their tribal patrons, their thick and unruly side-locks proclaimed their courage according to the conventions of their kinsmen. They lived on the outskirts of the eastern lands, where there were no other people except for a few Bedouin from the Dhū Ḥusayn tribe who lived nearby.

We found these Jews to be fervent in their religion as it had been taught to them by their ancestors, but there were also some rigorists like those we had found in al-Madīd and in Nihm.[2] Their livelihood was slightly easier
than that of the Jews of the Jawf, for the land of Khabb is not as harsh. They 146
even grow grapes and dates, although these fruits are insubstantial and quite unlike those of the blessed Wādī Najrān. By contrast, in the Jawf, may God have mercy on them, we did not see any fruit trees other than the *qurūd*, a kind of lote tree that is found in abundance.[3] The Bedouin bring this fruit to Ṣanʿāʾ, and it is sold in no other place. In and around Khabb, they gather date pits, soak them in water, and then crush them in a mortar until they break into pieces. They feed this to their flocks, which like it and become very fat. I had already been amazed at the abundance of fat on the sheep that was slaughtered for us, and they said that it was on account of these dates.

A CONFLICT OVER A BETROTHAL

That day, when those eight men had gathered at Saʿīd Ḥuwwah's house to greet us and celebrate our arrival, there was a conflict about a 4- or 5-year-old girl. One of them claimed that she had been betrothed to him in place of his wife, the mother of his children; but the girl's family denied this and would not acquiesce to the marriage on account of the bad character of his children. They presented their arguments before my teacher Joseph so that he could judge between them, but my teacher would not listen to them. "No doubt he does not know the law," I said to myself. They had brought out the book of our master Joseph Caro,[4] whose laws they followed, and were making arguments on the basis of the book without knowledge either of what it
147 was about or of how to give a ruling in accordance with it. By the end of the day, their conflict had become more violent. They threatened one another, drew their weapons, and were on the verge of a fight. At this point, one of them intervened to extinguish the fire of contention.

"Why should we fight in vain when we have this sage among us who knows all the law by heart?" he said. "Let us entrust him with the matter and he will judge between us."

Since I was afraid that they might fight, I rejoiced at this, also thinking that we would stand to improve our own position in the best possible way. But my teacher Joseph did not bat an eyelid, neither fearing their dispute nor troubled by the prospect of a brawl. So, in private, I asked him, "Why do you not heed them and judge them according to the book? If it was I who knew their law, I would have already issued them a judgment, and they would not be burdened with this dispute."

"What stake do we have in their dispute that would oblige us to judge between them?" he replied. "We are strangers. If we give judgment against one side, because of their obstinacy and brazenness, they will seize us and we have no idea what would then befall us. It is best for us to leave this alone. As for the judgment, however, the law is clearly explained in the book in such-and-such a chapter and such-and-such a section."

So I took the book in my hand, opened it where he had told me and, behold, there was their exact judgment, no more, no less. However, our brethren did not know of this solution. I was greatly amazed by my teacher's knowledge of the law.*

ENCOUNTERS WITH THE JEWS OF KHABB

After we had stayed with our dear brother Saʿīd Ḥuwwah for two days, he 148
traveled with us by night to a Jew's house in another village. This Jew welcomed us like the others had. A Jewish neighbor of his, a silversmith called Mūsā Jamīl, came to visit and served us date arrack. We had not seen any Jew with arrack since we left Ṣanʿāʾ because, at that time, a blight had damaged the crop. And I, poor wretch, was new to traveling and was not yet used to the food of the village Jews. In particular, I was not used to their preparation of meat, although my teacher informed me that it was most healthy and nourishing. However, when I tasted the arrack that he had brought us, I found it good and I greatly rejoiced. Afterward, when Mūsā Jamīl returned to his house, I followed him to ask him for some more and he gave me what remained, which amounted to 30 *dirhams* in weight.[5]

I then went to search Khabb for Himyarite inscriptions and remains but found none. I met Sālim Ḥuwwah, who complained of his distress at living in this land, even though he was a blacksmith and his work supported him well. He had so exasperated himself that he wanted to immigrate to the Land of Israel. I said to him, "How will you be able to live in the land of Canaan
when you are from an eastern land?" 149

"If God were to bring me there and I were to die the day after I arrived," he replied, "my wish would be fulfilled."[6]

Because he was an old man and was well versed in their books, I asked him about what he knew of the ancient Jews who lived in this land. He told me that all their books come from Ṣanʿāʾ and that they have no indigenous books or chronicles whatsoever. As for the Jews of contemporary Khabb, all are immi-

* Although Halévy does not mention this dispute, he does mention his involvement in another dispute in Khabb. Far from remaining on the sidelines, he says that he gave a ruling against a local *marī* who argued that Jews should not purchase butter from Muslims on the grounds that it might contain camel's milk. Although Halévy marshals Talmudic support for his view, his grounds for intervening appear to have been largely humanitarian. That is, he did not want to effectively deprive these Jews of butter, given that it was the sole seasoning available in the region. Joseph Halévy, "Voyage au Nedjran II: De Sana à Nedjran," *Bulletin de la Société de Géographie de Paris* 13 (1877), 468–69.

grants from Baraṭ, Ṣanʿāʾ, and elsewhere. Because there are few of them and they are spread out, they have no synagogue. This is all I learned from him.

⟨ CHAPTER 8 ⟩

AN ORDEAL IN THE DESERT

ENCOUNTERS WITH NON-JEWISH GUIDES

Afterward, they brought us to a village at the edge of the land of Khabb and took us to the home of Yaḥyā Ḥuwwah (the aforementioned Sālim's brother and the father of Saʿīd, at whose house we had first arrived). Even though he lived at the edge of Khabb, he was a merchant, and he kindly gave us everything we needed for our journey across the desert to Najrān. He served us arrack, of which I drank my fill, and even gave me snuff for the journey. He also asked a Bedouin to accompany us to Najrān, lead us to its Jews, and bring back word to him of our well-being. And it happened just like that.[1] He wrote a contract for the Bedouin and had it witnessed before his ruler.

At midday, we left with the Bedouin and his camel. After traveling for two or three hours through the mountains, because all of Khabb is mountainous, we no longer saw any people. At the end of the day, the Bedouin
150 slowed down, telling me that I should go ahead, leading the camel on which my teacher was riding, and that he would catch up. While I was leading the camel, not knowing the way and feeling afraid, I saw a Bedouin far in front of us who was watching us. Because our guide was not with us, I grew even more afraid. However, the Bedouin disappeared and we saw him again only when, as we came under a cliff, this bandit's head and rifle suddenly appeared at the other side.

"Stop, Jew!" he shouted. "Abandon your belongings and the camel and save your head!"

While he was threatening us and shouting, our guide arrived. Taking in the situation, he hid behind the cliff and lit the match cord of his rifle. The two of them shouted at one another while I crawled behind the camel. Then, I know not why, the bandit left us.[2] The sun then set, and we spent the evening on the mountainside. At the end of the night, we set out. When the sun

brightened over us, we reached the foot of the mountain and the open desert
was before us. And behold, before us was a young woman pasturing sheep.
Our guide greeted her and asked where the Bedouin were encamped. He
then stayed behind with her while I went on with the camel for two hours.
When he rejoined us, he had entirely lost his mind [over her].[3] We traveled
further, the sand shining as if it were gold, until we came upon six Bedouin
women whose beauty was even greater than that of the Bedouin woman
whom our guide had previously met and been enchanted by. We greeted 151
them and they went on their way. At the end of the day, we came upon the
Bedouin of the Dhū Ḥusayn tribe and spent the night with them. The next
day, our Bedouin guide changed his mind and no longer wanted to travel
with us to Najrān.[4] My teacher and I were troubled, for how would we fare
alone in these empty regions? After much trouble, a Bedouin agreed to accompany us for a fee, and a contract was written and witnessed like that
which had been written by Yaḥyā Ḥuwwah. The scribe was a judge and
sayyid from Ṣanʿāʾ who had come to them by way of Baraṭ.

HADHLŪL, THE NEW BEDOUIN GUIDE

Once Hadhlūl[5] the Bedouin had committed to accompany us, I rejoiced because he was brave and was from the Yām tribes, not from the tribes of Dhū Ḥusayn. While we were traveling, he told us that he had once had sons but that they had all been killed, some in raids, some in battles. I was amazed. How was it that he was neither distressed nor saddened on account of his slain sons?

We traveled, spending the night wherever the sun set.[6] In the end, our flour and water was used up. When the sun set on Thursday, Hadhlūl made his camel kneel and we sat down to eat.

"Oh, Hadhlūl," I asked him, "how much longer do we have to travel before we reach an inhabited place?"

"Tomorrow, the day after, and another half day," he replied.

Once I had absorbed what he had said, I was upset because the Sabbath
was near and, moreover, Pentecost (Shavuʿot) was on Monday. All this and 152
we had neither food nor water.

"Curse your father!" I reproached him. "You bound yourself in contract to take us to an inhabited place in a short time. Today, our food and water is exhausted, there is not a single person to be seen in this desert, and the day after tomorrow is the Sabbath. What will become of us?"

"I swear by my nose that I will spend the Sabbath with you," he rejoined. "And do not fear, I will get you food."

To certify their promises, the Bedouin have the custom of raising their right hand, placing a finger on their nose, and letting it slide from between their eyes to the end of their nose—this is their law. However, in the Ṣanʿā' region, they instead place a finger on their eyes.

"How will you get us food when there is not a tree or bush for us to eat from? I asked him. "There is nothing here but sand."

"Light a fire," he said, "and don't put it out until I return." And he left in the darkness of night.

My custom during this trip was to take a little of our flour and knead it in the corner of my waist wrapper. I did this because our guide had taken our kneading bowl and had drunk camel milk from it, making it unkosher, so we had let him have it.[7] I used to knead the flour in my waist wrapper and make it into two loaves of bread, one for me and one for my teacher. I would
153 light the fire, not with a European match, because these did not then exist in Yemen, but with a flint and gunpowder. I would stoke the fire until the sand and what was under it became hot, then I would scatter it and bury the loaves in the hot sand to bake. No sand would cling to them and they tasted better than the bread of my own land. That night, I lit the fire and kept it burning as Hadhlūl had asked. However, when he was late in returning, I scattered it and placed our remaining two loaves on it. While I was talking with my teacher Joseph about what we would eat, Hadhlūl arrived.

"Why did you put out the fire? Light it up!" he called out to us.

So I lit the fire a second time and saw by its light that he had two animals with him, similar to what we call *waḥar* and *lizaq* lizards—but these were bigger. He had hunted for them that night in the sand, and they were skewered on the staff he used to drive his camel. He put his staff on the flames until he had cooked them and they had swelled even larger than they had been. He then presented one to my teacher and one to me. I took it, broke it into pieces, and contemplated it while he ate.

"Eat this good food!" he said. "I have added to your provisions and you will need nothing further."

"May God brighten your countenance for sating our hunger with this," I replied, "but as for our thirst, with what will you quench it?" 154

"Do not fear," he said, "for we have a camel which will slake all our thirst."

But I was neither accustomed to eating lizards or mice nor to drinking camel milk. This Bedouin Hadhlūl, however, was one of the Bedouin who live on the edges of the land, who do without food and water for weeks or months on end by drinking only camel milk at the beginning and end of each day. They have no need of anything else, but, if they happen upon wheat, they gnaw on it like animals.

"Oh, Hadhlūl," I said, "your food and drink are of no use to us. Leave us here this very night and return to your companions, for death here is easier than death elsewhere after exhaustion."

"Even if I had to carry you between my teeth like a piece of meat," he said, "I would not abandon you in this desert unless I myself were to die. So long as I am alive on the face of the earth, I will spare no effort to protect you."

"I can tell that your words are true and that you would not abandon us in the desert," I said, "but what use to us are your efforts and protection when we are far from people? If you think that you're able to bring us to an inhabited place as soon as tomorrow, let's travel tonight and run and not spend the night or stop at all. That is our desire for which I will pay you half a riyal in addition to your wages."

Hearing this, he got up and said, "With God's help."[8] He readied his camel, my teacher mounted it, and we traveled the whole night until sunrise. 155
By this time, my strength began to break. The increasing heat weakened my nerves, while fatigue, hunger, and thirst destroyed me. When the sun beat harder, I took to walking a little and then stopping to rest. When this happened, Hadhlūl and his camel stopped until I resumed following him. My fatigue increased, and I became exhausted. At one point, after waiting for me, Hadhlūl called to me but I was no longer able to answer him. He walked back to me and said, "Come, get up!"

"Oh, Hadhlūl," I said to him, "by God, I beg you to leave me and go on your way because I am already lost."

When he saw that I was too exhausted to move, he struck me twice with his staff until I forgot my exhaustion and jumped up, either to beat him or to protect myself from his blows. He immediately grabbed my hand and led me to his camel to persuade me to ride on it with my teacher. Now camel riding did not agree with me because the movement crushed my bowels. So, before mounting, I took the kneading bowl, shook the sack of flour into it, then poured in the water from the waterskin, together with the mud and hair. I mixed them together and drank—from the very bowl from which I had previously been repulsed and had no longer kneaded in because it had been rendered impure with camel milk. After I had drunk what was left, I revived a little, my spirit returned, and my eyes lit up. Hadhlūl mounted me on the camel next to my teacher and we traveled onward.

156 Because of my teacher's amazing ability to endure hunger, thirst, and sitting on the back of a camel, he showed no signs of fatigue, nor did I hear a word of complaint from him throughout this arduous trip.

While we were riding fast on the camel, I saw something moving slowly in the distance, but I did not know what it was. "Oh, Hadhlūl," I said, "can you tell what it is that I see in the distance?"

Hadhlūl mounted the camel, scrutinized it, and then cried out, "People!"

We all rejoiced and pressed on until we converged and it turned out to be an old woman. We asked her what she was doing here, and she told us that she was lost in the desert, where she had been searching for the Bedouin to whom she had married her daughter.[9] We now felt even greater grief and sorrow. The old woman traveled with us until we met three Bedouin from the tribe of Yām who were passing by. We greeted them, and Hadhlūl asked them the way. They told us that we were close to an inhabited place and then left with the old woman. We continued on our way until, close to noon, I saw something moving and said to Hadhlūl, "Can you tell what this is?"

He looked at it and rejoiced, saying, "Praise God, this is a Bedouin camp!"

He led us toward it and, on Friday evening, we arrived. There was a well there to which the Bedouin, their wives, their children, and their beasts come from afar to draw water. Some of them, out of caution, had lit the match
157 cords of their rifles. Most were naked, except for that which covered their male and female parts. When they saw us, they stopped drawing water and came to greet us, stare, and ask questions. They gave us milk and water, telling us that we were on the edge of Wādī Najrān. They also told us that a Jew lived nearby.

A RELUCTANT HOST

We immediately hastened to the house of the Jew, Marī Maṭrūd, whom they had described to us. When we arrived there, I was still afraid of the Najrānī tribesmen, for I was not yet sure of the good character of the ones who had guided us to him. I knocked on the *marī*'s door.

"Who's that who beats on my door?" he said.

"It's your brother, open up," I replied.

He heard me but was silent. I waited for half an hour, thinking that he would open up and speak to us, but when he did not appear, I knocked a second and a third time. As if he had not heard us, he said, "Who's at the door who summons me on the Sabbath eve?"

"If you had gone to the tribesmen," our guide Hadhlūl said, "they would already have happily welcomed you."

I was no longer afraid of the tribesmen, but I was afraid for my teacher Joseph, so I banged violently on the door, paying no attention to Marī Maṭrūd's words, even when he threatened me with his weapon. When he opened the door to face us, I put my foot forward to enter the house, but he grabbed my hand, pulled me outside, and sat down. I became angry and said in Hebrew,[10] "O, evildoer, your Jewish brethren have come from afar to visit you, inquire after your well-being, and learn of your condition. Not 158
only have you not hastened to welcome and bring us under your roof, but you force us to stay outside! If today was not the eve of the Holy Sabbath, we would have expelled you from the diaspora community, I by the authority of the Jewish court of Ṣanʿāʾ and the sage by the authority of the rabbis of Jerusalem unto which all the eyes of Israel are lifted." Hearing my threat, he became submissive.

"Oh *marī*," he said, "we fear the Gentiles who do not permit us to host guests."

"You lie!" I told him. "The Gentiles are hospitable to guests. They serve them food and drink and anoint them. But you, God forbid, are not from the seed of Israel!"

After that, he said, "Welcome and greetings to the guest," and wanted to usher us in.

"Do us a favor," I said to him. "Ask your tribesmen friends to pay half a riyal to this Bedouin who accompanied us. After the Sabbath ends, I will pay you back and, don't fear, I have enough money to furnish our needs." This was done and, after he had been paid, Hadhlūl the Bedouin immediately returned home.

We entered Marī Maṭrūd's house, and he took us to the upper room, which was entirely bare.

"We would like to sanctify ourselves in honor of the Sabbath," I said.

For them, this term *sanctify* meant to wash oneself with water in honor of
159 the Sabbath. Marī Maṭrūd led us down from the upper room to the courtyard in front of his house. We washed our hands, feet, and faces and then returned to recite the Sabbath prayer. After we had completed our religious obligations, which fatigue, hunger, and fear made difficult, they served us two pancakes, which were as small as the ears of a mouse, and also brought us half a young chicken. As for coffee, they said, "Never on the Sabbath!"

We sat down and spoke with Maṭrūd and with another Jew who was sitting with him. The other Jew was hunched over and leaning against Marī Maṭrūd's wife, who was not sitting but reclining, her head raised on her right hand. She also chatted a lot with them. Tiring of this miserable gathering, I said, "Oh, Maṭrūd, we are fatigued from traveling and would like to sleep. Tomorrow we will have the whole day for long conversations."

"Yes," he replied, "but it is my desire to get up at night to go to pray at Marī Maʿīḍ's."

I was so pleased that I wanted him to repeat himself, so I asked, "What did you say?"

"Yes," he replied, "at dawn we'll go to pray at Marī Maʿīḍ's. It's nearby to us."

"May God be good to you," I exclaimed. "Tell us where we can sleep so that we can get up early."

He hurried to do so, making no objection. That night, the fleas gathered from everywhere in the house to welcome us and keep us company. They knew about our plans for the morning prayer, which meant that this was the
160 only night they would be able to dine on us. But neither they nor the sleepless night and fatigue upset me, for tomorrow we were to go to the synagogue of our brethren, the Jews of Najrān! And so I sat in battle with the fleas. When I drove them off my leg, they returned and attached themselves to my hand and back, when I drove them away from those, they returned to other

places.[11] This continued for most of the night until I said to myself, "Only prayer will save me from them," so I called to Maṭrūd.

"Let's get up and go to pray, for dawn has already risen."

"No," he replied, "go back to sleep. The cock has not yet crowed and it is still nighttime."

I returned to my afflictions—truly the fleas had a great feast that night. Finally, sleep overcame me, and then there was Maṭrūd, poking us and saying, "It's time to get up. The sun has already risen."

Having no further excuse to sleep, we got up, washed our hands and faces, and were on the road by the first light of day. When the sun had risen above us, we were still traveling through the palm trees and among a few houses of Wādī Najrān. I said to Maṭrūd, "Sir, don't you acknowledge the power of the day? You have caused us to travel beyond the Sabbath boundaries."

"Don't worry, *marī*," he said. "I have already made a Sabbath *eruv*."*

"You've done well," I replied, "but let's hurry so that we can arrive before mealtime."

I had not said what I had said in seriousness but only to induce him to speak. As for my teacher Joseph, although he observed most of what went 161
on, it seemed as though he neither saw nor heard it. In any case, if he did not write it in his notebook, he wrote it upon the tablet of his heart.

We passed through palm groves where we could not see the sun because of the many trees and their overlapping leaves. At the end of one grove, we saw five or six houses under which four or five girls were socializing. When we drew near them, they recognized what we were, but I did not recognize that some of them were our fellow Jews, since their clothing was the same as those of tribeswomen. I did not recognize what they were until they confirmed who we were, then fled the company of their friends and went inside one of the houses, from which they kept peeking out at us from the windows. I knew then that this was a Jewish home.

* Jewish law prohibits traveling more than 2,000 cubits from one's town on the Sabbath. An *eruv teḥumim* is a legal fiction that allows Jews to travel greater distances without technically violating the Sabbath restrictions. Zvi Kaplan, "Eruv," in *Encyclopedia Judaica* (Jerusalem: Keter, 1972), 6: 849.

A WARM WELCOME AND A HIDDEN SORROW IN WĀDĪ NAJRĀN

Marī Maṭrūd led us to this house and we entered. A girl sat outside the door to the main room, hiding her face in her head scarf as though her heart had been struck with the stick of shame. Inside the room was an old woman who sat with an air of sadness, and in a corner sat an old man who also seemed sorrowful. When we entered, the old man and woman rose to greet and welcome us. When I saw that, I assumed that this place was a synagogue and that the congregation had, as was customary, left after the prayers but would return for the Torah reading and conclusion of the service. I believed
162 that the veiled girl was there to hear the prayer. I began to recite the Tiqqun (nighttime liturgy) and finished with the morning prayer. After that, the old woman offered us a stone pot called a *madhalah*, which they make in Ṣaʿdah, and in which they had baked a kind of bread called *kubānah*.[12] She removed the *kubānah* from the *madhalah* and placed it in another earthenware bowl. She then parted the dough and poured the oil into the center. We all gathered for that breakfast: the two old people, the girls, the girl who was at the door of the room, Maṭrūd, myself, and my teacher. Because the breakfast was so tasty, I said to myself, "When I return to Ṣanʿāʾ, I will tell my family to prepare the *kubānah* only in this way."

After we had eaten, they served us coffee and dates. We then read the week's Torah portion, completed the remaining prayers, and studied a large section of the book *The Menorah*,[13] as is the custom of Yemeni Jews. After that, we continued to chat a little. Marī Maṭrūd wanted to return to his house, taking us with him, but I wanted to remain with Marī Maʿīḍ—because the name Maʿīḍ, derived from the word *recompense*, [is a sign of blessing], unlike the name Maṭrūd.[14] Marī Maʿīḍ then spoke up, "Marī Maṭrūd, today they are my guests."

"They were my guests before this and it would be disgraceful for me to abandon them," he replied.

He got up, grabbing our hands as though he truly wanted to force us to return with him to his bare and far-off house. The old man [Marī Maʿīḍ]
163 rose from his corner and, blocking the door, he said, "All of you are my guests. No one will ever leave my place."

We stood firmly by the master of the house, while Maṭrūd continued to insist, until he finally bade us farewell and departed. I now realized why he had brought us here for prayer and why he had pretended that our Jewish brethren in Wādī Najrān had a synagogue.* May God grant him his reward in this world!**

THE JEWS OF WĀDĪ NAJRĀN

Marī Maʿīḍ and I returned to talking about his own situation and that of his land. He said, "All the Najrānī Jews are protégés (*rubʿān*), that is, clients (*jār*), of the tribes. They can never own land or houses in Wādī Najrān. This is also the case for foreign tribesmen and for the Jawf *sharīfs*, who come every year for the harvest season. They cannot own anything in the wadi, although they do have certain places reserved for them to dwell in while they harvest the palms. After that, they abandon them and return to their land. Although the Jews have always lived here, their houses belong to the local tribes, but they do not pay rent. This is because the tribes of Yām are not oppressive to their clients and exceed all other tribes in the support that they give them.[15] If there is a need to sell a [Jew's] house, one of the owner's relatives buys it."

I have never seen a land as fertile as Wādī Najrān. This is because its wa- 164
ters are sweeter than others. They have many wells, and the water is as close as 12 cubits to the surface.

It takes two days to traverse the length of the wadi and half a day to traverse its width. Most of the wadi is shaded by palm trees. Each tree has between five and sixteen bunches of dates, and each bunch weighs between one-half and one Ṣanʿānī *qadaḥ*. Figs and grapes also grow in the wadi, but the people are so uncivilized that they harvest them while they are still unripe. Wheat is the most commonly cultivated grain. The wheat is so good that, when dough is kneaded, its oil can be seen.

While we were still chatting with Marī Maʿīḍ, the old woman, without budging from her spot, turned to her daughters and said, "Come for lunch. The guests are hungry!"

So, without delay, they hurried to get it ready, which was exactly what we

* That is, Ḥabshūsh realizes that Maṭrūd had pretended that the Najrānī Jews had a synagogue in order to rid himself of his guests by foisting them on Marī Maʿīḍ. In fact, Maṭrūd's "synagogue" was just the private home of the hospitable Marī Maʿīḍ.

** According to tradition, whatever good deeds the wicked perform are rewarded *in this world* so that they will entirely forfeit reward in the next. See, for example, *Sifre* on Deuteronomy 32:4.

wanted. The old woman took a skin, which seemed to be filled with ghee, and poured it into the *harīs*,[16] which contained meat.

"What are you doing?" I said. "Don't you know that the Law forbids mixing ghee with meat?"*

"God forbid!" they replied. "This is just animal grease! It's not ghee and it's not forbidden tallow."[17]

It was so good that I could not detect a difference in taste or smell. After the meal, they again served us dates.

CHAPTER 9

THE HONOR CODE OF THE NAJRĀNĪ JEWS

A FAMILY IN GRIEF

I made conversation, but they had no desire for it because their minds were elsewhere. I persisted, telling them pleasant and amusing stories to win their
165 hearts so that we could relax together in good cheer, but nothing availed. Instead, the old woman averted her eyes and gazed out the window, contemplating the palms that she had known all her life. While I chattered away, the young girl who sat outside the door would glance about furtively and then return to her former state. It was also difficult for Marī Maʿīḍ to respond to me, for he too had lost heart.

"They must surely be suffering from some great anguish," I said to myself, so I thought up a plan to find out what was grieving them. I interrupted what I had been saying to them, fell silent, put my hand over my face, shut my eyes, and mumbled some words to myself. I then got up, went to the window by which the old woman sat, and put my head out to examine the firmament of the heavens. I did this twice, reading the stars and raving on until I had beguiled them with this deceit and trickery.

Although eastern Yemenis[1] do not believe in these arts as much as western Yemenis, they certainly believe in them enough. The source of such beliefs are people who feign knowledge of jurisprudence. Even though

* Jewish dietary law prohibits the mixing of milk and meat.

Islamic law prohibits it, where there are many jurists, these beliefs are widespread. Although they are uncommon today in eastern Yemen, [in western Yemen] they are especially common in the Tihāmah plain, because of the town of Zabīd, and in Ḥudaydah, because of the towns of Bayt al-Faqīh and Marāwiʿah.

Thank God, having been immersed in the waters of insight by my 166
teacher Joseph, may God grant him long life and enlighten his heart, I can now ask the Lord's forgiveness for the deception with which I enticed their minds in order to know what was troubling them. This is what happened . . .

After I had grown quiet, having pushed the trickery to its utmost, the old woman asked, "Marī, what are you doing?"

"I am reading the stars and discovering the innermost secrets," I replied.

"And what have you discovered from these readings?"

"I know that your stars are those of great misfortune and that you are in great distress," I said. "But do not fear. Today is the Sabbath, on which neither work nor grief is permissible, but, God willing, when the Sabbath ends, we will find a remedy."

The old woman turned toward me crying, and the girl stuck her now unveiled face into the room to hear what was being said. The mother said, "How can you tell us not to fear and grieve when we are in a misfortune like no other—which also happened to the daughter of my paternal uncle, the daughter of my mother's uncle, and the granddaughter of my paternal uncle. There was nothing for it but to kill and bury them, for this is our law.[2] But as for us, the man of the house is too old and cannot slaughter and bury her by himself. So we have sent for our relatives in Ṣaʿdah, her father's nephews, to come and help us kill her so that we will be cleansed of our shame and disgrace."

Having learned their secret from her, my mind reeled at this calamitous
law that she said they follow. I said to them, "Surely God must have sent me 167
from my home, from Ṣanʿāʾ, to save her from this curse by extracting the fetus from her womb so that no one will know it was ever occupied. Don't worry and don't grieve because, with God's help, I will free her from this through my knowledge of these matters."

When the girl heard my words, she jumped up and, rooting herself at my feet with her arms around my knees, wept. "Marī, protect me! I have sinned and brought this judgment upon myself. Oh Marī, let me live or kill me, but don't make me wait any longer until my cousins come, for I don't know what they will do to me. Marī, I am at God's mercy and at yours. Don't give up on me while you can still fight for me. I am under God's protection and under yours."

When I saw her rooted at my feet, weeping for her life with a fiery heart, my guts burned with pity. Were my heart as hard as stone, on that day it would have run like wax with compassion. So I lifted her by the hand and said, "Do not fear, my sister, and do not grieve. God willing, I will save you from this."

Their hearts stilled by my words, the mother said to her youngest daughter, "Get up and give the *marī* the hatchet," which looked like a small axe. And her sister, whose soul had been grieving, took it in her hand and gave it to me. I took it from her, wondering what to do with it, because I had already made peace between them and there was no longer any need for either an
168 axe or a sword to kill her with. After turning it around to examine its length, width, sharpness, and sheen, I put it down, still wondering what they wanted me to do with it. The mother then told me, "Take it and strike that ledge on your left."

So I took the axe and turned to the ledge, which was so hard it seemed to be made of stone. I thought to myself, "What reason do they have for striking this stone bench on the Sabbath day when they know that it is forbidden on the Sabbath?"

The girl then took the hatchet from me and struck the ledge until it split. And, behold, there were dates pressed in their skins—the very best kind of dates that they call *ruṭab*. The skins had dried on the dates so that they had become as hard as stone. "Take some," the mother said, "for there is nothing like it." I knew then that they had placed their trust in me and that their grief had abated. Now that the girl no longer sat outside the door, I asked her, in front of her family, "Oh, Saʿīdah, how was it that Satan was able to seduce you when your father is Marī Maʿīḍ and your mother is from the family of Pinḥas ha-Kohen of Ṣaʿdah, which originated in Ṣanʿāʾ, and you yourself are not a foolish woman."

"Listen," she said, "I will tell you what happened to me."

This was her story. It was the custom in Najrān, when a Jew fell ill or something bad happened, for the Jews of all the villages to visit him until
169 his health returned or he died. If his health returned, they had what they

desired; if he died, the visitors sent for his friends to gather to perform the final rites. One month, Saʿīdah's father said to her, "Come, let's go to visit so-and-so, who is sick."

They took flour and ghee and went to the sick man's home, staying with him for five days until other Jews came to visit. Her father then said to her, "My daughter, I'm going to return home, but you stay here to help the sick man's wife and serve the guests."

"As you wish," she replied, and he went on his way while she stayed to serve them.

Two days later, six young men arrived, whose names she told me. That night after dinner, they sat up making merry before deciding to sleep. Some left the room to sleep, but one came to her while she was sleeping beside the sick man's wife. She let him, since he wouldn't have listened to her, and this situation resulted from it. She told herself that nothing would come forth from this one time. All this happened because she was ashamed lest his friends hear her cry out. This was the girl's story.

A STORY WITHIN A STORY: A SHARĪF ATTEMPTS TO VIOLATE THE HONOR OF A JEWISH WOMAN

The young traveler said: All these events happened before my teacher Joseph's eyes and he did nothing to interfere. I was pleased with myself for having done all I could to relieve them of their misfortune and also to im- 170
prove our own position in the best possible way.

To better understand the spirit of the villagers of this land, I will add some explanation of what happened last year at this time. Rābiʿah was a Jewish girl from Ḥazm Hamdān in the Jawf. At that time, she was only 5 years old and, because of her family's poverty, went about naked save for a leather strip to cover her genitals. In addition, her father, Sālim ibn Sulaymān, disguised her as a boy by shaving her head and leaving her with two side-locks like those of her brothers.

"Why did you give her side-locks?" I asked them.

"So that she will live," they replied.

And she did live. She grew up, married, rebelled against her husband, and became famous for her beauty throughout the land. One of the *sharīf*s of the Jawf heard of her famed beauty, so he rode to her house and knocked on her door. When she opened it, he tied his horse to the door and entered. He greeted her and she welcomed him, serving coffee as was their custom. He asked her for lunch.

"As you wish," she said.

When she brought him the bread, he grabbed her hand and tried to violate her.

"The meal first, oh *sharīf*, and then I will not deny you," she cried out. "Be patient and I will come to you."

So he believed her and was patient, but she left the room and locked the door.

When she got out of the house, she began to cry at the top of her voice,
171 "Woe, a disgrace, a disgrace!" until she had gathered a crowd.

"What's with you, oh Jewess, that you gather the people?" they demanded.

"I want my patron," she replied.

"Who is your patron?"

"So-and-so," she said.

When her patron arrived with his entourage, he said, "What's with you, oh Jewess, that you disturb the people, gathering them with your screams?"

"Listen everyone," she replied, "the Jawf tribesmen, whether or not they are *sharīfs*, have always followed law and tradition. The Jews have also followed both law and tradition as long as they have lived among the tribes. Today, someone came unexpectedly to my house and I welcomed him, as is our custom, but he then demanded from me my very self. If the pact between the Jews and the tribes and the tribes and the Jews has been dissolved, then tell us and we will find our own remedy; if not, should this matter not be acknowledged as infamy?"

Her words so moved the hearts of those present that they said to her, "Who is it who sought to offend you?"

"He who is at my house where I have imprisoned him," she replied, "and here is his horse."

They immediately fell upon the horse and hamstrung it. They then entered the house and brought him out, but they did little to him because they could not kill him on account of the fame of his family. They did, however, declare that anyone who offended the woman again would be killed like a snake. This is what happened in the village of Ḥazm Hamdān in the Jawf.

THE SANCTITY OF FETAL LIFE

Let us return to the house of Marī Maʿīḍ. It was at the end of that Sabbath
day, after we had been treated more graciously than strangers deserved, that 172
my teacher said, "Let's go for a stroll among the date palms."

"Right away," I said, and hurried to get up.

When he got outside, he said, "I see that today our situation has changed and that your speeches have brought us joy. Tell me about this, because I did not understand what they said."

"Did you not know that this family was in grief but, with God's help, I gave them relief?" I said.

"And what will their relief be?" he asked.

"I have expertise in medicines that I can burn as incense or serve as a potion and which have the property of expelling the fetus."

"Your words are astounding," he said. "Please tell me, who is your sheikh who taught you these sciences?"

"I have no sheikh," I replied, "but I learned from the mouths of the people and from books."

"Where will you get these medicines when you are on the outskirts of the country?" he asked. "You are not in the city where you can get what you need from the market."

"I know of certain trees and plants whose acrid sap can substitute for the medicines that I lack," I answered.

He continued to draw me out, inwardly ridiculing me while I responded sincerely, proud of my knowledge, although not with the pride and boastfulness that I had shown in Marī Maʿīḍ's home.

"When I was in Ṣanʿāʾ," he said, "I did not know that you were one of those men of science and, had I known, I would not have dared to bring you with me."

And he began to shoot bullets of abuse at me, strike me with the sword of 173
cursing, and pierce me with the lance of insult. I was astounded and offended
by his words, having never heard him speak like this as long as I had known
him. I said to myself, "Oh Lord, make me patient so that I can bear this."

"I will make this matter known," my teacher added, "in Ṣanʿāʾ, Holy Jerusalem, and in all villages in which Jews dwell."

I replied in a low and abject voice, which I do not usually use, "Oh sir, oh light of my eyes, please explain the reason for your anger, for I know that I am innocent of sin and that my intentions in this matter are only good."

"How can you say that you are blameless?" he replied, "and on what basis can you claim to be in the right when you would kill a sacred life and shed blood?"

"Heaven forfend that you should falsely accuse me of this, for whom have I killed and whose blood have I ever tried to shed, who was not first the aggressor?"

"Do you think it permissible to kill the fetus in the girl's womb?" he said. "Do you not realize that this is shedding blood?"[3]

"Oh my teacher," I replied, "If anyone other than you had said this, I would have called him a madman. Do you know nothing of what happened to us today? I thought that after what we heard from the girl and her mother and what happened before your own eyes, you would be fully apprised of their story."

I therefore told him, from beginning to end, of their grief and of their happiness, of their law and of their desires. I also told him about the women
174 whom [the mother] said had been killed.

At that time, because of my thoughtlessness and my upbringing among the Arabs, I was not concerned about that which was in a mother's womb. Indeed, because I had heard about the fear and shame resulting from a few such incidents in Ṣanʿāʾ, I felt grief for the girl who had thrown herself at our feet and who did not deserve this because of her decency and great beauty.

Once my teacher had heard from me about their circumstances and what they had said, he ceased being angry with me and turned his many wrathful words upon them, insulting and cursing them. "How can this be their law when it agrees with no other? Even a pagan would not rule according to this law, killing mothers together with their children. God, take vengeance upon these people even if they are Jews and this is their law. If they do not renounce the killing of the girl and do not abolish this vile law, I will make this matter known in each and every place in which Jews dwell until their vile deeds are clear to all."

After I had considered the matter and it became clear to me that he was correct and we were in error, I said to him, "You are correct. However, the old woman will ask how a bastard can be raised in her home when she is from a good family, and what will the people say who see him with them?"

"The Torah," he replied, "does not call him a bastard, but calls him kosher (legitimate), and this is also the teaching of the rabbis."[4] He again 175
became angry and said, "Let us return to them, and I myself will tell them that if they do not acknowledge the rabbis' words, they are not part of the community of Israel."

When I saw him readying for a fight, the matter troubled me, and I, the student, said to him, "Oh sir, oh my friend, your words are suitable for those who know the truth, but do not engage them with such threats, for we will do no more than tire ourselves and increase their grief. Rather, let us engage them strategically and find a way for them to attain insight."

"I cannot be forbearing," he said, "for there is no shame in upholding religion."

When we entered the house, his scolding, as well as the night, darkened their spirits. Their clouds of sadness returned, dimming their heavens. I remained perplexed, searching for something to improve their situation, and their grief became my grief.

AN ALTERNATIVE SOLUTION IS PROPOSED

The next day, as I was sitting with the mother and giving her words of comfort, it seemed as if we were one family.

"My mother," I said to her, "the words of the sage are correct, but do not grieve, for God will find a way."

"May God lead her to the grave before she gives birth to a bastard," she replied.

"If that is your fear," I said, "do not grieve, for I will be responsible for her."

"How can you be responsible for her when you are a traveler who will not marry her and the child will remain with me? What you say cannot be."

"That is no problem," I replied. "If that is what you desire, I will send 176
your daughter Saʿīdah to people I know in the Jawf. There I will take her for a wife, since there is no one here to conduct a marriage according to law and custom."

"I fear," she objected, "that you won't keep your word and will abandon my daughter when she is far away from me and her family."

"God forbid," I said. "I am not someone who makes empty promises—I am God-fearing."

After we had agreed on this, they rejoiced, and Saʿīdah took my hand and placed it between her eyes, saying, "I am your servant, for you have saved me from shame and death."

"God willing," I replied.

"What caused their grief to depart and made them happy?" my teacher questioned me.

I told him that, God willing, we had come to an agreement, which I then described.

"When this business of yours reaches the ears of your family and friends in Ṣanʿāʾ," he said, "you tell me what they will say about it. Will they praise you or shame you?"

"They will praise me," I replied, "and say that he has come upon a good prize like no other, an eastern girl—because the women of the east are famous throughout all of Yemen for their beauty."

"All right," he said, "I see that you have been seduced by her great beauty and grace," and he continued to praise her from the top of her head to her toenails.

"Oh sir," I replied, "I have not been seduced and my intentions are good.
177 I am proud to the core of this lovely woman."

"Do you not remember," my teacher angrily retorted, "that you left your house to serve God through our work, and now you want to involve me in other matters. Even if you leave her in the Jawf or elsewhere so that we can finish our travels, what will your family, your brothers, your sons, and your first wife say when you return to your house in Ṣanʿāʾ with a rival wife? Will this affair not be shameful and distressing for them? Will you not be forced to separate, not only from your first wife but also from your children? Will you not embroil your wife and children in conflict because of her? Such grief on her account! And your family will say, 'This is all the fault of the sage, Joseph Halévy.' But, oh people of Yemen, if you do not reverse this deed which you think is good but which is evil, I will not curtail my description of your vile deeds, either in the company of honorable people or in my book. I know that there are people among you who marry many women without considering the sin and misfortunes which befall them and their children."[5]

How many humiliations and how much cursing I heard until I made up my mind and felt ashamed of myself. "I understand that you are right and that your advice to me was correct," I said to him, "but I ask that you do me the courtesy of not revealing this affair to anyone, for it would be needlessly shameful for me." And I wholly and utterly abandoned the matter.

CHAPTER 10 178

PERSECUTION

THE DAḤḌAH MARKET

After Shavuʿot, we left Marī Maʿīḍ's house, but we were certain that we would later return. We arrived at the house of another *marī* who was a silversmith, but I no longer remember his name or where he lived. He served us date honey, the like of which I had never tasted. Nearby was a market called Daḥḍah,[1] to which I went to see the people and their merchandise and trades. When I entered, I found that it was like the other Bedouin markets, which have no houses or stalls. Their merchandise was Sawāḥilī or Ḥaḍramī cotton, undyed or dyed with indigo, but other fabrics were not to be found. This was the only merchandise that was brought from outside their land. For the rest, they made do with what grain, dates, and cattle they produced. It is rare for other merchandise to be imported, and few ask for it. Their salt comes from Ṣāfir, which is near Mārib, and this salt is also exported to the Ṣanʿāʾ region.

While I was observing all of this, I saw a Karrāmī[2] preacher at the edge of the market who was warning the tribesmen not to look at the women who were shopping. But I did not see a single tribesman showing him respect or heeding his words, and only the women were embarrassed by his shouting. When the sun grew hot, I became thirsty and did not know where I could get 179 a drink. When I came upon a Jew, I grabbed him, saying, "Come my brother, give me water, for you know that I am a stranger."

He took me to the center of the market where there was a woman selling water from two waterskins. He gave her a handful of dried dates from his bag, and she let me drink the water. He then took out another handful so that he could also drink, but no sooner had he put the skin to his mouth than the sound of war arose. The people gave out a great cry of alarm and fled. The Jew was so afraid that, forgetting he was drinking, he spat the water from his mouth and shouted at the top of his lungs, "Market! Market!"

He fled, shouting at someone fleeing behind him, "Is there no covenant between us? Why do you pursue me?" And, tossing his water bowl, he continued to flee. Within moments, I could no longer see even a single person in the market. Their merchandise, spread out on rugs, remained but had been trampled by everyone fleeing. I was still marveling at this when the men of the market returned, all of them crying out, "Market! Market! Market!"

But the last of these had not yet returned to his rug when there was again the sound of screaming and those in the market fled again. I stood where I was in the center of the market, for I already knew that they would not
180 interfere with me because I was a foreigner. I tried to work out where they had fled to, for they had fled in all directions. Because the Daḥḍah market is in a clearing surrounded by palm trees, the people had slipped in between them, and I was unable to see any of them except the warriors. These had let their turbans slip from their heads, flung about their hair, and climbed the nearby palms, which were not very high. Armed and perched in the palms, they fired rounds during the battle. After this commotion had lasted for a short time, these brave men descended from the palms and the people ceased their flight. Returning to the market, everyone cried out, "Market! Market!" By saying this, they meant that markets are protected areas.[3] Neither legal claims nor judgments are issued in the market, lest a fight break out. This is the case regardless of whether the claim involves a debt, a transgression, or even a murder. All the tribes unite against anyone who breaks this law of theirs. This is the same for the rest of the tribal markets of Yemen, except for those in the cities. As far as I remember, I saw no Jew in that market other than the one who gave me water. After that, I returned to my teacher and told him what I had witnessed.

THE PEOPLE AND ANTIQUITIES OF NAJRĀN

The people told us of one ruin and I went there, but I did not find it as amazing as the ruins of the Jawf. There were no sculpted stones, and I found 181
inscriptions on only two stones. Next to this ruin was a domed mosque. The Bedouin say that this is the grave of Thamūd, the brother of ʿĀd.[4] They say that he no doubt helped his brother build on the land, and, content with this, he did not build anything for himself and his companions in Wādī Najrān, for he trusted the strength of his companions. To this day, most of the tribesmen of Wādī Najrān are distinguished from the other eastern tribesmen by the considerable size of their bodies. For this reason, the Qurʾān calls them "the companions of Ukhdūd."[5]

The tribesmen say that their land had once been part Jewish and part Christian, and some places are still called by Jewish names.[6] To this day, these tribesmen belong to a different sect from those of the rest of Yemen. I saw at the house of their judge, whose name was Ibn Lughah,* documents by Qāḍī Sayyid Aḥmad al-Kibsī of Baraṭ concerning claims and disputes according to the rites of the Dāʾūdī and Sulaymānī sects.[7] The remarks I made to Ibn Lughah have slipped my mind, but they caused him to offer me a house and date palms. He said that if I would stay with him, he would give me one of his Jewish protégées as a wife, and even proposed a girl from the Jamal family, but I did not accept his offer. He then offered to host me for three months, or at least two, but I stayed only two days with him and then returned to my teacher. But, in my heart, I wanted to return to that land after we finished our work, for the tribesmen there were of good character and generous, and 182
the land was good. However, I was concerned about my family and children. Moreover, our brethren who live in Najrān are not able to stay healthy. Every year, or at least every two years, they are struck for months with sickness. What they earn, they spend on their sicknesses and even go into debt. So goes their life in that land.

After that, my teacher and I wanted to go to Barād[8] where the Karrāmī scholars of the Yām tribe are to be found, but that was not possible. After

* Halévy also reports meeting with Muḥammad Ibn Lughah, whom he describes as learned and as an "aristotélicien enragé," that is, "a rabid Aristotelian." Joseph Halévy, "Rapport sur une mission archéologique dans le Yemen," *Journal Asiatique* 6 (1872), 38–39.

I had contemplated the tall palms, which were 50 cubits high—too high to climb to the top—we decided to travel to Baraṭ.*

I had asked our brethren about the Jews of Baraṭ but did not learn anything from them. They only praised the tribes of Dan and Reuben and, like the rest of their brethren, told many tales of them. In Ṣaʿdah they say that the Najrānī Jews (that is, those who dwell in western Najrān, for example, in the village of Katāf and environs) are related to the ten lost tribes, and they call them after one tribe or another. There are, however, only a few families of these Jews. They have no books except for those brought there from Ṣanʿāʾ. I had asked Marī Maʿīḍ, to whom we had not returned, to show me his books. He presented me with a leather bag in which there were some
183 books—this was his holy ark. While I was browsing through them, I came across a copy of the New Testament.[9] I recognized the volume, for I had seen what it looked like before in Ṣanʿāʾ. I did not want to take it out in front of my teacher, but he realized what I was doing and said, "Take out what you're hiding from me!" So I took it out and asked Marī Maʿīḍ where it had come from. He said that he had, with great difficulty, bought it for 2 riyals from a tribesman who had acquired it in Ḥarāz. He had been amazed at how well it was printed and bound, but he did not know what kind of book it was. This is what we saw at Marī Maʿīḍ's house.

ON THE ROAD TO KATĀF

Marī Yaʿīsh al-Sulūs[10] engaged a tribesman, named Ḥunbukh, to accompany us to Katāf. Because he could not get a camel or donkey for my teacher, we all traveled by foot. We reached the mountain pass of al-Ḥudaydah when the sun had set and continued through the night by the light of the moon. As we dragged ourselves along with great fatigue between the mountainsides, Ḥunbukh the Bedouin suddenly hit me on my chest with his staff and pushed me backward until I tumbled over. I immediately turned and shouted at him, but he said, "Move back. It's going to kill you."

He came to me and pulled me next to him, but I didn't know what he was up to until he said, "The beast is in front of you, run!"

*As Goitein notes, this passage does not make sense, and it is possible that part of the manuscript has been lost. Ḥayyim Ḥabshūsh, *Ruʾyā al-Yaman (Masʿot Ḥabshūsh)*, ed. S. D. Goitein (Jerusalem: Ben-Zvi Institute, 1983), 162n14.

I then caught sight of a snake that looked like a big leather sack. Its eyes 184
were so large and round that they could frighten a fetus in its mother's womb. If this snake were to bite a human, nothing would save him, for its venom is like that of a viper. Neither weapons nor bullets can pierce it. To kill this snake, a brave person must approach it, spear it with a stick, pinning it so that it cannot flee, and then kill it. The people who are present must then gather wood around it and set it on fire. They call this kind of serpent *ḥayyah*.[11] After what we had seen of this snake, I remained on guard against it, day and night, during my travels.

ḤUNBUKH THE BEDOUIN CARRIES HALÉVY ON HIS BACK

My teacher's energy had been exhausted from traveling through the mountain pass of al-Ḥudaydah. He had suffered all sorts of torments because he did not have an animal to ride. Ḥunbukh the Bedouin did his utmost to help us, even carrying my teacher on his back. We traveled a long way like this until we saw the light of a fire. When we approached, we saw some *sharīf*s from the Jawf spending the evening by the side of the mountain road on their way to Najrān for the harvest. Ḥunbukh took my teacher down from his shoulders and went to spend the night with them. They spoke to him, and he boasted to them of how good he had been to us, even carrying one of us who had been exhausted on his back. They, however, rebuked him: "Do you not know that you are a Muslim who prays for the Prophet and that they are Jews? How can you let him ride on your back when you are forbidden even
to speak amiably with them? If you speak amiably with them, you will come 185
to share laughter with them; and the Law says that one who shares laughter with a Jew will not see the Prophet's face on the Day of Resurrection, for the Prophet will turn his back on him on account of his friendship with the Jew."

These were the words of the *sharīf*s of the Jawf, according to what Ḥunbukh told us. May God improve their minds! Had I not already met one such person from the Jawf—she who had said to her friend when I had knocked on their door, "Someone whose name should not be mentioned"—I would not have believed Ḥunbukh's account of them.[12] These *sharīf*s do not know that the Prophet had a Jewish neighbor with whom he spoke amiably

and that the Qur'ān says, "[Do not dispute with the people of Scripture]
except in the fairer manner."[13]

Ḥunbukh did not give credence to all their words, but neither did he trust
us. He accompanied us until, the next day, we reached a place whose name I
no longer remember and entered the house of a Jew. The tribeswomen there
surrounded and stared at us, asking where we were from and jokingly asking
us what sex we were.[14] One of them gracefully and flirtatiously extended her
hand toward my teacher, but he paid no attention to her and was disgusted
by her words. Then, in front of everyone, she tried to touch his chest with
her hand, but he pulled away, grumbling softly and snorting in disgust. The
186 woman was embarrassed, and her friends laughed at her. I heard one of
them say to another, "This is an angel, not a human being. Would that someone have a son by him so that he might look like him!"

AN OLD JEWISH MAN CHASES AWAY ROBBERS

Ḥunbukh had hired two tribesmen to take us to some other place, no doubt
it was to Katāf, where he was obliged to take us. However, after having taken
us partway, they fell upon us and tried to rob us, even though we clearly did
not have anything on us. I coaxed them until they brought us to the house of
a Jew. The Jew was very elderly, no doubt over 100 years old. He welcomed
us into his house, which had nothing but a sheepskin blanket and his new
wife—not the wife of his sons, some of whom I had met in Wādī Najrān and
who were also old men. The tribesmen who had brought us sat at the Jew's
door expecting a second payment in addition to what we had paid them
before. They sat and threatened us. When the old Jew realized what they
were up to and understood their threats against us, he stood up to them with
his weapon, which was his staff, and, shouting, he threatened, upbraided,
and cursed them. I was amazed at him, fearing it would turn into a fight
of which we would be the cause, but they fled from his scolding. I thought
about this Jew who threatened the tribesmen even though his strength had
187 already gone with age and he could only go about if supported by his staff or
by a wall. His stubbornness and courage remained, just as it had been taught
to him in his youth. As for my teacher Joseph, when he saw the tribesmen
fleeing, he scolded me for not threatening them and persuading them to

leave—for what could they have done to us? He also said that I was like a cat, whose nature is well known.

"Oh sir," I replied, "do not be amazed at the old man's courage and threats, for he is a son of this land and was raised among the tribesmen. In contrast, we are strangers in this land and do not know anything of their ways. Picking a quarrel with them would cause us nothing but trouble. There is nothing to shield us from grief except gentle coaxing."

When we ceased quarreling, we drank coffee and I asked the old Jew about himself. He told me that he was born to the al-Jamal family in Ṣanʿāʾ but had fled in the days of Imām al-Manṣūr ʿAlī.[15] This was the imām who was more glorious than all the others. All the ports of Yemen paid him tribute, and India sent him precious gifts of treasure. He had also acquired many maidservants and had therefore asked his doctor for a medicine that would increase his already substantial sexual potency. The doctor purchased the most glorious males of the most lustful animals and made them drink the most powerful aphrodisiacs. When their penises grew in arousal, the doc- 188
tor cut them off with a razor, combining them with other drugs to make a medicine more potent than the Nile lizard.[16] The imām took this medicine whenever he needed it. This story is told by concupiscent people who make the aforementioned imām its protagonist—this is one of the strange peculiarities of the Yemeni people. Owing to his maidservants, the imām had many sons, and the status of his maidservants' sons was debated and argued about by jurists and religious scholars.[17] Even though he had properly married the maidservants, they claimed that he had nonetheless brought shame to his descendants. Ishmael, the son of Abraham's maidservant, can be considered a prime example of this. The imām had built amazing buildings in Ṣanʿāʾ, which had cost him a lot of money, but, because of the great prosperity during his reign, he had paid no attention to this. They say that the cost of quarrying, chiseling, and hiring workers to lay each hewn stone was 1 riyal. The documents of that era attest to the great expense of everything.

THE ORPHAN DECREE DURING THE REIGN OF IMĀM AL-MANṢŪR ʿALĪ

Once Imām al-Manṣūr ʿAlī had ensconced his children in the palaces, he
gave the order to seize Jewish orphans and convert them to Islam—so that
they could dwell as servants and scribes in the palaces and castles under
which flowed the rivers of tears of their mothers and families.[18] The children
also grieved. Some people hid them in their houses until they reached matu-
189 rity; others helped their families to flee to places far away from Ṣanʿāʾ, such
as the Jawf and so forth. This old man had been one of these. He had come
from a rich and prestigious family but had lost his money, grown feeble, and
become an old man with his family dispersed throughout the land. When we
had finished drinking coffee with him, we set out for another place, without
any guide, until we reached the land of Wāʾilah. There we spent the night
with some Jews, one of whom said that he was originally from the al-Qiḥā
family in Ṣanʿāʾ.

A JEW DRESSED IN THE GARB OF A TRIBAL CHIEF

The next day, we went out alone to al-Maḥtawiyah, near Sūq al-ʿInān, in the territory of the Dhū Muḥammad tribe in the land of Baraṭ. On our way, we met a man riding a donkey who was dressed in the garb of a tribal chief. He wore a fringed cap from which locks of hair hung over his face, an indigo shawl around his shoulders, and a sleeved gown that was, like those of the tribesmen, tied around him with the belt that held his weapon. Because we took him for a tribesman, we humbled ourselves before him. He approached us, scrutinized us closely, and then said in the language of the Jews, "Shalom ʿaleikhem."

Quickly dismounting his donkey, he greeted us with an embrace, as was
190 their custom. He traveled with us for a little, and I spoke with him. He said
that he was originally from Ṣanʿāʾ, from the family of Pinḥas Ha-Kohen. I
asked him about his clothing, and he said that the custom of some Jews in
these places is to resemble the Arabs in their dress on the roads and in the
tribal markets, lest they be considered weak and are attacked. In times of
need, they will draw their swords on an attacker, even if it means killing him,
because this is a matter of pride for their tribal patrons who have their backs.
After bidding us farewell, he went on his way and we slowly went on our
away along the mountainsides of the land of Baraṭ.

THE ROAD TO AL-MAḤTAWIYAH

I was suffering greatly from traveling and fatigue, and the skin on my toes had been stripped time and time again by sharp rocks. We had not found any ancient remains or inscriptions,[19] although we had seen ancient graves, those which are called "the *durūm* of the unbelievers."[20] While we were traveling and I was bemoaning all this exhaustion for nothing, we suddenly saw an Arab fortress on a mountaintop.

"Climb up to that fortress to see what relics you can find," my teacher said.

"Sir," I replied, "I don't see anything there. Its architecture is in the Arab style. I don't see any trace of the ancients on its stones, and I am also very tired."

"No," he said. "I will sit here and you will climb up to that fortress." 191

"I'm afraid that someone might attack you if you sit alone," I replied.

"Don't fear and climb up," he answered.

Unable to oppose and disobey him, I climbed a little way up the mountain until I couldn't see him and he couldn't see me. I then sat down for the time it would have taken to climb all the way up and down. I was afraid to actually go up, lest the tribesmen see me and ask what I was doing in an empty fortress, which would have created problems for us—all for nothing. So I rested there for some time, then went down and said that I had visited the fortress but had found nothing there. He, however, did not believe me and argued with me.

We continued on our way, my heart sick with fatigue and worry about the road. I was so weary and sorrowful that, when we neared the village of al-Maḥtawiyah, I had to stop to sit down while we were still a good distance away. My teacher went ahead of me to the Jews and told them of my condition. When I was slow in joining them, they began to worry about me, so they sent a man to search for me on the road and invite me back. Finding me brooding by myself, he greeted me, took my hand, and soothed me with words. When he saw that my toes were so stripped of skin that I could not walk, he asked me why this was.

"This is because the mountains of your land quench their thirst on the blood of my feet and have delighted in my misery," I said.

"No doubt this is because you don't know how to travel through the mountains," he replied, "but I will teach you."

192 "May God reward you if you teach me this," I said.

Putting me on my feet, he walked eight to ten steps and then returned. His feet did not drag on the ground but remained slightly raised as he went. "Walk like I do and don't drag your feet," he said. By the time we left that place, I had learned how to do so and had forgotten my sorrow and weariness.

We arrived at the home of our dear and honorable brother, Dāwūd Jamīl, may God have mercy on him, who was famous for his generosity and good character. He welcomed us more warmly than we had ever been welcomed. Setting aside his work for the day, which was silverwork; he made the day into a holiday for us all. He slaughtered one of the best of his sheep for us. He then brought out his finest dried dates, crumbled up like sugar, and almonds, sesame seeds, and fried barley seeds. Then, mashing them together, he gave us our fill together with some excellent date arrack. We chatted and I asked him about what books he had, but I did not find anything that I was looking for. We were so carried away by his good manners and sweet words that we wished we could stay with him for at least two or three days. I was also amazed by the honor and respect that he had for his mother, an old woman who was no doubt over 70 years old, because he himself was nearly 60. He had put her in charge of all the household expenses and chores. His storeroom keys, which were made of wood, not iron, hung around her neck with
193 her jewelry, which consisted of *duqqah*, *labbah*, and *lāzim* necklaces.[21] A ring of iron also hung around her neck to prevent [bad spirits] from seizing her.[22] Dāwūd Jamīl also had two or three wives, but she was more energetic than they. She did not skimp on anything that would comfort us after the fatigue and sufferings of our journey. She also prayed to God to grant our wishes and return us home safely.

The next day, we decided to travel to the Jawf. They implored us to remain for as long as we liked, but we did not oblige them because we were eager to get back. They wanted us to go to the village of Rajūzah and to other villages in the vicinity, so that our brethren there could gather contributions for our trip. At that time, making a livelihood was easy for them because, after al-Mahdī ʿAbdallāh's death in 1849,[23] the Baraṭ tribesmen, known as the Bakīl, ruled over most of the regions that had previously paid tax to the government in Ṣanʿāʾ.[24]

OTTOMANS, EGYPTIANS, THE BAKĪL TRIBE, AND THE JEWS: A HISTORY

These events occurred after Ibrāhīm Pāshā, the nephew of the lord of Egypt, Muḥammad ʿAlī Pāshā, conquered and ruled over the Yemeni ports and advanced with his army toward the town of Taʿizz.[25] This is what happened in the days of al-Nāṣir, the imām of Ṣanʿāʾ.[26] This was the imām who, after his palace had been destroyed, found a book in it belonging to the Jewish Badīḥī 194
family, who used to serve al-Mahdī ʿAbdallāh [the previous imām]. Seeing that the book was of no use to him, whether to barter or to settle a debt, he sent officers to all the Jewish chiefs and notables, claiming that they had converted al-Mahdī from Islam and that this book was the proof. He ordered them to bring out the Torah scrolls from their synagogues and to burn them in his square. These Jews were then placed in stocks, ready for beheading, while camels were led carrying the scrolls from the synagogues. While these poor people were still in chains, the mediators arrived at a compromise. For the payment of a sum of 500 riyals, the Jews could keep their heads and the scrolls could stay in their arks—and this was done.[27] However, those who like to brag said that the Jewish leader had only paid the money to Imām al-Nāṣir after he had cast a powerful spell on him. So it was that, by the spell's special power, before a year had passed, the imām and his friends were killed in his home in Wādī Ḍahr.[28] ʿAlī ibn al-Mahdī,[29] whom we have previously mentioned, succeeded him and became imām for a second time.[30]

As for Ibrāhīm Pāshā, he was unable to annex the town of Taʿizz because the governor, who had been there before al-Nāṣir since the days of al-Hādī,[31] had declared himself imām and had marshaled soldiers, most of 195
them from the Baraṭ tribes.[32] When Ibrāhīm Pāshā appeared on the scene, there were great wars between them with savage killings until the Egyptian soldiers bribed the Yemeni soldiers with money. Moreover, because he was on the side of Ibrāhīm Pāshā, Muḥammad ibn Yaḥyā, whom I have previously mentioned,[33] continued to bribe the governor, who had declared himself imām and who was his paternal uncle. Soon the Egyptian soldiers were victorious and entered the city. [The governor] made peace with them, and the soldiers disbanded and dispersed. This is the custom of the people of Yemen—deception and betrayal—both toward their government and toward themselves.[34]

Shortly after this, the Egyptian armies received the order from their government to leave the country, and so they abandoned it.[35] The Bakīl tribes then deployed themselves throughout the region, ruling until they were expelled to their land of Baraṭ, which was unable to provide them with sustenance. Thus God saved the land and his servants through the shining of the sun of the world upon them [the Ottoman sultan] and with it the light of its moons [the Ottoman officials]. With His permission, I ask forgiveness of God, of His sun, and of his moons for mentioning that, due to the sins of his servants, some of the moons of the land are darkened on account of their distance from the rays of the sun. May God guide them toward
196 righteousness so that this land can flourish. May it not be neglected, even a little, and become desolate and empty for the owl and the jackal to inherit and dwell there. May God protect our sun and enlighten the hearts of our moons. Amen.

As for the Bakīl tribes, which were the backbone of the Ṣanʿānī government, they were no longer able to rule and plunder lower Yemen, so they returned to seek a livelihood from their own land.[36] However, their land was not able to meet their needs, for they were accustomed to receiving taxes and levies, which they squandered while they still held power.[37] Today they are poor, may God have mercy on the destitute, to say nothing of our brethren, who live in their region and are poorer than their patrons. May God open their minds so that they can learn to gain an honest and easy livelihood.

The author says: I told this story, which does not pertain to my goal, in order to allow the reader some repose from the fatigue of our journey in the land of Baraṭ.

SABBATH AT THE EDGE OF DHŪ ḤUSAYN TERRITORY

The day after our night at Dāwūd Jamīl's house, we traveled with a Jew whom they had sent to show us the road back to the Jawf. We reached a Jewish house at the edge of Dhū Ḥusayn territory and spent the Sabbath there. The house was unlike any I had ever seen. This is a description of it. The inner courtyard
197 measured 6 by 3¾ cubits. In the corner of one of its inner walls was the door to the main room, through which a person could enter only if he squeezed through it. This room was 3 cubits long and 3 cubits wide. The Jew's rug was the bare floor, and he had only a threadbare blanket to keep himself warm.

This was all that he and his wife and children had. He slaughtered a young and still unfledged rooster, both for us and in honor of the Sabbath. The weekday and Sabbath prayers were according to their proper order, not lacking a thing. After the Sabbath prayer and after he had given his children their lessons, we ate what food was left and he served us a small number of jujube fruit, which we liked and finished.

"Marī," he said, "if you still want more, come and take from the storeroom."

And since I wanted to see his storeroom and provisions, I asked, "Where is your storeroom and where is the key?"

"It has no key," he answered, "and the storeroom is right here in front of you in the courtyard."

I went outside and found a small opening, a span and a half in size, to a crevice in the ground which contained 4 or 5 *qadaḥ* of jujube fruit. This was his fortune and treasure, and this story illustrates the conditions of life in that region.

The next day we traveled and spent the evening with another Jew, who
told us that Harūn al-Ṣaʿdī of al-Ghayl, the alfalfa-eater,[38] had become pos- 198
sessed by *jinn*. Although he may have just been suffering from a fit of epilepsy, that was taken to be a manifestation of the *jinn* who possessed him. He had also told the Jews the names of the *jinn*, al-Baḥaye and al-Saba', and said that these two had revealed to him the secrets of the sciences and of what lay in people's hearts. Behold, after having eaten alfalfa like a donkey, today he is a great scholar! From the time he became possessed, he used to call for Ḥayyim Ḥabshūsh, the companion of the sage, saying that al-Saba' and al-Baḥaye urgently need him.

"He is still waiting for you on the road to the upper Jawf," [the Jew concluded.]

Consider, oh reader, the weak intellects of our brethren for whom the words of this sick man are the truth and on account of which both their men and women rejoice. And I, poor man that I am, was greatly saddened by this story and was even more saddened when I encountered him. At the end of the next day, we met him when we had drawn near to al-Ḥazm. He greeted us and wanted to burden me on the road with the burdens of melancholy people.

"I'm afraid of the tribesmen," I answered, "so don't speak to me here and don't accompany us. If God wills it, we'll meet in al-Ghayl."

He replied that the *jinn* and Umm Qālid[39] were bothering him on account of me and that al-Saba' and al-Baḥaye had told him about a great treasure in the ruin of al-Sawdā'. They had told him that he would not be permitted to take it out unless I was present.

"Go now!" I said to him, for I already feared his insanity. "I have taken
199 note of your words and will discuss this later."

When we reached Sālim ibn Saʿīd's house, we found that a letter from Yaḥyā al-Qārah in Ṣanʿā' had been delivered to him by our brethren in Baraṭ. It was addressed to Ḥayyim ibn Yaḥyā Ḥabshūsh the Ṣanʿānī, wherever he may be, but my teacher took it, opened it, and found that the letter itself was addressed to him. I asked him, "What is this and what is in it?" He said that it was from his wife, but he did not divulge its contents.

CHAPTER 11
THE BEDOUIN

PREPARATIONS FOR THE JOURNEY

My teacher asked Sālim ibn Saʿīd to find us a guide to Mārib, saying that we would undertake to pay him. He happened on a Bedouin named Murshid, who was already traveling to Mārib for his own business and contracted him to take us there by camel.[1] We left behind with Sālim all the transcriptions that we had made in these regions as well as two light stones, each of which bore a line of inscription. We had a total of 42 riyals, including the alms that we had gathered and the 5 riyals that Yaḥyā al-Qārah had sent from Ṣanʿā' to the Jawf. I hid them by sewing them into my belt. Sālim ibn Saʿīd promised that, when he came to Ṣanʿā' to get what he needed, he would bring
200 everything that we had entrusted to him together with the transcriptions that we had entrusted to Yaḥyā ibn Saʿīd. This was what we had hoped for. On the day that we departed, my teacher said to him, "If it happens that you do not come to Ṣanʿā', send a special messenger and I will pay him his wages, but do not let him give them to anyone but me or Marī Yaḥyā al-Qārah.

Even if you yourself come, do not hand them over to anyone other than me or Marī Yaḥyā."

When I heard him say this without mentioning me, I was greatly puzzled, for I did not know the reason for this. "It seems that this is a trick," I thought to myself, but I acquiesced and did not say anything.

At the end of the day, we traveled and spent the night near al-Ḥazm at the home of Murshid the Bedouin. The next day, he made us wait "until his camel arrived"; but we knew that he was delaying travel until the money from Baraṭ arrived, which he had to deliver to people in Mārib. This was a secret because, if anyone had known about it, they would have killed him and taken the money, which amounted to 800 riyals (the price of some Ḥadramī fabric destined for a merchant in Sūq al-ʿInān). After that, fearing for his money, he did not take us by way of the regular route [to Mārib]. Although he did not give us an explanation regarding either the money or the circuitous route, we were happy with the route because it meant that we did not run into the tribesmen.[2]

TRAVELING THROUGH RAGHWĀN AND THE TORMENT OF THIRST

While we were traveling in the desert, my teacher riding upon his camel, we came upon the remains of a building made of chiseled stone that seemed as though it was a channel for water.[3] Murshid the Bedouin then led us through 201
the Raghwān region, which, in our day, is on the eastern edge of the settled part of the Jawf. Beyond this, it is a twenty-day journey through the sands to Muskāt, meeting no one on the way. A short distance northeast of Najrān are al-Dawāsir and al-Aḥsāʾ, but there are no Jews in this region until one reaches Baṣrah. I will discuss the subject of Jewish settlement in Yemen in another place.[4]

We finally came to an impressive ruin near Raghwān, which was not like those of the Jawf.[5] I must have found two or three stone inscriptions there. We spent the night outside in the desert. The next day, we traveled among the sand dunes. We had used up the water that had been carried on the camel, and the heat of the sun increased our thirst. While we were traveling, seeing nothing but sand dunes, we suddenly noticed something approaching us in the distance. When it reached us, we saw it was a Bedouin with a cloth

wrapped over his mouth, a shawl around his head, a piece of cloth to cover his nakedness, and a rifle and dagger—nothing else. After we had greeted him, Murshid asked him what he was doing. He said that, for two days, he had been tracking the footprints of a wild animal that he wanted to hunt.
202 The Bedouin himself was like a wild animal, and he soon left on his business. Murshid led us through places of which he had no knowledge and which were empty of people. Each time I asked, "Murshid, where are the people?" He would reply, "Nearby." The sun then set, and there were no people and nothing for us to drink.

Thirst deranged me, and I picked a fight with Murshid for having taken the wrong road. My teacher forbade me from doing so, saying, "Why are you fighting with him? Do you think you're the only one who is thirsty? Are not he and I also thirsty? Murshid and I share the same fate, yet we remain patient. Be patient in your turn and God will soon deliver us."

His words brought me back to my senses and I mounted the camel beside him. When night fell, we were still searching left and right, seeking whence God's salvation would come.

When the night grew darker, we saw the light of a fire in the distance. We headed toward it, but it disappeared from view. We found no further trace of it until the second half of the night, when we heard the sound of a dog barking far away. We determined its direction and headed toward it until we drew near. All of a sudden, from every side, the light of rifle match cords flashed and the dogs howled louder. But once the Bedouin chief determined that we were not trying to raid them, we did not see the flash of match cords again.
203 Then, still keeping their distance, they called to us, "Who are you?"

"We are only guests," Murshid replied.

Once they discovered who we were, they emerged from where they had hidden in preparation for war, extinguished their match cords, and welcomed us. They even let us into their camp and hastened to prepare a porridge of sorghum, milk, and ghee. When we arrived, I asked them for water.

"Be patient!" they said. "Wait until you eat and we serve you coffee."

"Give me water!" I exclaimed. "I'll take coffee later!"

So they gave me a wooden bowl filled with water and, although I drank, the fire of my thirst was not extinguished until my teacher forbade me to drink any further, saying, "You will harm yourself with this much drinking of water when we have only just arrived from the road. Wait until we have coffee and then you can drink."

DINNER WITH THE BEDOUIN

They brought us dinner, and we ate it together with Murshid. I do not ever remember having been so hungry as on that night. I ate and yet did not feel sated. My companions were satisfied and had removed their hands from the food, while I sat gobbling down porridge. And, although I had devoured the porridge with its ghee, I sat hungry and restless, as though I had eaten nothing at all. That night I was afraid and felt ashamed of myself in front of the Bedouin and my companions. I removed my hands from the food, even though I still trembled with desire for the meal. I had eaten enough for three days without knowing what had become of it.

After we had dined in the tent by the light of the fire, they took us outside the encampment so that they could all speak with us. There, they welcomed us a second time and served us milk coffee. They asked us for news of the 204
Arabs from whom we had come and about what had happened to us on our journey, how we had fared in the desert, the purpose of our travels, and many other questions. This was their custom, because they were cut off from other people.

By the light of the moon under the starry heavens, we sat on a hair-rug that they had spread, drinking milk coffee and conversing with them. Murshid was at one end, surrounded by Bedouins who were listening to what he told them; I sat at the other end, talking with others. Suddenly, some Bedouins turned and fled to the opposite side of the encampment, drawing their daggers. I sat where I was, astonished at their flight, while they shouted at me, "It's a scorpion! Flee lest it kill you!"

But I did not listen to their words and instead thought about where their flight had begun from. And behold, it had been from where Murshid and his Bedouin friends had been sitting. So, I jumped to where he had been sitting and, by the light of the moon, searched for what they had fled from. Meanwhile, they continued to shout at me, afraid lest it bite me. When I saw something, the like of which I had never seen, move under the edge of the carpet, I boastingly called out, "I am Abū Yūsuf!" Then I brandished a stick, stabbed the carpet and pressed down.

"Do not fear and arise," I said, "for I have already killed it." But I did not 205
release the stick from it until they had struck it with their daggers.

They then praised me greatly, saying, "This man is not from the mountains but from the plains."*

After that, we spoke for a little and then lay down. We did not neglect to pray, even though we were in the desert.

A MEETING WITH A LOCAL JEWELER

The next day, I set out to examine the region and its inhabitants. I found large areas filled with rock salt and realized that this was the place to which salt had first been brought from Mount Ṣāfir. They call this salt Māribī salt. They bring salt from this place, known as al-Faḍī, to Mārib and from there to all the markets.[6] They also told me that one of their countrymen was a jeweler who worked with silver. I went to him and found that of all the tools of the silversmiths, he had only a hammer, anvil, bellows, tongs, and scissors to cut with, nothing else! I further discovered that he was entirely ignorant of how to smelt away the dross. His work was merely that of hitting a riyal with a hammer until it became thin, then cutting it into the smaller coins that Bedouin women use to adorn their burkas. Other than this, he knew nothing of silversmithing. Despite all this, he was not content with the prestige of the title of jeweler. Instead, he sought further prestige by smoking fake tobacco in his hookah, something that even the Bedouin chiefs do not usually
206 do. When I saw his lead hookah vase with its reed pipe and him smoking as though it contained real tobacco, I greatly desired to smoke tobacco, because I was very fond of it as snuff. When my supply ran out in the desert, my teacher Joseph used to laugh at me. "Ḥayyim," he said, "sniff up the sand in place of your snuff!" But I withstood that desire, just as I have withstood other things. I said to the silversmith, "Give me two puffs on the hookah."

"Help yourself," he said, and gave me the reed. Filled with great desire, I drew in one breath. Then, at the second breath, no smoke remained.

"By God, give me fresh tobacco!" I said.

"You're welcome to it," he replied and, passing me the bowl of tobacco, he said, "Place it on the hookah yourself."

* That is, the tribesmen flattered him by saying that he was, like them, from the desert, not from the mountains.

So, I took it and saw that it was the barley bran they call *ḥassah*. "Curse your father!" I said. "I ask you for tobacco and you give me *ḥassah*."

"What else is there?" he replied. "This is what we smoke."

So I contented myself with smoking this bran until my head ached and I returned to my teacher.

A BEDOUIN BATTLE

We had already asked the Bedouin about the region and my teacher had taken notes. I sent our guide Murshid back to al-Ḥazm with a letter in the name of my teacher for Sālim ibn Saʿīd. The letter said that we were near Mārib, that is, at al-Faḍī, and that we had rested and were in good health. The letter further urged, "You are to apply your mind to what we commanded you and are not to hand over what we deposited with you to anyone but me, Marī Yaḥyā al-Qārah, *or my companion Ḥayyim Ḥabshūsh*—to no others. And peace!"*

[Murshid] departed that day, that is, the day after we arrived [at al-Faḍī]. 207
We, however, waited for them to prepare a meal for us. These Bedouin had a fortress in which they stored their supplies. Two Bedouin women opened the gate and brought out some flour for our meal. As they were about to lock the gate after them, an old Bedouin who wanted to enter the fortress tried to push them aside, but the Bedouin women pulled him away and he was not able to enter. They, however, could not make him go away, nor could they lock up, because he had stuck one foot inside. While they were quarreling, their voices slightly raised, another Bedouin came and stabbed him in his belly, causing him to immediately fall to the ground. The women raised their voices in a scream of battle. Then, before we knew it, the flame of war had been kindled and the heavens trembled with screaming, yelling, and gunfire. Bullets flew in all directions while we sat where we were on the sand in front of the fortress, the glare of the sun roasting us with its heat. Everyone hid and we saw nothing but the smoke of gunpowder. Half a day passed and we still did not have the meal for which we had delayed our departure. The battle had not ceased,

* Ḥabshūsh's letter "in the name of my teacher" appears to be an underhanded maneuver to get even with Halévy for his earlier trickery. Because Halévy had effectively told Yaḥyā ibn Saʿīd not to hand over the transcriptions that had been entrusted with him to Ḥabshūsh, the latter now sends Yaḥyā a letter that cancels that order. See [200] in this chapter.

and we were unable to flee or even to raise our heads for fear of being shot. I said to my teacher, "Let's get up and go. Perhaps God will be kind to us and
208 we won't be destroyed by the heat of the sun, hunger, and thirst."

"I followed your counsel and heeded your advice when we left Ṣanʿāʾ on the road to Nihm," my teacher said, "and God opened the doors to the Jawf, Wādī Sabaʾ, and elsewhere for us. We discovered things in these places of which no traveler has told. Initially, I had no intention of traveling to these places and had not known of them, for my goal was to travel to Mārib following the way described by the first traveler.* (The latter said that the people there had nearly killed him and then, to see if he was dead or alive, had lifted his head by his ear and let it fall. The meaning of this for the tribesmen is that if the head falls to the ground, the traveler has already died and, if not, he is still alive and they proceed to stab and kill him. Knowing their trick, the poor wretch let his head fall, so they left him and he fled.) But, as for us, God has made our road easy in these empty places to which no one would believe we ever reached. It was because of God's kindness that my luggage was detained in Ḥarāz, for it stopped me from traveling directly to Mārib—just because I had no luggage! In any case, had I entered Mārib with my luggage, I would not have been safe from their iniquity. Poverty has benefited us better than riches, so let us travel and trust the way to God."

These were the words of my teacher when we were in the middle of the sands.

ALONE IN THE DESERT

We got up and left the encampment, that is, al-Faḍī. We slipped between the
209 Bedouin who were fighting one another, and they let us pass, their bullets missing us and passing into sand or into flesh. And we know no more of what happened.

At sunset, we saw a house constructed from the stones of the ruins on top of which it was built. I climbed up to it in search of inscriptions on its outer walls. As I was checking the last corner, I suddenly saw a frightening looking Bedouin. He was old, had a stick in his hand, and was sitting on his knees under a corner of the house. When we noticed one another, we were both

* That is, Thomas Arnaud, who visited Mārib in 1843.

afraid. In fear, he drew his dagger and I brandished a stick to protect myself. My teacher, who was below me, could not see any of this. The Bedouin said, "Curse your father, what creature is this?"

"Greetings," I replied. "I am a stranger and was looking for the door to this house to ask the family to spend the night with them."

I already knew where the door was and that the house was uninhabited, but how else was I to answer the Bedouin? After we had greeted one another and spoken about the news of the Arabs from whom we had come, he said, "There are no people in this place. I am sitting here to watch over the camels that are pasturing in the wadi."

"And where will I be able to find people?" I asked.

"Leave here and go there," he answered, "you will find people ahead."

I said goodbye and returned to my teacher. I told him what had hap- 210
pened to me, but I did not know if he believed me or was making fun of me.

While we were traveling through the wadi in which the camels were pasturing, a young Bedouin came and threatened us, shouting, "Halt! Hand over what you have and your lives will be saved!"

Turning to him, I said, "Curse your father! What can you steal from me, for I have nothing that you want? There is nothing for you to take except my life."

The two of us fought. He could not overpower me, but I could not free myself from him, and we had no weapons. At that moment, the Bedouin whom I had met at the house arrived. I rejoiced at the opportunity to seek his protection, for he was like a patron to me.

"This ruffian is blocking my way even though I'm a stranger and have nothing on me. He just wants to fight, nothing else," I said.

The Bedouin whom I had asked for protection replied, "Don't worry, I will save you from anyone in my land who stands against you. However, this young man is my son and I sent him to take the 'provisions' that you have, nothing more. Because our Lord has given you to me as a gift, my son and I have more right than others to whatever 'provisions' you have"—and the meaning of this for them was money.

"Curse your fathers!" I said to them. "If we had any 'provisions,' we would not have brought them into this desert and, if we had any, we would
have handed them over to you out of the goodness of our hearts without any 211
fighting and killing. However, if your goal is to rob us of our flour and ghee,

which is not enough to last us even a single day, you will not get it except by killing us. We prefer death to losing our provisions and dying of hunger when we are in the desert and there is no one to help us. If we fight for our lives, surely the Lord will grant us victory and kill you for the sin of standing against us, who are but strangers and wretches."

"I don't want flour or anything else except 'provisions,'" he replied, "so take your utensils from your bag and put them where we can see them."

I believed him, so I lowered the sack from my shoulder, held it in my left hand and, with my right, took out some of the things. There was nothing but 100 dirhams of flour, 60 dirhams of ghee, a ball of wool, a small prayer book, and our phylacteries. While I was still counting out what was in it and showing it to them, the Bedouin youth snuck up on us, snatched the sack with what was in it from my hand, and fled. I ran after him and grabbed him, and already I tasted death. The father came to make peace between us, but, when the boy saw the needle stuck in my torn wrap, he swore that he would not free me unless I gave it to him.

"I will not give it to him," I exclaimed, "for with what will I patch my
212 garments while I am in the desert? Even if you were to pay me its price, I would never sell it."

After much trouble, I agreed to give it to him as payment for showing us the way, and that was that. He traveled with us for most of the night, although I still had not handed it over. Finally, he asked me to give it to him so that he could return home, for he feared the Bedouin who lived where we were, as there was a blood feud between them. I handed him the needle as payment and he immediately returned.[7] We continued on our way until, at the break of dawn, we reached some Bedouin tents and sat down at the gate of their mosque. At sunrise, they went to pray while each one boasted, "Today, these are my guests!" Then we were approached by a ruffian who, after having spoken with us, told his companions that we were gypsies,[8] not Arabs. When they all left the mosque, one by one, they were no longer sympathetic to us and not one of them paid us any attention. Finally, a Bedouin invited us to his home and prepared two loaves of bread for us. We ate a little and saved the rest. He also served us coffee. When we left him, we saw one or two ruins, but I no longer remember what inscriptions we discovered in those places.

❨ CHAPTER 12 ❩
THE CITY OF MĀRIB AND RETURN TO ṢANʿĀʾ

ENTERING MĀRIB

We approached Mārib from the east, walking among the tamarisk trees. We came to its eastern gate, and then, as though we had not seen it, made our way along the outer wall until we came to the southern gate and entered.[1] 213
As we entered the city, we saw five or six people, one of whom was a man whose appearance proclaimed him to be a person of authority. When he saw us, he asked about us, and then they too entered. We asked about him, and they said that he was Emir al-Jazzār, the emir of Mārib. We made our way from that gate to the western gate and sat down for a moment in front of it.

The Bedouin tribesmen then gathered there, and so, before we knew it, we were surrounded by them. We did not know it then, but that was their meeting place. We returned to the center of the city, and one tribesman who knew me from Ṣanʿāʾ invited us to his home.[2] He gave us two loaves of barley bread and a jar of coffee as charity and then left for the meeting place. We ate one loaf and stored away the other. While we were drinking coffee, my teacher said, "As soon as you can, go and search for what you can find around the city so that we can leave immediately, for I have no desire to stay here even for a single hour."

So I left and transcribed what few inscriptions I found, five or six stones, and returned to him within the hour. We left the city while the tribesmen were still in the meeting. We saw a place that looked like the ruins of Banāt ʿĀd,[3] which the tribesmen call the Mosque of Solomon. It is located outside the western gate of the city, and next to it is the well from which they draw water. All of this is inside the ancient ruin, and even the new city is built over 214
part of it.

A STORY ABOUT GOLD EXTRACTED FROM THE DUST OF MĀRIB

People had told us about Ibn al-Aʿraj from Ṣanʿāʾ, who dug in the ruins of Mārib, washed away the dust, and brought forth gold, silver, and the like,

which he sent to be sold in Ṣanʿāʾ. We came across some of the holes that he had dug and from which he had scraped out the dust. I knew this man, and he was one of the poorest devils there were in Ṣanʿāʾ. His livelihood was in buying the sweepings from artisans' workshops and washing them to extract the copper, lead, or silver wasted by the artisan. When harsh circumstances afflicted the metalsmiths, especially the silversmiths in Ṣanʿāʾ, this Ibn al-Aʿraj used to scrape the stalls in which the Jews worked, dig in them as deep as the height of a man, and then wash away the dust. After having finished most of them, he dug in the ʿAqīl market, from one side to another, until he finished it. He then went to do the mint, located in the fortress of Ṣanʿāʾ, and finished that as well. He then went to Mārib, working there until he died. This story about Ibn al-Aʿraj took place in 1868.[4] To this day, the Mārib Bedouin come to Ṣanʿāʾ with, more or less, 10 to 20 dirhams of gold and silver,
215 all of it refined. Most of the gold that they bring is set in small beads. This
is what we saw and even bought from him. God knows how much gold and silver the Sheban tribes had, but it has remained with them with the passing of time until this very day and has not been used up.

NO JEWS LIVE IN MĀRIB

Let us return to the mosque they call the Mosque of Solomon, son of David. They say that there are Arabic inscriptions on its inner pillars. The *sharīfs* of Mārib know Solomon only by his mosque. They do not know the people of Solomon's nation who returned with the Queen of Sheba, dwelled in her land and traded there with the help of their king.[5] Today, no Jews dwell in Mārib. Two or three years ago, there was a Jew there from Ṣanʿāʾ by the name of Sālim Sharʿabī, but, when the famine struck, he became bankrupt and fled Mārib. The Mārib tribesmen say that all Jews plunder the property of the tribes because they are not afraid of sinning. God preserve us from this accusation! An evildoer is an evildoer, regardless of whether he is a tribesman or a Jew.

THE MĀRIB DAM

After we had passed some time in front of that mosque, we went to the well and filled our waterskins. We then traveled without a guide along the road to the dam. We saw some places built from chiseled stone. No doubt they were

the graves of the ancient Arabs, not the buildings of the Sheban tribes. In 216
that place, we also saw broken and crushed bones that time had not entirely destroyed. Despite torrents of rain, they remain on the road to this very day. Most of them were like those I had come across in the Jawf at the Maʿīn ruins, although these had not been burned by fire like those at Maʿīn.

Leaving that place, we entered between the great walls in front of the Mārib dam, which is between two mountains, until we drew near to it.[6] We saw an amazing dwelling on the mountain slope by the side of the dam. We climbed up to it but found that it had neither door nor window, nor did it have a path leading to it. So we searched below it for what inscriptions we could find but found nothing but two or three lines engraved on the mountain underneath it. We had also come upon some inscriptions on our way there from Mārib.

We traveled from that dwelling along a road cut by rain torrents until we reached a slightly raised place that blocked our path. I tried to lift my teacher so that he would be able to climb up to the high step that blocked us. After much effort, I succeeded and we traveled until we left that mountain, traveling on the Mārib road to Ṣirwāḥ. When night fell, we spent it alone in the desert. 217

DANGER AND CONFLICT IN ṢIRWĀḤ

The next day we set off for Ṣirwāḥ. Two Bedouin tried to rob and kill us, but God saved us from them by means of some other travelers we met on the road.[7] At the end of the day, which was a Friday, we reached the first houses of Ṣirwāḥ. We entered the courtyard of a house, but found that no one lived there except some shepherds who were spending the night there with their flocks. These two tribesmen were with two young naked girls—nothing covered their skin except a leather thong and one of them was about 20 years old! We took out some flour, and they made it into two loaves for the Sabbath. We then spent the night with the tribesmen. In the morning, they went to pasture their flocks while we stayed where we were, detained by the Sabbath. After reciting the Sabbath prayers, my teacher and I sat down to talk. At midday, I left the house in which we were staying to look around the area and found that, although we had not known it, we had reached the ruin of Ṣirwāḥ. I entered the castle that still stood just as it had been built by the ancients. Inside it, two or three tribesmen lived together with their families,

who were weaving carpets from wool. I sat with them, and we spoke about their affairs and the affairs of the world while I contemplated a large stone on which there were many lines of inscriptions. I knew then with certainty
218 that this was the place that my teacher had meant when he said that there was a well in Ṣirwāḥ on which there were many inscriptions.[8] However, this was not really a well but one of the halls of Sheba that have inscriptions protruding from their stones.

I sat with them for a while, then walked about a little before returning to my teacher and telling him what I had seen. "We should stay here for a day or two until we finish our work, for I have seen that there are many inscriptions," I told him.

"No," he replied, "we won't need to stay any longer. Let's work together and so what you would do alone in two days, you and I will do together in one."

"It is not possible for you to work," I said, "because the tribesmen will see you and we will bring great misfortune upon ourselves and will not be safe from their evil."

"No," he said, "we will work together, and we will not stay any longer in this place."

I argued with him, but he would not listen, so I said, "Don't you know that all the work was my responsibility? Now, all of a sudden, you want to ruin us. If you're doing this because of my fee, don't pay me for this place and I will still finish the work as usual. If not, know that I will not be your guide, for I can see that this will bring us harm. If you do not change your mind, God willing, tomorrow morning I will bring you to the site, but will then immediately go on my way. I will not stay with you, for I greatly fear both for you and for me."

Although he hardened his heart and did not respond to my words, this
219 thing was from God! Early on Sunday morning, we went to the castle.[9] The gate was locked and the tribesmen were still asleep, but I knocked on the door until they woke up and opened it for us. We entered, and I asked them for bread and coffee. My teacher and I sat next to the inscribed stone that I had spotted and told him about. The Bedouin began their wool weaving while I told them about Asʿad, his grandmother Bilqīsah, and their riches, about Haram ibn Maʿīn and his paternal aunt Bakbakah and of their fame,

and about the Mārib dam and its fertile valleys. One of them then interrupted, "Don't tell us about Asʿad and Bakbakah. Tell us about the treasure troves of Zahrā the daughter of al-Azhar, the queen of this castle, if you are indeed a miracle worker."

"I am not a miracle worker, and I don't know anything about such things," I said, "but no doubt everything concerning this treasure is inscribed on this stone."

"There is no doubt that it is set out on it," they replied. "The Jews know the books, so don't fear and do tell. Don't hide anything from us."

"The truth is that I do not know," I said, "but it is possible that my companion might be able to glean something from it."

Turning to my teacher, I said, "Look, oh companion, at this inscribed stone. If you understand what is written on it, read it, or at least copy it down and investigate it. Perhaps the King of Kings will provide us with something from the castle of Zahrā, the daughter of al-Azhar." 220

When I saw that my teacher Joseph had taken out pencil and paper and had begun to copy it, I left him and headed out of the castle toward the ruins to search for what inscriptions I could find there. I came upon many and transcribed them. After three or four hours, I came across a long stone with many inscriptions that was sunk in the ground. Sitting under the remains of the wall to which this stone belonged, I began to transcribe it. While I was busy with this, a Bedouin appeared in front of me. He was searching for me and calling out, "Oh Jew, oh Jew," but he did not notice that I was right in front of him. Hiding my pencil and paper in my sleeve, I got up and said to him, "What do you want from me?"

"What are you doing here?" he asked.

"I was only sleeping," I replied.

"Get up," he said, "the tribesmen have tied up your friend and want to kill him, and we've already been searching for you for a long time."

Looking toward the castle gate, I saw that many tribesmen had gathered there. They had seized my teacher, and the paper on which he had written his transcriptions was in their hands. Fearing for my own transcriptions, I turned away from them and sat down, as if to relieve myself. Then, while pretending to search for some stones to wipe off the filth, I found a place between two stones to hide my transcriptions—I did this in front of them all,

although they did not realize it. Then, approaching them, I said, "Oh tribesmen, oh blessed assembly, why do you gather against us, striking us with fear? We are wretches and strangers, and you are the most mighty and famous of
221 the tribes, renowned for welcoming guests and honoring strangers. Yet today, not only have you not treated us like this, but you have also made us fear you by gathering against us, and we do not know the reason for this."

"A certain chief entered the castle and found your friend transcribing from the stone," they replied. "'Stop what you're doing!' the chief said. But your friend did not listen to him. Not so much as turning around to face the chief, he hurried on with his work and transcribed the stone. The chief wanted to hit your friend over the head with his hatchet and, had the tribesmen not grabbed his hand and seized the transcription, he would have killed him."

"God preserve us, oh tribesmen!" I replied. "Satan tempts people so that they can become fuel for the flames of hell. Noble tribesmen, guard yourselves from these terrifying misfortunes by not violating the stranger and the wretch, especially those in your territory. The truth is that, even now, my friend does not understand anything you say to him because he is a foreigner and also because he knows no Arabic whatsoever. Because God did not want you to commit a sin, he was kind to you and let you save this poor man, who is like a lamb in your hands, from disaster. Fear God and do no evil, even with words!"

"Don't protect yourselves with cunning and deception," one of them answered. "We already know what your business is and that you are sorcerers. We won't kill you, but we will tie you up and bring you to Chief So-and-So who is with the Bedouin in such-and-such a place—a two-day journey from here. We'll give him the writing that was copied, and whatever judgment he makes, you will get."

222 Some of them, however, said, "Let them go. They are poor people and shame on us for interfering with them." "Don't believe them!" said another. "They are pigs and today is the third day that they have been staying here. No doubt there is something that we don't know about."

They did not cease threatening and frightening us until it was time for the afternoon prayer, or maybe even later. All my energy had been exhausted in trying to convince them, but to no avail, and my situation had become oppressive. Raising my voice, I said, "May God not have mercy on those who seek to afflict us. It is true that we have been here for three days, but we came at the end of Friday and were detained by the Sabbath. Today we planned to travel away and came to this place to ask the tribesmen for a little bread and a cup of coffee so that we could leave immediately. But there is no power and no might save in God, the great and the exalted! We are still waiting for them to give us food as charity so that we can travel, but we have received nothing but slanderous accusations. And now, either kill us and redeem us from our troubles, or leave us be so that we can go on our way. We no longer even want provisions from you. But, if you know the law of the tribes, let us eat to revive our spirits from hunger and, afterward, bind us and bring us to any place you wish, or do what you want to do."

Speaking to one another, they said, "This Jew is correct. Shame on us for denying them food. Who among us will take responsibility for feeding them? Afterward, we will tie them up and bring them to the Bedouin."

"I will take responsibility for feeding them," one of them said. 223

Grabbing our hands, he led us away. He brought us to his house, which was outside the castle, and told his wife to make us wheat bread.

While we were waiting, I so engaged this tribesman in conversation that he showed us from his window the road by which we could flee, and it was a road avoided by travelers. After an hour, without the tribesmen noticing, we left his house and set out. I took the transcriptions that I had hidden with me, but my teacher's transcriptions remained with the tribesmen.

Fearing the pursuit of their ruffians, we did not travel on the road suggested by the tribesman until we reached the village of al-Ḥarajah, the first Jewish village of the Ḥarīb region in the territory of the Banū Jabr. We entered and found that they were poor, may God have mercy on them. Finding nothing among them, we left by way of Wādī Ḥarīb and entered another village called al-ʿĀriḍah. We found Jews there, the most famous of whom was Sālim al-Mashriqī. We entered his house, and he welcomed and greatly honored us, even urging us to stay with him for two or three days, but my teacher would not oblige. I would have liked to have stayed with him on account of our exhaustion and the fear that we had experienced.

THE STORY OF THE MURDER OF SHUKR AL-MASHRIQĪ

And you, [dear reader,] who are following the story of our alarming journey,
224 bear with me so that we can explore the laws and statutes of the tribes. Know

that had the ancients not bound them to observe the tribal law called the Ṭāghūt, the strong would have destroyed the weak and, in time, the Yemeni people would have perished due to their remoteness from the government.

This is what befell the al-Mashriqī family in the year 1887.[10] After the death of the aforementioned Sālim al-Mashriqī who had hosted us, his son Shukr succeeded him and, like his father, became famous among the tribes. That year was one of famine, as it frequently is in this land. When Shukr al-Mashriqī saw that he no longer had grain to lend to the tribesmen who were his friends, as was his custom, he gathered the best weapons that he had taken as mortgages and placed them on his donkey. He thought he would travel from the territory of the Banū Jabr tribe to that of the Banū Siḥām. There, he would mortgage these weapons—two guns and three swords—with the famous chief of Khawlān, Ḥizām ibn Ṣāliḥ, and receive in return 15 to 20 *qadaḥ* of grain to satisfy the needs of his customers during that difficult time.

However, some bandit tribesmen got wind of his plans and lay in ambush for him. While he was traveling on the road, trusting in the protection of God and his patron, they fell upon him, bound him to a tree by the roadside, and stuffed his mouth with the kerchief that was tied to his head above his
225 keffiyeh. They seized what was on the donkey, that is, the weapons that I mentioned, and all the rest. But they did not take the donkey, lest they be discovered on account of someone identifying it. The next day, some tribesmen passed by that place and saw the donkey, which they recognized.

"This the donkey of al-Mashriqī the Jew," they said. "No doubt he has been killed and this is why his donkey has been abandoned in a field."

They immediately searched around for him until they found him slain and bound to a tree with the kerchief stuffed in his mouth. Seeing this and recognizing him, they raised a cry of distress with wailing and lament until they had fetched the tribesmen and Jews from all around. But they did not know who had killed him, so the Jews of the Banū Siḥām buried him.

Afterward, his uncle, Yūsuf al-Mashriqī, came with the women and children of his family and encamped at the grave of Ṣāliḥ ibn Ḥusayn al-Nīnī, their deceased patron who had been one of the famous chiefs of Khawlān, for the man had been slain in his territory. When Chief Ḥizām learned that the slain man's uncle was encamped, crying and lamenting, at the grave of his father, Ṣāliḥ al-Nīnī, he brought sheep to appease the al-Mashriqī family so that they would leave the grave. He feared that the tribesmen would shame him, saying, "He has treated his client dishonorably because he did not have the power to protect him, even in his own territory."

He promised them that he would spare no effort to discover who had committed the crime. But the Jew responded, "We will not budge from this grave until our deceased patron, Ṣāliḥ ibn Ḥusayn, rises from his grave to 226
hand over the killer, dead or alive. If he cannot keep his clients safe, we will find our own way to do so."

From the moment the death had been discovered, Chief Ḥizām had not ceased to investigate who was guilty of it. When he saw that the Jews would not leave his father's grave and that, because the man had been slain in his territory, he was seen as responsible for the blood of the Jew in the eyes of his allies, the Banū Jabr tribesmen, he contacted a bandit with whom he was acquainted. He offered him a reward of a camel-load of grain if he would go to the land of Khawlān to spy on and investigate the bandits there to discover what had happened to the Jew. So this bandit, disguised as a purchaser of grain, saddled his camel and went to the land of the Banū Siḥām, which bordered that of the al-Nīnī family. While taking the road by Wādī Banū Jabr, he entered a house on the pretext of making inquiries about grain. There, he found the murderers fighting over the booty taken from al-Mashriqī. They told him that they were appointing him to divide the spoils between them and would give him a reward from the booty. So, he divided the spoil but did not take a reward. Returning to Chief Ḥizām, he told him that the criminals were from the Banū Jabr tribe [the Jew's patrons!], not from the Banū Siḥām tribe or from any other. When Chief Ḥizām examined their deception, how . . . [the manuscript here is fragmentary and corrupt] . . . This is their law.

[SEVERAL PAGES OF THE MANUSCRIPT ARE MISSING[11]]

TRAVAIL ON MOUNT ASHJA‘ 232?

We return to our travels, to Sālim al-Mashriqī's house, which is on the western edge of Banū Jabr territory, near Mount Ashja‘. The very day we reached our brother Sālim, my teacher said, "Let's travel, but let's agree not to speak to any of the tribesmen who greet us, question us about our route, where we are from, who we are, and what we have with us, because, on account of giving these answers, our travel will be delayed. And moreover, we have no need to speak with them."

"Sir," I responded, "there is no sense in this, even if we are a little delayed, for we are already close to Ṣanʿāʾ. Your suggestion that we not acknowledge the tribesmen who greet us is untenable, for we are weak foreigners in their land."

"No," he continued, "we will travel and we will not listen to their words, speak to them, or even greet them."

His words were very hard on me, but I said to myself, "May God's will be done!" So I said to him, "I will not disobey you. Let's travel."

We went and were like those who do not hear and do not see but are dragged along the way.

When the tribesmen who till the land saw that we were foreigners, they called out to inquire after us, as is customary, but we neither returned their greeting nor acknowledged them until we reached the foot of Mount Ashjaʿ. They had already called out to us . . .

[A PAGE OR MORE OF THE MANUSCRIPT IS MISSING]

234 . . . the covenant that is between us."*

"How can I speak to my companion about remuneration?" I asked him. "What would I say to him, given that we have been in foreign parts for several months and have nothing with us? Moreover, an important man like you, who is a *ḥājj*** and a pilgrim, cannot make empty speeches like these. It is your duty to give us alms from what God has provided you so that you will receive a great reward."

"Are there not oaths of God between us that prevent you from hiding anything from me?" Ḥājj Ḥusayn replied.[12] "As for this companion of yours, Ibn Muslimānī says that, in Ṣanʿāʾ, they say he came from the Port of Aden and that he is a Christian, not a Jew. They say that he is a spy who seeks to

* After the gap in the manuscript, we find Ḥabshūsh in the middle of a conversation with a Muslim man named Ḥājj Ḥusayn.

** A *ḥājj* is someone who has performed the pilgrimage to Mecca.

discover the weaknesses of this land for his government and who will write about its mountains, lands, wells, towns, villages, and markets.[13] This matter is well known in Ṣanʿāʾ, where they are already searching for you. Now tell him what I have said to you so that we can observe his answer."

When I heard these words, I was overcome with deadly fear, both for him and for myself. I felt numb and my strength left me. I said to myself, "I will trust in God!" I then replied, trembling with fear, "Oh Ḥājj Ḥusayn, oh Ḥājj Ḥusayn! It is possible that you are right but, until now, nothing has led me to believe what you have told me. Rather, he claimed that his journey was on account of a brother who had been lost for several years. People had told him that he was to be found in eastern Yemen and, in every place we visited, we questioned the people about him and gave them a description of him. In 235
this way, he explained his journey. But give me a little time—for we are travel companions—and I will confront and question him this evening. If you are correct, even if only in part, I swear by God that it will be I, and no one else of woman born, who shall kill him. Or, at the very least, I will be the first to stab him; then whoever wishes to can kill him. As for money, we will never find any on him!"

But he cut me off. "Don't give me words of deception and delusion, as is the way of the people of Ṣanʿāʾ. If you speak truly and are traveling with us, give us your things and we will be friends after that."

This dispute happened when the caravan had already set out, together with us, up the mountainside. I turned to my teacher and informed him of all that this man from Mārib had said, concluding, "We have nothing to fear unless they see our transcriptions. Give them to me. I will hide them so that we will no longer suffer from his accusations and have to be afraid."

On our travels, I had always kept these transcriptions by my side in a small bag. However today, by chance, my teacher had taken them with him. He began to argue and insult me, saying that we were despicable and vile beings who flee at the slightest noise, fear our own shadows, and are weak-hearted. He said that these tribesmen were not chiefs who could give us orders and suggested that we should simply up and leave them.

"Heroism will avail us nothing on Mount Ashjaʿ unless you hand over the inscriptions to me," I replied.[14] "After you do that, I will do anything you say. 236
The inscriptions are still mine, for you have given me no payment. And how

can you say that they are not chiefs? Don't you know that even a child of the tribesmen can do as he likes with us? Who would concern himself with us and who would support our claim when we are foreigners?"

He returned the inscriptions to me and, after hiding them, I went back to Ḥājj Ḥusayn and said, "It is impossible for me to speak with my companion about anything while we're still on the road, but when we stop for the evening, I will try to broach the matter strategically. As for our things, he will give them to you, but know that we have nothing with us."

He did not respond to me. No doubt, he thought that I was speaking nothing but words of delusion. I spent a little longer at the caravan until I saw that he was weary of my speeches. Then I went to my teacher, who was a little in front of the caravan, and said, "What are your thoughts about this ruffian who is interfering with us?"

"I already told you," he replied. "Let's up and leave them and their speeches."

So we climbed the mountain, ahead of the tribesmen, reaching the top when the sun was about to set. And there, at the top, were five tribesmen with their guns lit, ready to fire.

"They somehow managed to overtake us," I said to my teacher, "and now they're sitting on the mountaintop in our path ready to apprehend us."

When I reached them, I greeted them and sat down to talk with them,
237 and they returned my greeting. My teacher continued on the road until we could no longer see him. When the caravan reached the top, I said to the tribesmen, "I want to follow my companion so that he will not get lost."

And it was there that we separated from Ḥājj Ḥusayn and the caravan.*

A WELCOME STOPOVER AT A JEWISH HOME

We pressed on in the darkness of night until we saw the light of a lamp in front of us. We headed for the light until we reached the house that had the lamp. I knocked on the door.

"Who's at the door? Who calls on us at night? We are Jews!" they said.

"We are your brethren and have come to be your guests!" I answered happily.

* Given this non sequitur, it appears that some lines are missing from the manuscript.

Candle in hand, they immediately came down to open the door for us. They took us inside, but they were perplexed because our appearances and form of conversation were different from theirs. In this house, there was a meal at which many people were present, but I did not know whether it was for a wedding or for a funeral.[15]

They served dinner, and we sat down to talk with them. Among them were two men from Ṣanʿāʾ whom I recognized, but they did not recognize me.

"It seems that I recognize you but can't identify you. Tell me your name," one of them said.

"I am Ibn al-Futayḥī[16] from the land of the Jawf," I said, "but I dwelled for a time in Ṣanʿāʾ."

He remained confused. I hid my name so that news of our return would not escape before I could find out what our fate would be in Ṣanʿāʾ.

TWO FALSE MESSIAHS (SHUKR KUḤAYL I AND II)

Early the next day, my teacher said, "Let's travel to Tanʿim and, after that, enter Ṣanʿāʾ."

"I can't appear together with you in Tanʿim," I replied, "because I fear 238
the Jewish followers of the man who claims that he is [Shukr] Kuḥayl.[17] Last year, I debated and fell into conflict with them."

"Don't fear," he said, "come with me and we will finish our work. Afterward, we will trust in God."

I obeyed him, although I was in great danger. I feared the false messiah and his followers who had at one time intended to kill me.

[Dear reader], if you wish to learn about the "messiahs of Yemen" who appeared in my era and whom I knew in the flesh, let us deviate from our path, that is, the path through al-Sirr from the village of al-Sharafah to Tanʿim, to return to the land of Ḥarīb. There we will ascend Mount al-Ṭiyāl, in the territory of the Banū Jabr, and tarry there, for this is the place in which the first Shukr Kuḥayl was killed. He was the yeast and the second Kuḥayl was the dough. In 1859,[18] as I already mentioned at the beginning of this book, poverty and famine prevailed, the state was neglected, and the power of its rulers waned. In that year, Aḥmad al-Ḥaymī was the sheikh of Ṣanʿāʾ.[19] The name of the imām was Ibn Wazīr, and he lived in the land of al-Sirr.[20]

In those days, a wretched Jew left Ṣanʿāʾ to declare himself the harbinger of the awaited messiah. This was the beginning of his work. He was one of those weak people who, on account of their insufficient intellects, are not able to make a living by dint of their own skill. This was his skill: the repair of damaged water containers—he didn't even know how to make new water containers, and that is very easy work! He claimed to be an ascetic. Most of his insights into the books of received wisdom (the Kabbalah) were received from no sheikh or authority at all. When his hallucinations increased, he began to write letters and dots on a piece of paper. On the Sabbath he, accompanied by some people, brought it to the study house of one of the Jewish sages. He even invited the notables of the congregation, wanting them to listen to his words. But one of them rebuked and so ridiculed him that those who had come would no longer listened to a thing he said. As for the piece of paper, he left it with someone there, who could not discern any meaning in it.

After that, he divorced his wife so that he could travel among the villages and warn the people to return to God and repent of their bad deeds. He did not cease doing this until he had passed through most of the Yemeni villages, even reaching the port of Aden and greatly confusing the minds of the poor wretches there. He then returned to the land of Ḥarīb, wishing to live on Mount al-Ṭiyāl in the territory of the Banū Jabr, and dwelled there for two years. He also summoned the sons of Dan to come from the east to Ḥarīb, but he exchanged the *n* for the *m*, for sons of blood (*dam*) came. His blood was spilled by bullets and they brought his head to Ṣanʿāʾ.

[MANUSCRIPT ENDS]

GLOSSARY

Ashkenazi. A Jew of central or eastern European descent.

buqshah. A small copper coin.

Dāʿī. The title given to important religious leaders of the Ismāʾīlī movement.

dirham. A unit of weight measuring approximately 3 grams. Also the name of a silver coin.

Ḥājj. A title given to someone who has performed the pilgrimage to Mecca.

hijrah (adjective, *muhajjar*). An area that has received a tribal guarantee of protection.

Hujar (nominal adjective, *Hujrī*). A sacrosanct caste whose members often served tribes as judges and healers.

imām. In *A Vision of Yemen* this term is used to describe the office or title of the religio-political leader of Zaydī Muslims.

jinn. Invisible beings, either harmful or helpful, who interfere with the lives of human beings.

jizyah. The poll tax that, according to Islamic law, the "People of the Book" are required to pay in exchange for religious toleration.

marī. A title meaning "my master" that was often used by scholars and teachers. Sometimes, *marī* was used as the equivalent of "rabbi," a title that was not used in nineteenth-century Yemen; sometimes it was merely used as a term of respect.

miracle worker. This term translates the Arabic term *ṣāḥib kitāb* (literally, "possessor of a book") and its Hebrew equivalent *baʿal ḥefets* (literally, "master of the will"). The miracle worker works his magic by sitting alone at night reading magical texts. If he is able to control the *jinn* who spring forth from them, they become his servants and he can use their power.

parnas. The head of the Jewish community.

qadaḥ. A unit of measure. One Ṣanʿānī *qadaḥ* is equal to approximately 41 kilograms.

Qarār (nominal adjectives, *Qarawī* and *Qarārī*). The name of a pariah caste in Yemen.

riyal. A silver coin.

roṭl. A unit of measure that, in Ṣanʿāʾ, weighs about half a kilogram

sayyid. In Yemen *sayyid* refers to an individual who claims descent from Ḥasan or Ḥusayn, the grandsons of the Prophet Muḥammad. Used interchangeably with the term *sharīf*.

shamlah. A woolen shawl. The garment had many uses. In addition to being worn around the shoulders, it was sometimes used as a blanket, sometimes for carrying things, and sometimes as a Jewish prayer shawl.

sharīf. In Yemen *sharīf* refers to an individual who claims descent from Ḥasan or Ḥusayn, the grandsons of the Prophet Muḥammad. Used interchangeably with the term *sayyid*.

sheikh. Literally, an "elder." Depending on context, a sheikh can be a tribal leader, a community leader, or a religious authority. The word is used by both Jews and Muslims.

uqqah. A unit of measure equal to approximately 1¼ kilograms.

Zaydī Islam. The sect of Shiʿism to which most Muslims in Yemen belonged.

NOTES

Page references in square brackets refer to the pagination of Glaser's manuscript of *A Vision of Yemen*. These page numbers can be found in the margins of this translation. Ḥayyim Ḥabshūsh, *Ru'yā al-Yaman*. Austrian Academy of Sciences, Glaser Collection, A 1009, Tagebuch XVI a.

PART 1: INTRODUCTION

Ḥayyim Ḥabshūsh and the European Explorers

1. Ḥayyim Ḥabshūsh, *Ru'yā al-Yaman (Mas'ot Ḥabshūsh)*, ed. S. D. Goitein (Jerusalem: Ben-Zvi Institute, 1983), 81; and Joseph Halévy, "Voyage au Nedjran," *Bulletin de la Société de Géographie de Paris* 6 (1873), 249.

2. Few guides wrote about their experiences with orientalists. For some examples, see E. Mittwoch, *Aus dem Jemen: Hermann Burchardts letzte Reise durch Südarabien* (Leipzig: Deutsche Morgenländische Gesellschaft, 1926); Harvey Goldberg, "The Oriental and the Orientalist: The Meeting of Mordecai HaCohen and Nahum Slouschz," *Jerusalem Studies in Jewish Folklore* 22 (2002), 145–57 (Hebrew); and Lucette Valensi, *Mardochée Naggiar: Enquête sur un inconnu* (Paris: Stock, 2008).

3. On the phenomenon of orientalism in general, see Suzanne Marchand, *German Orientalism in the Age of Empire* (Cambridge, UK: Cambridge University Press, 2009), xvii–xxxiii.

4. See, for example, Halévy, "Voyage au Nedjran," 19, 586–87.

5. Ḥabshūsh, *Ru'yā al-Yaman*, i.

6. Ḥabshūsh, *Ru'yā al-Yaman*, 166–74.

7. Ḥabshūsh, *Ru'yā al-Yaman*, 177.

8. Ḥabshūsh, *Ru'yā al-Yaman*, 177.

9. The Arabic transliteration is *Ru'yat al-yaman bayna Ḥabshūsh wa-Halīfī*, ed. S. Naïm Sanbar (Ṣan'ā': Markaz al-buḥūth wa'l-dirāsāt al-yamanī, 1992). The French and Italian editions are *Yémen*, trans. Samia Naïm Sanbar (Paris: Actes Sud, 1995); and *Immagine dello Yemen*, trans. Gabriella Moscati Steindler (Naples: Istituto Orientale di Napoli, 1976).

10. Ḥabshūsh, *Ru'yā al-Yaman*, 5, 215. For an overview of these ancient Yemeni civilizations, see Christian Robin, "Arabia and Ethiopia," in Scott Fitzgerald Johnson, ed., *The Oxford Handbook of Late Antiquity* (Oxford: Oxford University Press, 2015), 247–334. On the magical properties imputed to these inscriptions, see Esther van Praag, "Introduction to Jewish Silversmiths in Yemen Before Operation 'On Eagles' Wings,'" *Tema* 10 (2007), 97–126.

11. Ḥabshūsh, *Ru'yā al-Yaman*, 7–8.

12. Ḥabshūsh, *Ru'yā al-Yaman*, 9.

13. S. D. Goitein, *The Yemenites: History, Communal Organization, and Spiritual Life*, ed. Menahem Ben-Sasson (Jerusalem: Ben-Zvi Institute, 1983), 164 (Hebrew).

14. For example, Ḥabshūsh, *Ru'yā al-Yaman*, 165–66. A short note, apparently by Ḥabshūsh, endorsing the efficacy of a medical treatment, appears in a composition on practical magic. There is no reason to suppose, however, that the work itself is by Ḥabshūsh, as is assumed in the National Library of Israel catalog; see *Segulot ve-Keme'ot* (Nahariya: Menaḥem and Sa'idah Ya'akov Collection), no. 240, 79b.

15. Ḥayyim Ḥabshūsh, "History of the Jews in Yemen," ed. Y. Qāfiḥ, *Sefunot* 2

(1958), 246 (Hebrew). Because Jews were not allowed inside this mosque, it is not clear whether these manuscripts were brought outside for him to read or whether Muslims consulted the manuscripts in the mosque for him and then reported to him on their findings.

16. Yehiel Hibshoosh, *The Ḥabshūsh Family* (Tel Aviv: Self-published, 1985), 1: 54 (Hebrew); and Yosef Tobi, *The Jews of Yemen* (Leiden: Brill, 1999), 175.

17. Ḥabshūsh, "History of the Jews," 247.

18. Meir Ben Isaac Auerbach, *An Open Letter Addressed to Sir Moses Montefiore* (London: Wertheimer, 1875), 136.

19. Yehuda Nini, *The Jews of Yemen, 1800–1914* (New York: Harwood Academic, 1991), 87. Tobi estimates that 90 percent of the city's Jewish population was killed in the siege; see Y. Tobi, "A Hebrew Chronicle on the Ṣanʿāʾ War Between the Turks and the Yemenis," *Proceedings of the Seminar for Arabian Studies* 32 (2002), 295.

20. "Yaḥyā Ḥayyim Ḥabshūsh [*sic*] Murdered in Ṣanʿāʾ," *Davar* (April 13, 1938), 6 (Hebrew).

21. On Yemeni immigration to Israel, see Tudor Parfitt, *The Road to Redemption: The Jews of Yemen, 1900–1950* (Leiden: Brill, 1996); and Ari Ariel, *Jewish-Muslim Relations and Migration from Yemen to Palestine in the Late Nineteenth and Twentieth Centuries* (Leiden: Brill, 2013).

22. These three self-published books are *Bidur* (Jerusalem, 1998), *Shene ha-Meʾorot* (Tel Aviv, 1987), and *She'erit ha-Peletah be-Teman* (Tel Aviv, 1990), respectively.

23. Hibshoosh, *Ḥabshūsh Family*, 1: 33–35, 46–47. This story is confirmed in another source; see Amram Qoraḥ, *Seʿarat Teman* (Jerusalem: Mosad Ha-Rav Kook, 1954), 55–57.

24. Hibshoosh, *Ḥabshūsh Family*, 1: 35–36, 45–46, 86–87. Cf. Qoraḥ, *Seʿarat Teman*, 53–54.

25. Hibshoosh, *Ḥabshūsh Family*, 1: 41.

26. Hibshoosh, *Ḥabshūsh Family*, 1: 47–48.

27. Hibshoosh, *Ḥabshūsh Family*, 1: 40–41, 48–49.

28. Hibshoosh, *Ḥabshūsh Family*, 1: 26.

29. Hibshoosh, *Ḥabshūsh Family*, 1: 51.

30. Hibshoosh, *Ḥabshūsh Family*, 1: 33–51.

31. French government documents list Halévy's birthdate as either September 15 or October 14, 1827. Halévy to Monsieur le Garde des Sceaux, November 7, 1871, Archives Nationales de France, Dossiers de Naturalisation, 1908, x. 72, Halévy, Joseph.

32. Y. Kantorovitz, "Rabbi Joseph Halévy: Biographical Material," *Ha-Mevasser* (Istanbul) 49 (Kislev 21, 1911), 707 (Hebrew); and Nahum Sokolow, "Professor Joseph Halévy," in Nahum Sokolow, *Personalities* (Jerusalem: Ha-Sifriyah Ha-Tsiyonit, 1958), 2: 350 (Hebrew).

33. Kantorovitz, "Rabbi Joseph Halévy," 707. According to Kantorovitz, Halévy fled with Adolf Arosdi (born Schnabel), a refugee who established the first department store chain in the Middle East. There is exhaustive documentation of Jewish soldiers who fought with Kossuth. One was Josef Löwy (Hungarian spelling of Joseph Halévy), born 1828, in Neustadtl-an-der-Waag, Hungary. It is possible that Löwy and Halévy refer to the same person, given the closeness in birth year. It is also possible, however, that Halévy went by a different name in Hungary. See Béla Bernstein, *Negyvennyolcas Magyar Szabadságharc és a Zsidók* (Budapest: Tábor-kiadás, 1939), 31, 247. On the refugees, see Kemal Karpat, "Kossuth in Turkey: The Impact of Hungarian Refugees in

the Ottoman Empire," in Kemal Karpat, *Studies on Ottoman Social and Political History* (Leiden: Brill, 2002), 169–84.

34. Joseph Halévy, "Here I Am, Send Me!" *Ha-Magid* 6 (February 8, 1865), 46 (Hebrew).

35. A. Navon, "La foundation de l'école de l'Alliance à Andrinople," *Paix et Droit* (April 1, 1923), 14. Cf. Kantorovitz, "Rabbi Joseph Halévy," 707. Halévy says that he began writing Hebrew poetry in Adrianople in 5614 (October 1853–September 1854), a year earlier than the date given by Navon; see Joseph Halévy, *Maḥberet Melitsah va-Shir* (Paris: A. M. Lunts, 1894), 201.

36. Navon, "Foundation de l'école," 14.

37. Shlomo Haramati, *Three Who Preceded Ben-Yehuda* (Jerusalem: Ben-Zvi Institute, 1978), 20 (Hebrew).

38. Haramati, *Three Who Preceded*, 13–15. On Halévy's relationships with local families, see A. Elmaleh, "The 'Student' and 'His Rabbi': The Friendship Between the Learned Sage, Rabbi Abraham Danon, and the Famous Orientalist, Professor Joseph Halévy," *Otsar Yehude Sefarad* 7 (1964), 43–48 (Hebrew).

39. On the "civilizing mission" of the Alliance, see Daniel Schroeter, "Orientalism and the Jews of the Mediterranean," *Journal of Mediterranean Studies* 4 (1994), 183–96. Cf. André Kaspi, ed., *Histoire de l'Alliance israélite universelle de 1860 à nos jours* (Paris: A. Colin, 2010).

40. Aron Rodrigue, *French Jews, Turkish Jews: The Alliance Israélite Universelle and the Politics of Jewish Schooling in Turkey, 1860–1925* (Bloomington: Indiana University Press, 1990), 51, 95; Salomon Reinach, "Joseph Halévy," *Revue Archéologique* 5 (1917), 240; and Joseph Halévy to Alliance Israélite Universelle, June 27, 1867, AIU Archives, Turquie I, G 1 a.

41. Kantorovitz, "Rabbi Joseph Halévy," 708.

42. S. Markus, "History of the Bekhmoharar Rabbinical Dynasty," *Mizraḥ u-Me'arav* 5 (1930), 175 (Hebrew).

43. Halévy discusses his excommunication in *Recherches bibliques* (Paris: Leroux, 1907), 133–34. Other factors may also have contributed to his fall from favor in Adrianople. Soon after his arrival, he married a local woman from a prominent family, with whom he had four children; they then divorced. The children remained with their mother after he left, although he kept in contact with them. Halévy occasionally intervened with the Alliance on their behalf. A series of letters detail his attempts to prevent the Alliance from blocking his daughter Dinah's marriage by relocating the couple to posts in separate towns. Halévy to Loeb, December 9, 1883; and Halévy to Alliance Israélite Universelle, September 23 and 29, 1883, AIU Archives, France XI, A 79. On the Alliance's interest in its employees' marriages, see Erol Haker, *Edirne, Its Jewish Community, and Alliance Schools, 1867–1937* (Istanbul: Isis Press, 2006), 77–78. Earlier, Halévy intervened to secure his son a place at the Alliance's preparatory school in Paris. Halévy to Alliance Israélite Universelle, February 15, 1878, AIU Archives, France XI, A 79. Cf. Archives Nationales de France, Dossiers de Naturalisation, 1908, x. 72, Halévy, Joseph.

44. In his application for residency in France, Halévy claimed that he was born to Dutch parents and, reportedly, even initially came to France on a Dutch passport. Perhaps then he was indeed genealogically connected to the Sephardic culture that he so admired, distantly descended from those Jews of Sepharad who had famously settled in Amsterdam in the wake of Ferdinand and Isabella's expulsion of 1492. Archives Nationales de France, Dossiers de Naturalisation, 1908, x. 72, Halévy, Joseph. Cf. Reinach, "Joseph Halévy," 239.

45. For a favorable account of Halévy's oriental mannerisms, see Reuben Brainin, "Professor Joseph Halévy," *Ha-Eshkol* 4 (1902), 257–64 (Hebrew). Cf. S. Posnansky, "Note on Three Sages of Israel," *Ha-Zefira* (March 29, 1917), 3 (Hebrew). For references to unfavorable impressions, see Reinach, "Joseph Halévy," 242. When Halévy first arrived in France, one source correctly identified him as Hungarian. See "Procès-verbal du 22 janvier 1869," *Bulletin de la Société de Géographie* 17 (1869), 95.

46. On the problem of determining Halévy's location during the 1860s, see Shlomo Haramati, *Sod Siaḥ: Spoken Hebrew Between the 16th and 19th Centuries* (Tel Aviv: Yaron Golan, 1992), 76–77n257 (Hebrew). Halévy clearly returned to Adrianople after his excommunication for a significant amount of time. In an 1865 letter to the Alliance, he reports that, at the time of writing, he had been in Adrianople for five months. Joseph Halévy to the Alliance Israélite Universelle, Nisan 14, 5625 (April 10, 1865), AIU Archives, Turquie I, G 1 a. Yakir Giron, Istanbul's chief rabbi, described Halévy as the head of a school in Adrianople in a letter dated June 1865: "Letter," *Ha-Magid* 9.43 (November 8, 1865), 340 (Hebrew). However, by 1867, Halévy had returned to Romania. Halévy to the Alliance Israélite Universelle, June 3, 1867, AIU Archives, Turquie I, G 1 a.

47. A. Chouraqui, *L'Alliance Israélite Universelle et la renaissance juive contemporaine, 1860–1960* (Paris: Presses Universitaires de France, 1965), 110–11, 148, 160; N. Leven, *Cinquante ans d'histoire: L'Alliance Israélite Universelle (1860–1910)* (Paris: F. Alcan, 1911), 1: 156, 237; and M. Laskier, *The Alliance Israélite Universelle and the Jewish Communities of Morocco* (Albany: State University of New York Press, 1983), 61.

48. Joseph Halévy, "A Word in Due Season," *Ha-Magid* 6 (April 3, 1862), 109 (Hebrew).

49. Haramati, *Sod Siaḥ*, 47.

50. Kantorovitz, "Rabbi Joseph Halévy," 709.

51. Joseph Halévy to the President of the Alliance Israélite Universelle, April 3, 1867, AIU Archives, France XI, A 79. Halévy notes that Abraham Geiger, a founder of the Reform movement, received him warmly. During this period, Halévy also traveled to Constantinople to solicit support for the Alliance from its Karaite community. "Séance du 22 juillet 1867," *Bulletin de l'Alliance Israélite Universelle* (July–December, 1867), 4.

52. Rodrigue, *French Jews*, 51. Cf. Joseph Halévy to Alliance Israélite Universelle, June 27, 1867, AIU Archives, Turquie I, G 1 a. In a brief description of the Jews of Aden, Halévy describes them in terms similar to those he uses for Polish Jews; see Joseph Halévy, "Aden," *Ha-Levanon* (November 22, 1869), 358–59 (Hebrew).

53. Halévy, "Here I Am," 46–47.

54. Although most Europeans were unaware of the plight of Abyssinian Jews in 1848, scattered accounts of them did exist and so it is possible that Halévy's date is correct. See Menachem Waldman, *Beyond the Rivers of Ethiopia: The Jews of Ethiopia and the Jewish People* (Jerusalem: Misrad Ha-Bitaḥon, 1989), 109–16. (Hebrew).

55. Halévy to the Alliance Israélite Universelle, February 10, 1865, AIU Archives, Turquie I, I J 1.

56. Waldman, *Beyond the Rivers*, 156–68; and Steven Kaplan, *The Beta Israel (Falasha) in Ethiopia* (New York: NYU Press, 1992), 138–40.

57. On European intervention in Ethiopia, see D. Crummey, "Tewodros as Reformer and Modernizer," *Journal of African History* 10 (1969), 457–69.

58. Halévy, "Travels in Abyssinia," trans. J. Picciotto, in A. Löwy, ed., *Miscellany of Hebrew Literature* (London: Society of Hebrew Literature, 1872), 2: 207–8.

59. Joseph Halévy, "Travels in Abyssinia," 2: 193.

60. Halévy, "Travels in Abyssinia," 2: 215.

61. Halévy, "Travels in Abyssinia," 2: 215.

62. Halévy, "Travels in Abyssinia," 2: 191.

63. Although Halévy usually did not attempt to influence Abyssinian Jewish customs, at one point he attempted to persuade them to abandon their use of amulets; see Halévy, "Travels in Abyssinia," 2: 223. His objectivity as an anthropologist of the Abyssinian Jews is prejudiced only by the fact that his most detailed descriptions are of those Abyssinian customs that most closely resemble biblical ones. Joseph Halévy, "Excursion chez les Falacha, en Abyssinie," *Bulletin de la Société de Géographie* 17 (1869), 270–94.

64. Joseph Halévy, "Rapport au comité central de l'Alliance israélite universelle concernant la mission auprès des Falachas présenté dans la séance du 30 Juillet 1868," *L'Universe Israélite* 80 (1868), 131.

65. Kaplan, *Beta Israel*, 142, 207n130.

66. Halévy to Alliance Israélite Universelle, November 15, 1868, AIU Archives, France XI, A 79; J. Faïtlovitch, *Quer durch Abessinien* (Berlin: Poppelauer, 1910), 1–2, 10, 77–79; and Joseph Halévy, "Une lettre amharique des Falachas ou Juifs d'Abyssinie," *Revue Sémitique* 14 (1906), 94–95n2. Halévy was notified by telegram of the man's death; see letter to Halévy, January 14, 1872, AIU Archives, France IV, L 6.054.

67. E. Trevisan Semi, *Jacques Faitlovitch and the Jews of Ethiopia* (London: Valentine Mitchell, 2007), 19–20, 29.

68. T. Parfitt, "Rabbi Nahoum's Anthropological Mission to Ethiopia," in T. Parfitt and E. Trevisan Semi, eds., *The Beta Israel in Ethiopia and Israel* (London: Curzon, 1999), 1–14.

69. Paul Dresch, *Tribes, Government, and History in Yemen* (Oxford: Oxford University Press, 1989), 217–18; and Ḥusayn b. Aḥmad al-Sayyāghī, *Ṣafaḥāt majhūla min tārīkh al-Yaman* (Ṣanʿāʾ: Markaz al-Dirāsāt al-Yamanīyya, 1978), 125–26.

70. On hostility to foreigners in nineteenth-century Yemen, see D. Varisco, "Introduction," in Eduard Glaser, *My Journey Through Arḥab and Ḥāshid*, trans. D. Warburton (New York: American Institute for Yemeni Studies, 1993), vii; and Zahra Dickson Freeth and H. Winstone, *Explorers of Arabia from the Renaissance to the End of the Victorian Era* (New York: Holmes & Meier, 1978), 16. As British explorer D. G. Hogarth noted, although "it was always possible to explore the inner reaches of India, Africa and much of Asia without bothering even with the rudiments of language," travel in Yemen not only required speaking Arabic fluently but also passing "as a native, if not of Arabia then of part of the Islamic world." D. G. Hogarth, "Problems in Exploration," *Geographical Journal* 32 (1908), 552.

71. Requests from the Académie for governmental funding for Halévy's journey refer to him as "an Israelite sage from Adrianople" and emphasize his rabbinic learning. Halévy's own letter to the minister of public instruction emphasizes his attachment to France, his work ethic, and his scholarly credentials but also his traditional Jewish knowledge. Secretary of the Académie des Inscriptions et Belles-Lettres to Minister of Public Instruction, June 18, 1869, Archives Nationales, F/17/2974; and Halévy to Minister of Public Instruction, June 28, 1869, Archives Nationales, F/17/2974.

72. Noah Gerber, *Ourselves or Our Holy Books? The Cultural Study of Yemenite Jewry* (Jerusalem: Ben-Zvi Institute, 2013), 56 (Hebrew); and Y. Tobi, "Joseph Halévy and the Study of the Jews of Yemen," *Peʿamim* 100 (2004), 30 (Hebrew).

73. On travelers' disguises, see Hilal al-Hajri, *British Travel-Writing on Oman* (New York: Peter Lang, 2006), 54.

74. Hogarth, "Problems in Exploration," 552; and Ḥabshūsh, *Ru'yā al-Yaman*, 26–32.

75. Yehi'el Brill, "Assorted News," *Ha-Levanon* (May 21, 1873), 304 (Hebrew). Cf. Jacob Saphir, *Even Sapir* (Lyck: Meqitse Nirdamim, 1866–1874), 2: 162–63. On one occasion in 1875, however, Halévy did forward a letter from Yemen to the Alliance that outlined the difficult circumstances under which Yemeni Jews lived. See Joseph Halévy, "Israélites de Turquie," *Bulletin de l'Alliance Israélite Universelle* (January 3, 1876), 8–10.

76. André Dupont-Sommer, "Ernest Renan et le Corpus des inscriptions sémitiques," *Comptes-rendus des séances de l'Académie des Inscriptions et Belles-Lettres* 112 (1968), 539.

77. On Renan's views, see Maurice Olender, *The Languages of Paradise: Race, Religion, and Philology in the Nineteenth Century* (Cambridge, MA: Harvard University Press, 1992), 51–81.

78. Ernest Renan, "Conférence faite a l'Alliance pour la propagation de la langue française," in Ernest Renan, *Oeuvres completes* (Paris: Calmann-Lévy, 1961), 2: 1091.

79. Ernest Renan, "Le Judaïsme comme race et comme religion," in Renan, *Oeuvres completes*, 1: 361–74.

80. Paul Lawrence Rose, "Renan Versus Gobineau: Semitism and Antisemitism, Ancient Races and Modern Liberal Nations," *History of European Ideas* 39 (2013), 530, 536; and Tzvetan Todorov, *On Human Diversity: Nationalism, Racism, and Exoticism in French Thought* (Cambridge, MA: Harvard University Press, 1994), 142.

81. David Norman Smith, "Judeophobia, Myth, and Critique," in S. Daniel Breslauer, ed., *The Seductiveness of Jewish Myth* (Albany: SUNY Press, 1997), 123–54; and John Efron, *German Jewry and the Allure of the Sephardic* (Princeton: Princeton University Press, 2016), 219–23. Renan's negative views of Islamic thought, articulated in his public debate with the political and religious thinker Jamal al-Dīn al-Afghānī, had similar ramifications among some Muslims. See Monica Ringer and A. Holly Shissler, "The al-Afghani–Renan Debate, Reconsidered," *Iran Nameh* 30 (2015), xxviii–xlv.

82. Halévy said, "Despite the impersonal and respectful tone of my article of 1874, my theory has earned me countless afflictions. They organized a relentless persecution against me. I was prevented from making presentations at the Institute, they ousted me from the Society of Jewish Studies and, through denigration and slander, they did everything to deprive me of my position at the École des Hautes Études. And to make this happen more easily, they began to declare my theory ridiculous, knowing that ridicule kills quickly in France." Joseph Halévy, "Réponse ouverte à M. le Professeur C. Bezold," *Revue Semitique* 17 (1909), 198–99. Interestingly, Halévy wrote insulting poems in Hebrew about his chief adversary, Jules Oppert; see Halévy, *Maḥberet Melitsah va-Shir*, 169–75.

83. Jerrold Cooper, "Sumerian and Aryan: Racial Theory, Academic Politics, and Parisian Assyriology," *Revue de l'Histoire des Religions* 210.2 (1993), 205. After his death, Halévy's theories were rejected by all but Jacob Pereman, who seems to have adopted them for similar ideological reasons; see Jacob Pereman, *One Hundred Years of Assyriology, 1857–1957* (Tel Aviv: Hotsa'at Sefarim be-Yisra'el le-Mada'e ha-Mizraḥ ha-'Atiq, 1957) (Hebrew). Interestingly, Halévy took part in a similar debate on whether Hittite languages (now thought to be Indo-European) were Semitic. See L. de Lantsheere, *De la race et de la langue des Hittites* (Brussels: Goemaere, 1891), 83–89.

84. Joseph Halévy, "Rapport sur une mission archéologique dans le Yemen," *Journal Asiatique* 6 (1872), 13–15.

85. Halévy, "Rapport sur une mission archéologique," 50–52.

86. Ernest Renan, "Séances du mois d'octobre," *Comptes-rendus des séances de l'Académie des Inscriptions et Belles-Lettres* 15 (1871), 373–74. Halévy's Legion of Honor was awarded in 1905. Archives Nationales, F/17/25675; and Archives Nationales, LH/1259/20.

87. Two major publications resulted from Halévy's journey: "Rapport sur une mission archéologique dans le Yemen," *Journal Asiatique* 6 (1872), 5–98, 129–266, 489–547; and "Voyage au Nedjran," *Bulletin de la Société de Géographie de Paris* 6 (1873), 5–31, 249–73, 581–606. Cf. Y. Tobi, "An Unknown Study by Joseph Halévy on His Journey to Yemen," *Proceedings of the Seminar for Arabian Studies* 35 (2005), 287–92.

88. British Admiralty, *Handbook of Arabia* (London: Stationery Office, 1920), *passim*.

89. Fakhry wrote, "The journey of Halévy remains unique in the history of the exploration of Yemen, because none before him and none after him until the present time, could visit Nedjran, El Gōf and Mārib together. Glaser visited Mārib only, and El ʿAzm saw a few sites in the neighbourhood of Mārib, while Tewfik was unable to go anywhere beyond El Gōf. It is supposed that my visit to El Gōf and Mārib in 1947 can be compared with that of Halévy, but I am the first person to admit that I have not seen half of the sites seen by Halévy, and I have not been to Nedjran." Ahmed Fakhry, *An Archaeological Journey to Yemen (March–May 1947)* (Cairo: Government Press, 1952), 23.

90. The role of these emissaries, from the first to the nineteenth century, has been documented in Abraham Yaari, *Emissaries of the Land of Israel* (Jerusalem: Mosad Ha-Rav Kook, 1977) (Hebrew).

91. "Letter of the Ṣanʿānī Jews to the Anglo-Jewish Association (4 April, 1875)," in Y. Tobi, *The Jews of Yemen in the 19th Century* (Tel Aviv: Afikim, 1976), 238 (Hebrew).

92. Fakhry, *Archaeological Journey to Yemen*, 26. Cf. Barbara Flemming and Jan Schmidt, *The Diary of Karl Süssheim (1878–1947)* (Stuttgart: F. Steiner, 2002), 55.

93. Mark Wagner, *Like Joseph in Beauty: Yemeni Vernacular Poetry and Arab-Jewish Symbiosis* (Leiden: Brill, 2009), 237; and S. D. Goitein, "Who Was Eduard Glaser?" in A. Tsadok, ed., *Shevut Teman* (Tel Aviv: Mi-Teman le-Tsiyon, 1945), 149 (Hebrew).

94. In 1890, in a memorandum to the German Jewish philanthropist Baron Moritz von Hirsch, a proponent of Jewish agricultural colonies, Glaser floated the idea of establishing a Jewish colony in Yemen. In 1896, Theodor Herzl, the founder of political Zionism, discussed the memorandum in his diary, writing, "[Its] contents . . . shows excellent thinking. This Glaser is a man to remember. . . . He possesses considerable knowledge of the Orient, and he may even have a talent for military organization. . . . Glaser is to be cultivated." Theodor Herzl, *The Complete Diaries*, trans. H. Zohn (New York: Herzl Press, 1960), 2: 448–49. If Herzl here planted the seed for a relationship with Glaser, it never flourished. By 1897 they were publicly feuding over where to establish the Jewish state, with Glaser proposing northeastern Yemen and Herzl Palestine. Glaser argued that a Jewish state could never prosper on a land that was also a religious battleground. One needed a home with as few connections as possible to both Christianity and Islam. Palestine, holy to both religions, clearly did not fit this bill. It would be better for Jews to suffer exile than to create a state prone to interreligious conflict. In contrast, northeastern Yemen, unlike Palestine, was sparsely populated and had the additional advantage of being agriculturally fertile. Glaser, perhaps characteristically, finished his argument by suggesting that Herzl was in fact a British agent sent to weaken

the Ottomans. Only this, he asserted, could account for the irrational choice of Palestine. Herzl was reportedly so angry that he wanted to challenge Glaser to a duel, but he was dissuaded by friends. In the end, he dispatched the matter with a brief note in *Die Welt*: "We do not find these disputations and allegations sufficiently interesting to prolong the debate further." Herzl, "Zur 'Berichtigung' von Eduard Glaser," *Die Welt* 8 (February 25, 1898), 3; quoted in E. Rosenberger, *Herzl as I Remember Him* (New York: Herzl Press, 1959), 139. On the dispute between Herzl and Glaser, see Yosef Zurieli, "A Jewish State in Yemen: The Secret Plan of Eduard Glaser," *Nativ* 9 (1997), 57 (Hebrew); Yosef Zurieli, "Herzl and Glaser's Plan for a Jewish State in Yemen," *Pe'amim* 65 (1995), 57–76 (Hebrew); and Y. Nini, "Yemen, 'The Promised Land': Eduard Glaser and His Letters to Theodore Herzl," *Zionism* 5 (1979), 299–309 (Hebrew).

95. Walter Dostal, *Eduard Glaser: Forschungen im Yemen* (Vienna: Österreichische Akademie der Wissenschaften, 1990), 1–12.

96. Dostal, *Eduard Glaser*, 17.

97. Eduard Glaser, *Mittheilungen über einige aus meiner Sammlung stammende sabäische Inschriften nebst einer Erklärung in Sachen der D. H. Müllerschen Ausgabe der Geographie Al-Hamdānī's* (Prague: Self-published, 1886). For Müller's reply, see David Heinrich Müller, "Über meine Ausgabe der Ṣifat Ǧazīrat al 'Arab von al-Hamdānī," *Petermann's Mittheilungen* 32 (1886), 117–21. In 1887 Glaser wrote a bitter and unpublished poem about Müller titled "König David Heinrichs Glück und Ende." See Archiv der Österreichische Akademie der Wissenschaften, Sammlung Glaser, A 1014, f. 10. However, the two scholars were reconciled shortly before Glaser's death; see Fritz Hommel and D. H. Müller, "Erklärung von Fritz Hommel, E. Glaser und D. H. Müller," *Wiener Zeitschrift für die Kunde des Morgenlandes* 22 (1908), 180–83. Glaser's conflicts with Europeans were numerous; for another example, see Luca Beltrami, *Eugenio Griffini Bey (1878–1925)* (Milan: Allegretti, 1926), 27.

98. Carlo de Landberg, *Études sur les dialectes de l'Arabie méridionale* (Leiden: Brill, 1913), 2.2: x. Like Glaser, de Landberg felt embattled. He complained of persecution at the hands of the "Bani Isra'il of Austria," by which he meant Jewish scholars at the University of Vienna. De Landberg, *Études sur les dialectes*, 2.1: 263n2.

99. Goitein, "Who Was Eduard Glaser?" 151–52; and Siegfried Lichtenstadter, "Eduard Glaser," *Jahrbuch für Jüdische Geschichte und Literatur* 12 (1909), 171–72. The manuscripts that Glaser collected form the nucleus of several important collections; see David Hollenberg, Christoph Rauch, and Sabine Schmidtke, "Introduction," in David Hollenberg, Christoph Rauch, and Sabine Schmidtke, eds., *The Yemeni Manuscript Tradition* (Leiden: Brill, 2015), 3.

100. For example, early in his career, Glaser turned down the prestigious offer of a fully funded research trip to southern Africa so as not to be distracted from his goal to visit Yemen. Dostal, *Eduard Glaser*, 18.

101. Eduard Glaser, "Reise nach Marib," in D. Müller and N. Rhodokanakis, eds., *Sammlung Eduard Glaser* (Vienna: Alfred Hölder, 1913), 1: 99.

102. Marchand, *German Orientalism*, 123.

103. Dostal, *Eduard Glaser*, 110.

104. Glaser, "Reise nach Marib," 1: 121.

105. Jeff Meissner, "Eduard Glaser's Gravestone in Munich," *AIYS Newsletter* 23 (October 1987), 7; and Max Maas, "Zum Gedächtnis Eduard Glasers," *Ost und West* 18 (1918), 172.

106. Dostal, *Eduard Glaser*, 19.

107. Caesar Farah, "A German Plan of Reform for Ottoman Yemen," in *CIÉPO: VIIe Symposium Actes* (Ankara: Türk Tarih Kurumu Basimevi, 1994), 47, 55. On Glaser's diplomatic activities, see Caesar Farah, *The Sultan's Yemen: Nineteenth-Century Challenges to Ottoman Rule* (London: Tauris, 2002), 105, 149–53.

108. Thus, although Glaser's assistants were paid by the Ottomans, this was only because the effectiveness of his disguise depended on his being perceived not only as a *faqīh* but also as an Ottoman official. Glaser, accordingly, reimbursed the Ottomans in full. Dostal, *Eduard Glaser*, 110.

109. On European Jewish admiration for the Ottomans, see B. Lewis, "The Pro-Islamic Jews," *Judaism: A Quarterly Journal of Jewish Life and Thought* 17.4 (fall 1968), 391–404. Glaser appreciatively noted that the "interests of science and those of the sublime Turkish government are the same in South Arabia." Glaser, *My Journey Through Arḥab and Ḥāshid*, 17.

110. Dostal, *Eduard Glaser*, 26–29.

111. Fakhry, *Archaeological Journey to Yemen*, 26.

112. For a bibliography of the Halévy-Glaser debate, see C. Robin, "Le Judaïsme de Ḥimyar," *Arabia* 1 (2003), 99. Although Robin dismisses Halévy's view, other scholars have differed in this assessment. See A. Beeston, "Judaism and Christianity in Pre-Islamic Yemen," in Joseph Chelhod et al., *Le peuple yéménite et ses racines* (Paris: Maisonneuve et Larose, 1984), 277–78.

113. For Ḥabshūsh's statement that Glaser was a non-Jew, see Ḥabshūsh, "History of the Jews," 281. Nini's contention that Ḥabshūsh's reference to Glaser as a non-Jew is the insertion of a later copyist does not seem warranted; see Y. Nini, "The Polemic on the Kabbalah Conducted by Yemeni Scholars at the Beginning of the 20th Century," *Michael* 14 (1997), 226 (Hebrew). A Yemeni polemical text unconvincingly claimed that Jews knew Glaser to be a Christian because spies sent to the bathhouse had discovered he was uncircumcised. See *Sefer Emunat Ha-Shem* (Jerusalem: Ḥayyim Zuckerman, 1937), 2. Cf. Goitein, "Who Was Eduard Glaser?" 149; and Wagner, *Like Joseph in Beauty*, 237. It seems likely that both Jews and Muslims, with the exception of Yaḥyā Qāfiḥ, believed Glaser to be a Muslim.

114. Ḥabshūsh, *Ru'yā al-Yaman*, i.

115. For example, Ḥabshūsh, *Ru'yā al-Yaman*, i, 80, 178. According to a letter Goitein received from the scribe of the Glaser manuscript, Ḥabshūsh had saved the running invoices that he had prepared for Halévy and was able to use them as a memory aid when writing *A Vision of Yemen*. Shlomo Dov Goitein, *Travels in Yemen: An Account of Joseph Halévy's Journey to Najran in the Year 1870* (Jerusalem: Hebrew University Press, 1941), 6n8.

116. Ḥabshūsh, *Ru'yā al-Yaman*, 161.

117. Ḥabshūsh, *Ru'yā al-Yaman*, 172–73, 187.

118. Ḥabshūsh, *Ru'yā al-Yaman*, 75, 147.

119. Ḥabshūsh, "History of the Jews," 281n219; and Ḥabshūsh, *Ru'yā al-Yaman*, 6.

120. See, for example, Ḥabshūsh, *Ru'yā al-Yaman*, 187, 232.

121. Ḥabshūsh, *Ru'yā al-Yaman*, 144.

122. Ḥabshūsh, *Ru'yā al-Yaman*, 80, 114–15, 155, 190–91.

123. H. von Maltzan, "Gefälschte Inschriften in Arabien," *Westermann's Jahrbuch* (1872), 557–58; and Franz Praetorius, "Himjarische Inschriften," *Zeitschrift der Deutschen Morgenländischen Gesellschaft* 26 (1872), 417–40.

124. C. Phillips and St. J. Simpson, "A Biographical Sketch of Britain's First Sabaeologist, Colonel W. F. Prideaux, CSI," *Proceedings of the Seminar for Arabian Studies* 37 (2007), 208.

125. Joseph Halévy, *Études sabéennes* (Paris: Imprimerie Nationale, 1875), 237. Ḥabshūsh is first referred to by name in 1882; see J. Mordtmann and D. Müller, *Sabäischer Denkmäler* (Vienna: Academy of Sciences, 1883), 9. Cf. "Siegfried Langer," *Mittheilungen der Österreichischen Geographischen Gesellschaft* 25 (1882), 372; and Eduard Glaser, *Südarabische Streitfragen* (Prague: Self-published, 1887), 18.

126. Halévy, "Voyage au Nedjran," 252.

127. Goitein, *Travels in Yemen*, 10. Glaser was careful to credit Ḥabshūsh and expressed surprise that Halévy did not, noting that Halévy "kept Ḥayyim Ḥabshūsh's name secret for unknown reasons." Glaser, "Reise nach Marib," 1: 165. It is ironic that the French Geographical Society tasked Halévy with translating a report by Mardochée Aby Serour, the native guide of Charles de Foucauld. "Extraits des procès-verbaux des séances," *Bulletin de la Société de Géographie* 10 (1875), 552.

128. Ḥabshūsh, *Ru'yā al-Yaman*, 8.

129. H. St. John Philby, "Halévy in the Yaman," *Geographical Journal* 102 (1943), 123.

130. Philby, "Halévy in the Yaman," 124.

131. Elisa Bianchi, *Un finto rabbino, una subdola guida, un diario che riappare: viaggio in Yemen di Joseph Halévy* (Milan: Guerini e Associati, 2003), 259. In a similar vein, Ahmad Dallal denies Ḥabshūsh's agency by claiming that European influence prejudiced his objectivity. Ahmad Dallal, "On Muslim Curiosity and the Historiography of the Jews of Yemen," in J. Montville, ed., *History as Prelude: Muslims and Jews in the Medieval Mediterranean* (Lanham, MD: Lexington, 2011), 94. Cf. Wagner, *Like Joseph in Beauty*, 7n19.

132. Ḥabshūsh, *Ru'yā al-Yaman*, 237, 128.

133. Ḥabshūsh, *Ru'yā al-Yaman*, 195.

134. Efim Rezvan, *Russian Ships in the Gulf, 1899–1903* (Reading, UK: Ithaca Press, 1993), 3.

135. Eduard Glaser, *Skizze der Geschichte und Geographie Arabiens* (Berlin: Weidmannsche Buchhandlung, 1890), 2: 357–87. Cf. Dostal, *Eduard Glaser*, 35.

136. Zurieli, "Jewish State in Yemen," 57.

137. It was Halévy's experience in Abyssinia that changed his views on Zionism. Before the voyage, like the Alliance, he opposed Zionism, even urging action against the "Zionist danger" in Anatolia (Halévy to Alliance Israélite Universelle, July 3, 1863, AIU Archives, Turquie VIII, E 156). In Abyssinia, however, he saw Jews who endured such great suffering that they were convinced that they were witnessing the dawn of the messianic era. Groups of them, including children and the elderly, began to journey toward Zion, most dying along the way. Appalled, Halévy began to urge the Alliance to consider the advantages of their relocation to Palestine (letter from Halévy to Alliance Israélite Universelle, November 24, 1867, published in "Lettres d'Abyssinie," *Archives Israélites* 29 [1868], 175). Later, after returning from Yemen, Halévy helped to found the Parisian chapter of Ḥibbat Zion. Hillel Barzel, *A History of Hebrew Poetry*, Vol. 1, *The Chibbat Zion Period* (Tel Aviv: Sifriyat Po'alim, 1987), 332–35 (Hebrew). On the Alliance's attitude toward Zionism, see Catherine Nicault, "Face au sionisme (1897–1940)," in André Kaspi, ed., *Histoire de l'Alliance israélite universelle de 1860 à nos jours* (Paris: A. Colin, 2010), 189–226.

138. Indeed, their lives were so evocative and dramatic that they all became grist for novels. Halévy was the inspiration for the titular character of A. H. Navon's *Joseph Pérez* (Paris: Lévy, 1925). Glaser was the main character in Jean-Jacques Langendorf's *La nuit tombe, Dieu regarde* (Genève: Zoé, 2000). Ḥabshūsh appeared as Ḥayyim al-Futayḥī in Shalom Medina, *The Messiah from Yemen* (Tel Aviv: Avner, 1977), 180 (Hebrew).

139. Morris Jastrow Jr., "Joseph Halévy," *The Nation* 104.2700 (March 29, 1917), 379. For a preliminary bibliography of Halévy's works, see Michela Andreatta, "Vers un bibliographie de Joseph Halévy," in D. Friedmann, ed., *Recontres avec les Juifs d'Éthiopie* (Paris: Alliance Israélite Universelle, 2007), 65–82.

The People and Politics of Yemen

1. Aviva Klein-Franke, "The Jews of Yemen," in W. Daum, ed., *Yemen: 3000 Years of Art and Civilisation in Arabia Felix* (Innsbruck: Pinguin, 1987), 265–66. Cf. Reuben Ahroni, *Yemenite Jewry: Origins, Culture, and Literature* (Bloomington: Indiana University Press, 1986), 20–37.

2. Bat Zion Eraqi Klorman, "The Forced Conversion of Jewish Orphans in Yemen," *International Journal of Middle East Studies* 33 (2001), 23.

3. Some have argued that translating *qabīlah* as "tribe" is inexact, although most scholars of Yemen retain the term in the absence of convenient alternatives. On this issue, see Isa Blumi, *Rethinking the Late Ottoman Empire* (Istanbul: Isis Press, 2003), 43–56.

4. Paul Dresch, *Tribes, Government, and History in Yemen* (Oxford: Oxford University Press, 1989), 38–47. The notion of descent is often fictional. Thus Dresch remarks that Yemeni tribes are "best thought of not as cohesive groups . . . but as geographically based." Because of this, switching tribes is possible when necessary. Paul Dresch, "Aspects of Non-State Law: Early Yemen and Perpetual Peace," in P. Dresch and H. Skoda, eds., *Legalism: Anthropology and History* (Oxford: Oxford University Press, 2012), 146.

5. Dresch, *Tribes, Government, and History*, 74; and Robert Serjeant, "South Arabia," in C. A. O. Van Nieuwenhuijze, ed., *Commoners, Climbers, and Notables* (Leiden: Brill, 1977), 232.

6. Dresch, *Tribes, Government, and History*, 118; and Serjeant, "South Arabia," 228.

7. Najwa Adra, "The Concept of Tribe in Rural Yemen," in S. Ibrahim and N. Hopkins, eds., *Arab Society* (Cairo: AUP Press, 1985), 276–77; and Shelagh Weir, *A Tribal Order: Politics and Law in the Mountains of Yemen* (Austin: University of Texas Press, 2007), 137.

8. On the Qarār, see Ḥayyim Ḥabshūsh, *Ru'yā al-Yaman (Mas'ot Ḥabshūsh)*, ed. S. D. Goitein (Jerusalem: Ben-Zvi Institute, 1983), 82–83, 138–41; and Joseph Henninger, *Arabica Varia: Aufsätze zur Kulturgeschichte Arabiens und seiner Randgebiete* (Freiburg: Vandenhoeck und Ruprecht, 1989), 281–86. On other categories of "weak" people, see Thomas Stevenson, *Social Change in a Yemeni Highlands Town* (Salt Lake City: University of Utah Press, 1985), 42–63.

9. Andrey Korotayev, "North-East Yemen," in Dmitri M. Bondarenko and Andrey V. Korotayev, *Civilizational Models of Politogenesis* (Moscow: Russian Academy of Sciences, 2000), 213.

10. Yemeni Muslims sometimes explain the harmony between tribal law and Islamic law thus. Tribal law governs values pertaining to honor, such as generosity, courage, strength, and devotion to agriculture. Sometimes referred to as the law of protection, it brings order by negotiating rights of access to land and by regulating hospitality and claims of refuge. Islamic law, it is said, cannot be in conflict with these aims and occupies a different sphere. P. Dresch, "Guaranty of the Market at Ḥūth," in R. Serjeant, ed., *Arabian Studies* (Cambridge, UK: Cambridge University Press, 1990), 84–86. On the interplay between the two systems, see Martha Mundy, "Women's Inheritance of Land in Highland Yemen," *Arabian Studies* 5 (1979), 154–74.

11. Ḥabshūsh's view was also held by other Jews; see Mark Wagner, *Jewish and Islamic Law in Early 20th-Century Yemen* (Bloomington: Indiana University Press, 2014), 5.

12. George Hourani, *Arab Seafaring in the Indian Ocean* (Princeton, NJ: Princeton University Press, 1995), 5; and Gus van Beek, "The Land of Sheba," in J. Pritchard, ed., *Solomon and Sheba* (London: Phaidon, 1974), 41.

13. D. G. Hogarth, "Problems in Exploration," *Geographical Journal* 32 (1908), 6–7.

14. For example, "Yemen Türküsü" (The Lament of Yemen).

15. Thomas Kuehn, *Empire, Islam, and Politics of Difference: Ottoman Rule in Yemen, 1849–1919* (Leiden: Brill, 2011), 109.

16. Kuehn, *Empire*, 56, 190.

17. Ahroni, *Yemenite Jewry*, 149.

18. Ahroni, *Yemenite Jewry*, 151; and Ḥabshūsh, *Ru'yā al-Yaman*, 60–63.

19. Ḥabshūsh, *Ru'yā al-Yaman*, 98–100.

20. Yosef Tobi, "The Yemeni Jewish Community Under Turkish Rule (1872–1918)," in Yosef Tobi, *The Jews of Yemen* (Leiden: Brill, 1999), 85–108.

21. For an overview of European travelers to Yemen, see Aviva Klein-Franke, "Yemen," in J. Speake, ed., *Literature of Travel and Exploration* (New York: Fitzroy Dearborn, 2003), 1303–7.

22. Walter Langlois, *In Search of Sheba* (Knoxville, TN: Malraux Society, 2006), 232.

23. Langlois, *In Search of Sheba*, 232–34.

24. On the motivations of European Jewish travelers in the Islamic world, although not in Yemen, see Daniel Schroeter, "Orientalism and the Jews of the Mediterranean," *Journal of Mediterranean Studies* 4 (1994), 183–96.

25. Yehuda Nini, *The Jews of the Yemen, 1800–1914* (New York: Harwood Academic, 1991), 154–72; and Abraham Yaari, *Emissaries of the Land of Israel* (Jerusalem: Mosad Ha-Rav Kook, 1977), 144–51 (Hebrew).

26. Noah Gerber, *Ourselves or Our Holy Books? The Cultural Study of Yemenite Jewry* (Jerusalem: Ben-Zvi Institute, 2013), 28–51 (Hebrew).

27. T. Parfitt, *The Lost Tribes of Israel: The History of a Myth* (London: Weidenfeld & Nicholson, 2002), 213–45; Zvi Ben-Dor Benite, *The Ten Lost Tribes: A World History* (Oxford: Oxford University Press, 2009), 85; and Bat-Zion Eraqi Klorman, *The Jews of Yemen in the Nineteenth Century: A Portrait of a Messianic Community* (Leiden: Brill, 1993), 100–103. On Yemeni Jewish beliefs about the lost tribes, see Yehuda Ratzaby, *Yemeni Paths* (Tel Aviv: 'Am 'Oved, 1988), 244–51 (Hebrew). As late as the 1920s, rumors about the lost tribes continued to circulate; see T. Parfitt, *The Road to Redemption: The Jews of Yemen, 1900–1950* (Leiden: Brill, 1996), 26.

28. M. Adler, *The Itinerary of Benjamin of Tudela* (London: Henry Frowde, 1907), 72 (Hebrew), 48–49 (English).

29. Ḥabshūsh, *Ru'yā al-Yaman*, 9; and Erich Brauer, *Ethnologie der jemenitischen Juden* (Heidelberg: Carl Winter, 1934), 8.

30. Paul Fenton, "Moses Shapira's Journey to the Yemen," in Eilat Ettinger and Danny Bar-Maoz, eds., *Mittuv Yosef: Yosef Tobi Jubilee Volume* (Haifa: University of Haifa, 2011), lxviii–lxxxi; and Ḥabshūsh, *Ru'yā al-Yaman*, 128.

31. Mahalal Ha-'Adani, *Between Aden and Yemen* (Tel Aviv: 'Am 'Oved, 1947), 103–8 (Hebrew); Reuben Ahroni, *The Jews of the British Crown Colony of Aden* (Leiden: Brill, 1994), 109; Ḥabshūsh, *Ru'yā al-Yaman*, 3; and Alan Verskin, "Moshe Ḥanokh ha-Levi," in N. A. Stillman, ed., *Encyclopedia of the Jews in the Islamic World* (Leiden: Brill, forthcoming). Some sources suggest that Ḥanokh ha-Levi was an Ottoman, not a European, Jew.

32. See Aviva Klein-Franke, "J. Wolff and H. Stern: Missionaries in Yemen," in Paul Starkey and Janet Starkey, eds., *Interpreting the Orient: Travellers in Egypt and the Near East* (Reading, UK: Ithaca Press, 2001), 81–96.

33. Ḥabshūsh, *Ru'yā al-Yaman*, 183.

34. Qur'ān 9:29.

35. On the origins and early development of the pact, see Milka Levy-Rubin, *Non-Muslims in the Early Islamic Empire* (Cambridge, UK: Cambridge University Press, 2011).

36. Bernard Haykel, *Revival and Reform in Islam* (Cambridge, UK: Cambridge University Press, 2003), 121.

37. Aḥmad b. Yaḥyā Ibn al-Murtaḍā, *Kitāb al-Azhār* (Beirut: Dār Maktabat al-Ḥayāh, 1973), 322. Translation taken with modification from A. Shivtiel, W. Lockwood, and R. Serjeant, "The Jews of Ṣan'ā'," in R. Serjeant and Ronald Lewcock, eds., *Ṣan'ā': An Arabian Islamic City* (London: World of Islam Festival Trust), 421.

38. Yosef Tobi, *The Jews of Yemen* (Leiden: Brill, 1999), 78–79.

39. Aḥmad b. Yaḥyā Ibn al-Murtaḍā, *'Uyūn al-Azhār* (Beirut: Dār al-Kitāb al-Lubnānī, 1975), 528; and P. van Koningsveld, J. Sadan, and Q. al-Samarrai, *Yemenite Authorities and Jewish Messianism: Aḥmad ibn Nāṣir al-Zaydī's Account of the Sabbathian Movement* (Leiden: Leiden University, Faculty of Theology, 1990), 90.

40. In one such *ḥadīth*, Muḥammad said, "May God fight the Jews and the Christians! . . . Two religions shall not remain in the land of the Arabs." Mālik b. Anas, *al-Muwaṭṭa'*, ed. M. 'Abd al-Bāqī (Cairo: 'Īsā al-Bābī al-Ḥalabī, 1951), 2: 892–93. Many authorities reported that Muḥammad made these statements on his deathbed. Because this elevated the injunction to a last wish, it had the effect of canceling his earlier statements in favor of toleration. Y. Friedmann, *Tolerance and Coercion in Islam* (Cambridge, UK: Cambridge University Press, 2003), 90–93.

41. Haykel, *Revival and Reform in Islam*, 118; Y. Tobi, "Conversion to Islam Among Yemeni Jews Under Zaydi Rule," *Pe'amim* 42 (1990), 105–26 (Hebrew); and S. D. Goitein, *The Yemenites: History, Communal Organization, and Spiritual Life*, ed. Menahem Ben-Sasson (Jerusalem: Ben-Zvi Institute, 1983), 169 (Hebrew).

42. Van Koningsveld et al., *Yemenite Authorities*, 90–91.

43. Van Koningsveld et al., *Yemenite Authorities*, 95; and Eraqi Klorman, *Jews of Yemen in the Nineteenth Century*, 37–38.

44. Jane Hathaway, "The Mawza' Exile at the Juncture of Zaydī and Ottoman Messianism," *AJS Review* 29 (2005), 118; Ḥayyim Ḥabshūsh, "History of the Jews in Yemen," ed. Y. Qāfiḥ, *Sefunot* 2 (1958), 262–65 (Hebrew); and Ḥabshūsh, *Ru'yā al-Yaman*, 69–70.

45. Shivtiel et al., "Jews of Ṣan'ā'," 392; and M. Zadoc, *History and Customs of the Jews in the Yemen* (Tel Aviv: 'Am 'Oved, 1967), 54 (Hebrew).

46. Yehuda Ratzaby, "The Mawza' Exile," *Sefunot* 5 (1961), 339–95.

47. Yosef Tobi, "The Attempts to Expel the Jews from Yemen in the 18th Century," in Ephraim Isaac and Yosef Tobi, eds., *Judaeo-Yemenite Studies: Proceedings of the Second International Congress* (Princeton: Institute of Semitic Studies, 1999), 41–64.

48. Joseph Sadan, "The 'Latrines Decree' in the Yemen," in J. Platvoet and K. van der Toorn, eds., *Pluralism and Identity* (Leiden: Brill, 1995), 175; and Ḥabshūsh, "History of the Jews in Yemen," 274–75.

49. Haykel, *Revival and Reform in Islam*, 126.

50. Nini, *Jews of the Yemen*, 26.

51. On the decree, see Eraqi Klorman, "Forced Conversion," 23–47; and Kerstin Hünefeld, *Imām Yaḥyā ad-Dīn und die Juden in Ṣanʿāʾ* (Berlin: Klaus Schwarz, 2010), 50–55; Tobi, "Conversion to Islam," 119–22; Wagner, *Jewish and Islamic Law*, 43–44; and Ḥabshūsh, *Ruʾyā al-Yaman*, 188–89.

52. Eraqi Klorman, "Forced Conversion," 23.

53. Hathaway, "Mawzaʿ Exile," 111.

54. Yosef Tobi, "Jewish-Muslim Relations in the Tribal Regions in North Yemen," in Y. Tobi, *The Jews of Yemen* (Leiden: Brill, 1999), 145–51.

55. Ḥabshūsh, *Ruʾyā al-Yaman*, 189–90.

56. Ḥabshūsh, *Ruʾyā al-Yaman*, 63.

57. Ḥabshūsh, *Ruʾyā al-Yaman*, 71.

58. For an exception, see Lawrence Rosen, "Muslim-Jewish Relations in a Moroccan City," *International Journal of Middle East Studies* 3 (1972), 445.

59. Abraham Ovadia, *In the Paths of Yemen and Zion* (Tel Aviv: Afikim, 1985), 35 (Hebrew); and Bat-Zion Eraqi Klorman, *Traditional Society in Transition: The Yemeni-Jewish Experience* (Leiden: Brill, 2014), 9.

60. Dresch, *Tribes, Government, and History*, 118.

61. Ḥabshūsh, *Ruʾyā al-Yaman*, 58–59; and Bat-Zion Eraqi Klorman, "Yemen: Muslim and Jewish Interactions in the Tribal Sphere," in M. Laskier, ed., *The Divergence of Judaism and Islam* (Gainesville: University Press of Florida, 2011), 128.

62. Eraqi Klorman, "Forced Conversion," 24.

63. Tobi, "Jewish-Muslim Relations," 154.

64. Ḥabshūsh, *Ruʾyā al-Yaman*, 62.

65. Ḥabshūsh, *Ruʾyā al-Yaman*, 135.

66. Ḥabshūsh, *Ruʾyā al-Yaman*, 87. Cf. Ettore Rossi, "Il diritto consuetudinario delle tribù arabe del Yemen," *Revista degli Studi Orientali* 23 (1948), 7.

67. Friedmann, *Tolerance*, 47–50.

68. Bat-Zion Eraqi Klorman, "Yemen: Religion, Magic, and Jews," *Proceedings of the Seminar for Arabian Studies* 39 (2009), 130.

69. Ḥabshūsh, *Ruʾyā al-Yaman*, 13–26. Cf. Ḥabshūsh, *Ruʾyā al-Yaman*, 165–66, 219.

70. Ḥabshūsh, *Ruʾyā al-Yaman*, i.

71. Dresch, *Tribes, Government, and History*, 217–18; and Ḥusayn b. Aḥmad al-Sayyāghī, *Ṣafaḥāt majhūla min tārīkh al-Yaman* (Ṣanʿāʾ: Markaz al-Dirāsāt al-Yamaniyya, 125–26.

72. Nini, *Jews of the Yemen*, 10.

73. Quoted in Dresch, *Tribes, Government, and History*, 219.

74. Caesar Farah, *The Sultan's Yemen: Nineteenth-Century Challenges to Ottoman Rule* (London: Tauris, 2002), 84–85.

75. Eraqi Klorman, *Jews of Yemen in the Nineteenth Century*, 55–56.

76. Ḥabshūsh, "History of the Jews in Yemen," 249; translation taken with modification from H. Lenowitz, *The Jewish Messiahs* (Oxford: Oxford University Press, 1998), 261.

77. On these messianic claimants, see Eraqi Klorman, *Jews of Yemen in the Nineteenth Century*, 104–57.

78. Jacob Saphir, *Iggeret Teman ha-shenit* (Vilna: Ha-Levi Levinson, 1873), 6; and Ḥabshūsh, "History of the Jews in Yemen," 237–38.

79. Ḥabshūsh, *Ruʾyā al-Yaman*, 237–38.

80. Ḥabshūsh, *Ruʾyā al-Yaman*, 50.

81. Without question, after Ḥabshūsh's death, Ottoman influence on Yemeni Jews,

and particularly on the Dor De'ah movement, became much stronger as Jewish institutions in Istanbul built ties with Yemen. See Mark Wagner, *Like Joseph in Beauty: Yemeni Vernacular Poetry and Arab-Jewish Symbiosis* (Leiden: Brill, 2009), 222; and Menashe Anzi, "The Jews of San'ā' at a Time of Change: From the Ottoman Conquest to Their Migration to Israel," Ph.D. dissertation, Hebrew University of Jerusalem, 2011 (Hebrew).

82. Bat-Zion Eraqi Klorman, *The Jews of Yemen: History, Society, and Culture* (Tel Aviv: Open University, 2004), 29 (Hebrew).

83. Schroeter, "Orientalism," 188; and Y. Zurieli, "The Alliance and the Jews of Yemen," in S. Schwarzfuchs, ed., *L'"Alliance" dans les communautés du basin méditerranée* (Jerusalem: Misgav Yerushalayim, 1987), 20–30 (Hebrew).

84. Ḥabshūsh, "History of the Jews in Yemen," 281n219. Halévy also claimed that he had persuaded the Ṣan'ānī rabbinate to reject the Kabbalah. Joseph Halévy, "Voyage au Nedjran," *Bulletin de la Société de Géographie de Paris* 6 (1873), 249–50.

85. Ḥabshūsh, "History of the Jews in Yemen," 285.

86. For an overview of the Dor De'ah movement, see Eraqi Klorman, *The Jews of Yemen: History*, 26–73. Members of Dor De'ah came to be known as Darda'im, and its opponents as 'Iqshim.

87. Eraqi Klorman, *Traditional Society in Transition*, 22–23.

88. Once in motion, the Dor De'ah movement was no doubt influenced by other modernizing movements, both Ottoman and Arab. Eraqi Klorman, *Traditional Society in Transition*, 34.

89. Eraqi Klorman, *Jews of Yemen: History*, 42; and Mark Wagner, "Jewish Mysticism on Trial in a Muslim Court: A Fatwā on the Zohar—Yemen 1914," *Die Welt des Islams* 47 (2007), 207–31.

90. Ḥabshūsh, *Ru'yā al-Yaman*, 138; and Albert Hourani, *Arabic Thought in the Liberal Age, 1798–1939* (Cambridge, UK: Cambridge University Press, 1983), 78.

91. Ḥabshūsh, *Ru'yā al-Yaman*, 215.

92. Ḥabshūsh, *Ru'yā al-Yaman*, 128.

93. Ḥabshūsh, *Ru'yā al-Yaman*, 77–78.

94. Ḥabshūsh, *Ru'yā al-Yaman*, 185.

95. Ḥabshūsh, *Ru'yā al-Yaman*, 57–58, 182.

96. Ḥabshūsh, *Ru'yā al-Yaman*, 215.

97. Ḥabshūsh, *Ru'yā al-Yaman*, 29.

98. Ḥabshūsh, *Ru'yā al-Yaman*, 126.

99. Ḥabshūsh, *Ru'yā al-Yaman*, 76–77.

100. Ḥabshūsh, *Ru'yā al-Yaman*, i.

101. Ḥabshūsh, *Ru'yā al-Yaman*, 148.

A Note on the Text and Translation

1. Archiv der Österreichische Akademie der Wissenschaften, Sammlung Glaser, A 1013.

2. Shlomo Dov Goitein, *Travels in Yemen: An Account of Joseph Halévy's Journey to Najran in the Year 1870* (Jerusalem: Hebrew University Press, 1941), 3. For Rhodokanakis's correspondence, see Archiv der Österreichische Akademie der Wissenschaften, Südarabische Kommission, nos. 280/1936 and 111/1937.

3. The precise relationship of these fragmentary texts to the Glaser manuscript is not clear. They do not seem to be copies but stem from the same set of author's notes. For an examination of this issue, see Goitein's introduction to Ḥayyim Ḥabshūsh,

Ru'yā al-Yaman (Mas'ot Ḥabshūsh), ed. S. D. Goitein (Jerusalem: Ben-Zvi Institute, 1983), xxiii; Shlomo Dov Goitein, "A Hebrew-Arabic Manuscript on the History of the Jews of Yemen," *Kiryat Sefer* 14 (1938), 256–70; and Goitein, *Travels in Yemen*, 12–14. Of the fragments, Goitein's edition makes greatest use of Schocken Library manuscript 16944.

4. For a discussion of the manuscripts, see Goitein, *Travels in Yemen*, 12–14; and Shlomo Dov Goitein, "An Arabic-Hebrew Book on a Tour in Yemen in 1870," in F. I. Baer et al., eds., *Magnes Anniversary Book* (Jerusalem: Hebrew University Press, 1938), 89–96 (Hebrew).

5. Glaser's manuscript of *A Vision of Yemen* can be found at the Austrian Academy of Sciences (Glaser Collection, A 1009, Tagebuch XVI a).

6. Shlomo Dov Goitein, *The Yemenites: History, Communal Organization, and Spiritual Life*, ed. Menahem Ben-Sasson (Jerusalem: Ben-Zvi Institute, 1983), 164 (Hebrew).

7. According to Ḥabshūsh, Glaser preferred Arabic because he thought that a text written in the dialect of Ṣanʿāʾ would be of use to European researchers. Ḥayyim Ḥabshūsh, *Ru'yā al-Yaman (Mas'ot Ḥabshūsh)*, ed. S. D. Goitein (Jerusalem: Ben-Zvi Institute, 1983), 41. Cf. Wolf Leslau, "Linguistic Observations on a Native Yemenite Document," *Jewish Quarterly Review* 36 (1946), 261–79.

8. For a convenient overview of Judeo-Arabic, see Geoffrey Khan, "Judeo-Arabic," in Lily Kahn and Aaron D. Rubin, eds., *Handbook of Jewish Languages* (Leiden: Brill, 2015), 22–63.

9. Joseph Tobi, "The Hebrew-Aramaic Component in Written Yemenite Judeo-Arabic Literature," in S. Morag, M. Bar-Asher, and M. Mayer-Modena, eds., *Vena Hebraica in Judaeorum Linguis: Proceedings of the 2nd International Conference on the Hebrew and Aramaic Elements in Jewish Languages* (Milan: Universita degli Studi di Milano, 1999), 399–415; and Shachmon Ori, "Yemenite Judeo-Arabic," in N. A. Stillman, ed., *Encyclopedia of the Jews in the Islamic World* (Leiden: Brill, 2010), dx.doi.org/10.1163/1878-9781_ejiw_SIM_000717.Tobi notes that Goitein overstates the Ṣanʿānī colloquial element in Ḥabshūsh's work.

10. On this, see Y. Tobi, "Translation of Proper Names in Medieval Judeo-Arabic Translations of the Bible," *Bulletin of the Israeli Academic Center in Cairo* 21 (1997), 18–22.

11. Such a form of proper name translation is not without precedent in other languages. Increase Mather, the famous American Puritan minister, also has a translation of Joseph as his first name.

PART 2: *A VISION OF YEMEN* BY ḤAYYIM ḤABSHŪSH

Author's Note

1. Hebrew year 5653.

2. On this Jerusalem-based newspaper, see Menuḥah Gilboʿa, "*Ha-Tsvi/Ha-Or* (1884–1915)," in Menuḥah Gilboʿa, *Lexicon of Hebrew Periodicals in the 18th and 19th Centuries* (Jerusalem: Mossad Bialik, 1992), 308–13 (Hebrew).

3. Ḥabshūsh's custom, when writing in Arabic, is to translate Hebrew names rather than offering their Arabic equivalents. For example, although the Arabic equivalent of the name Joseph is Yūsuf, Ḥabshūsh prefers to translate the name as Yazīd, meaning "increase," according to the meaning of the name in Hebrew.

4. AH 1287.

Chapter 1

1. Imām al-Mutawakkil Muḥsin ibn Aḥmad al-Shahārī made numerous attempts between 1854 and his death in 1878 to be recognized as the Zaydī imām, but he was never universally recognized as such. See ʿAbd al-Wāsiʿ b. Yaḥyā al-Wāsiʿī, *Taʾrīkh al-Yaman* (Cairo: al-Maṭbaʿa al-Salafīya, 1927), 92–106; and Caesar Farah, *The Sultan's Yemen: Nineteenth-Century Challenges to Ottoman Rule* (London: Tauris, 2002), 85–104.

2. On this incident, which occurred in 1863, see Joseph Tobi, *The Jews of Yemen in the 19th Century* (Tel Aviv: Afikim, 1976), 234 (Hebrew). The ha-Levi al-Shaykh family was one of the most prominent Jewish families of Ṣanʿāʾ. They were descended from Marī Yaḥyā al-Shaykh, who was believed to have led the Jews back to Ṣanʿāʾ after their seventeenth-century exile to Mawzaʿ.

3. That is, the individual who was to become the widely recognized Zaydī imām, Imām al-Manṣūr Muḥammad ibn Yaḥyā Ḥamīd al-Dīn (r. AH 1307–1322/1890–1904), who died in a rebellion against Ottoman rule. Farah, *Sultan's Yemen*, 155.

4. A silver coin of the highest value.

5. The Ottomans ruled Ṣanʿāʾ from 1872 to 1918. On the Jews during this period, see Joseph Tobi, "The Yemeni Jewish Community Under Turkish Rule (1872–1918)," in Joseph Tobi, *The Jews of Yemen: Studies in Their History and Culture* (Leiden: Brill, 1999), 85–106.

6. On these events, see ʿAlī b. ʿAbdallāh al-Iryānī and Amat al-Malik Ismāʿīl Qāsim al-Thawr, *al-Mawqif al-Yamanī min al-ḥukum al-ʿuthmānī al-thānī maʿa taḥqīq makhṭūṭat al-Durr al-manthūr fī sīrat al-Imam al-Manṣūr Muḥammad b. Yaḥyā Ḥamīd al-Dīn* (Damascus: Dār al-fikr, 2008), 314–22.

7. Genesis 25:14, referring to the names of three sons of Ishmael.

8. Jeremiah 19:6.

9. Hebrew year 5620.

10. On the chaos in Ṣanʿāʾ during the 1850s and 1860s, see Yehuda Nini, *The Jews of the Yemen, 1800–1914* (Chur, Switzerland: Harwood Academic, 1991), 38–56.

11. What follows is the omitted portion of Ḥabshūsh's short sermon on alms giving: "This misery of ours is the poverty referred to when Scripture says, 'If your brother becomes poor and reaches out to you . . . ' (cf. Leviticus 25:35). But instead, you seize 'whatever he needs' (Deuteronomy 15:8), even if it is worth just a penny. Another verse says, 'If you assess him as being poor' (Leviticus 27:8). So, although you were told of his broken back, you [pretend] his trouble is hidden from you. You [pretend] that he anoints his face in oil morning and evening, that his tears are but kohl smudging his cheeks, and that his clothing is beautiful cotton, although it is worn and torn—so confused is your heart. Search and investigate well, and lo it is true: Silversmith, blacksmith, tanner, peddler, potter, day laborer, dung collector, vagrant, and bachelor—all seem rich too. [4] You say to yourself, 'How does this person earn his living? I will do the same for my family.' And if you had not already struck with your axe at the tree of his livelihood, you would slander them. If he were a silversmith, you would say, 'He debases his silver.' If he had some other trade, you would say, 'He counterfeits his copper coins.' If his hands were not stained by his work, you would say, 'He stole.' And if the respect of your peers was important to you, you would harm his reputation, saying, 'He has come into some wealth'—and then an opportunist would find a means to exploit your claims to collect his debt. These are the four terrible judgments (cf. Ezekiel 14:21)—but poverty is worse than all of them."

12. Yaḥyā ʿUmaysī was a scholar and merchant with a reputation for great philanthropy. Moshe Gavra, *Encyclopedia of Yemeni Sages* (Bnei Brak: ha-Makhon le-ḥeqer ḥakhme Teman, 2001), 1: 445–46 (Hebrew).

13. Moshe Ḥanokh ha-Levi, a merchant of Turkish or perhaps Russian origin, was one of the most prominent Jews of Aden and had an immense impact on the religious life of the city. He earned a living by importing religious books from Europe. Alan Verskin, "Moshe Ḥanokh ha-Levi," in N. A. Stillman, ed., *Encyclopedia of the Jews in the Islamic World* (Leiden: Brill, forthcoming).

14. On Sulaymān b. Yosef al-Qārah (d. 1889), see Shalom Gamli'el, *The Jewish Sages of Yemen* (Jerusalem: Mekhon Shalom le-Shivṭe Yeshurun, 1992), 161 (Hebrew). On Yaḥyā b. Yosef al-Qārah (d. 1882 or 1887), see Gamli'el, *Jewish Sages*, 163; and Gavra, *Encyclopedia of Yemeni Sages*, 1: 551. When writing in Hebrew, Ḥabshūsh gives the title of rabbi to several Yemeni scholars who would have been known locally by the title of *marī*, which means "my master." See the Glossary for more on this term.

15. Sālim al-Shabazī (d. 1679) was a major Yemeni poet, kabbalist, and geomancer. Mark Wagner, "Major Themes in the Poetry of Rabbi Sālim al-Shabazī," in Jonathan Decter, ed., *Studies in Arabic and Hebrew Letters in Honor of Raymond P. Scheindlin* (Piscataway, NJ: Gorgias Press, 2007), 227–49.

16. A modified version of Psalms 32:5. His "sins" refers to his interest in mysticism and magic.

17. On Jewish amulets, see Esther van Praag, "Introduction to Jewish Silversmiths in Yemen Before Operation 'On Eagles' Wings,'" *Tema* 10 (2007), 97–126. Cf. Joseph Halévy, "Voyage au Nedjran," *Bulletin de la Société de Géographie de Paris* 6 (1873), 24.

18. Al-Ḍāhirī's *Sefer ha-Musar*, written circa 1580, is perhaps the greatest work of Yemeni Jewish belles-lettres; see Zechariah al-Ḍāhirī, *Sefer ha-Musar*, ed. Yehuda Ratzaby (Jerusalem: Ben-Zvi Institute, 1965). On the translation of the title, see Adena Tanenbaum, "Kabbalah in a Literary Key: Mystical Motifs in Zechariah alḌāhirī's *Sefer HaMusar*," *Journal of Jewish Thought and Philosophy* 17 (2009), 96–97.

19. In Europe, Halévy was known for his rigid adherence to biblical style. Shlomo Haramati, *Three Who Preceded Ben-Yehuda* (Jerusalem: Ben-Zvi Institute, 1978), 40–41 (Hebrew).

20. An awkward construction drawing on phrases from Psalms 18:35 and 2 Samuel 22:37.

21. Mārib was one of the great ancient cities of Yemen and is sometimes referred to as the "Paris of the ancient world."

22. Ḥabshūsh uses a traditional Jewish ritual invocation to express this.

23. Habakkuk 1:8.

24. On Yemeni Jewish beliefs about the lost tribe of Dan, see Yehuda Ratzaby, *Yemeni Paths* (Tel Aviv: ʿAm ʿOved, 1988), 244–51 (Hebrew).

Chapter 2

1. On these tensions, see Husayn al-ʿAmri, *The Yemen in the 18th and 19th Centuries* (London: Ithaca Press, 1985), 85.

2. According to Halévy, he himself traveled to Ghaymān after his illness to collect inscriptions. Joseph Halévy, "Voyage au Nedjran," *Bulletin de la Société de Géographie de Paris* 6 (1873), 30.

3. It was common for Yemeni Jews to be employed in the manufacture of gunpowder. Yosef Tobi, "Jewish-Muslim Relations in the Tribal Regions in North Yemen," in Y. Tobi, *The Jews of Yemen* (Leiden: Brill, 1999), 147.

4. These were traditional occupations of traveling Jews. On Jewish professions in general, see Mark Wagner, *Jewish and Islamic Law in Early 20th-Century Yemen* (Bloomington: Indiana University Press, 2014), 96–100.

5. Literally, "My complaint will not be with you, but with my patron." Jews used this phrase to threaten those who sought to harm them with punishment from their patrons.

6. Cf. Zechariah 12:10.

7. As'ad al-Kāmil (d. 400–45 CE), the king of Ḥimyar about whom many legends are told, was reported to have converted to Judaism. Christian Robin, "Arabia and Ethiopia," in Scott Fitzgerald Johnson, ed., *The Oxford Handbook of Late Antiquity* (Oxford: Oxford University Press, 2015), 266.

8. Psalms 25:14.

9. Isaiah 40:28.

10. Isaiah 10:14.

11. Adapted from Psalms 132:4.

12. Ḥabshūsh refers to God as *ma'avir rishon rishon*, an expression usually interpreted to mean that God forgives a person's first offense. See, for example, *Babylonian Talmud, Rosh Ha-Shanah* 17b.

13. Ḥabshūsh uses the word *'aravim*, but, as Goitein notes, its meaning in this passage is "villagers" or "tribesmen." Ḥayyim Ḥabshūsh, *Ruʾyā al-Yaman (Mas'ot Ḥabshūsh)*, ed. S. D. Goitein (Jerusalem: Ben-Zvi Institute, 1983), 15n18.

14. Ḥabshūsh's intent in translating Muḥṣunah's name as "the pleasant one" is to indicate that her given name does not fit her description. However, his translation is erroneous. Whereas Muḥsunah can be translated as "the pleasant one," Muḥṣunah means "the chaste one."

15. The reference is to Judges 15:15–17.

16. A *qarqūsh* (pl. *qarāqish*) is a hood usually made of brocade. A *ṣūna* is a woman's head covering made of cloth that is wrapped, not tied. M. Piamenta, *Dictionary of Post-Classical Yemeni Arabic* (Leiden: Brill, 1997), 395, 291.

17. Proverbs 31:10.

18. A common phrase usually used in reference to the exodus from Egypt. See, for example, Exodus 6:1–6 and Psalms 136:12.

19. On this formula, see Sara Sviri, "Words of Power and the Power of Words: Mystical Linguistics in the Works of al-Ḥakīm al-Tirmidhī," *Jerusalem Studies in Arabic and Islam* 27 (2002), 216.

20. According to shared Jewish and Islamic traditions, the Seal of Solomon was the signet ring possessed by King Solomon that gave him the power to command the world of spirits; see Gershom Scholem, *The Messianic Idea in Judaism* (New York: Schocken, 1971), 257–81.

21. Jeremiah 18:15.

22. Halévy includes two transcriptions bearing the same text from Ghaymān. However, one is written from right to left, the other from left to right. Joseph Halévy, "Inscriptions Sabéennes," *Journal Asiatique* 19 (1872), 132 (inscription 3) and 134 (inscription 16).

23. A scribe and son of the noted scholar Judah ben Joseph Jizfān (d. 1837). Moshe Gavra, *Encyclopedia of Yemeni Sages* (Bnei Brak: ha-Makhon le-ḥeqer ḥakhme Teman, 2001), 1: 63–64 (Hebrew).

24. Psalms 5:9.

25. That is, the five imāms recognized by Zaydī Shiʿism.

26. Psalms 42:8.

27. Echoing Proverbs 25:13.

Chapter 3

1. Ḥabshūsh uses the Hebrew term *parnas* and the Arabic term *ʿāqil* interchangeably. They denote the head of the Jewish community. On this position, see Yehuda Nini, *The Jews of Yemen, 1800–1914* (New York: Harwood Academic, 1991), 105.

2. That is, a European Jew.

3. On Joseph ben Shalom Badīḥī, see Moshe Gavra, *Encyclopedia of Yemeni Sages* (Bnei Brak: ha-Makhon le-ḥeqer ḥakhme Teman, 2001), 1: 32 (Hebrew). On Sar Shalom ben Aharon Ha-Cohen al-ʿIrāqī, see Aharon Gaymani, "New Sources on the Work of R. Shalom al-Irāqī in the Communities of 19th-Century Yemen," *Peʿamim* 55 (1993), 134–44 (Hebrew). The identity of the Ashkenazic sage is not traceable.

4. This is, perhaps, a reference to al-Mahdī al-ʿAbbās b. al-Ḥusayn (r. AH 1160–89/1747–75).

5. This mark, sometimes referred to as a *zabība* (literally, raisin), is a bump on the forehead caused by frequent prostrations and is seen as a sign of great piety.

6. Because Ḥabshūsh wrote these lines in Aramaic, I have placed them in italics.

7. Leviticus 21:10.

8. Paraphrase of Lamentations 3:30.

9. That is, Baruch ben Samuel of Pinsk (d. 1834); see Yehuda Ratzaby, "Baruch ben Samuel," in *Encyclopaedia Judaica*, 2nd ed. (Detroit: Macmillan Reference, 2007), 3: 189–90.

10. On this event, see Y. Tobi, *The Jews of Yemen in the 19th Century* (Tel Aviv: Afikim, 1976), 265 (Hebrew).

11. Goitein suggests that Ḥabshūsh is referring to Eliyahu Ḥayyim, who died in 1893 in Raḥbah, not Raymat Waṣāb. See Ḥayyim Ḥabshūsh, *Ruʾyā al-Yaman (Masʿot Ḥabshūsh)*, ed. S. D. Goitein (Jerusalem: Ben-Zvi Institute, 1983), 28n13.

12. For Halévy's description of his clothing, see Joseph Halévy, "Rapport sur une mission archéologique dans le Yemen," *Journal Asiatique* 6 (1872), 14.

13. The *seʾah*, a biblical unit of measurement, is equal to about 7⅓ metric liters.

14. Saʿīd al-ʿArūsī (d. 1909) was a central figure in the Jewish Enlightenment movement in Yemen; see Saʿīd al-ʿArūsī and Y. Qafih, "Metsuqot Teman," *Sefunot* 5 (1961), 399–400.

15. See, for example, *Bereishit Rabbah* 48:14.

16. *Bustān al-sulṭān* in Arabic.

17. Muḥsin b. ʿAlī Muʿīd held de facto control of Ṣanʿāʾ from 1862 to 1872. Franck Mermier, *Le cheikh de la nuit* (Arles: Actes Sud, 1997), 42–54.

18. Ḥabshūsh includes the following notes on the building al-Jāmiʿ al-Kabīr: "This building is very ancient and, according to what they say, it was built by order of Fāṭimah, a daughter of their prophet. Over time, this mosque has received many endowments from all the regions of Yemen. These endowments include land, fields, vineyards, gardens, orchards, forests, springs, rivers, wells, whole villages, houses,

shops, and inns, wherever they may be. They also bequeath their books and other things. They therefore have a parable, 'If Ṣan'ā' is destroyed, this mosque will rebuild it from its great wealth, but if this mosque is destroyed, the Ṣan'ānīs will not be able to rebuild it.' The roof of the mosque is supported by stone columns which stand inside it. There is a large open-air courtyard in its center so that they might have *a ladder set upon the earth, the top of it reaching heaven* (Genesis 28:12), and there, according to their visionaries, is the gate of heaven. At the foot of the ladder, in the center of the courtyard, are two tombstones belonging to their saints. In this mosque, there are boundary markers pointing northward, which, according to their faith, were set there by their Lawgiver. They therefore sanctify and praise this boundary, which is called al-Masmūrah and al-Manqūrah. Because of their awe of this place, it is here that their judges administer the swearing of oaths for those who are required to make serious oaths. When Jews need Gentiles to swear an oath, they request that the judge administer the oath to the Muslim in this mosque at this boundary while the Jew stands outside the entrance to witness the Muslim's oath. The northern gate is never opened, except for their supreme kings, and upon it is a memento of the Sabaeans—two engraved copper tablets with Sabaean inscriptions. No one in the city knew about them, but I noticed them and pointed them out to travelers who came after the sage Joseph." On the building, see Hana Zabarah, "The Great Mosque of Sana'a: An Architectural History," *al-Masār* 10 (2009), 15. On Jewish exposure to al-Masmūrah and al-Manqūrah, see Mark Wagner, *Jewish and Islamic Law in Early 20th-Century Yemen* (Bloomington: Indiana University Press, 2014), 26.

19. Cf. Psalms 118:11.

20. For Halévy's description of his treatment in Ṣan'ā', see Joseph Halévy, "Voyage au Nedjran," *Bulletin de la Société de Géographie de Paris* 6 (1873), 18–19.

21. Isaiah 23:8. Ḥabshūsh is making a Hebrew-Arabic pun. "Crowning city" in Hebrew sounds like "apothecary" in Arabic.

22. *Shayṭān* (pl. *shayāṭīn*), which literally means "devil," can also mean either "bandit" or "ruffian" in Yemeni Arabic. Ḥabshūsh uses the word in both of these senses, and so I have translated it differently depending on context. Moshe Piamenta, *Dictionary of Post-Classical Yemeni Arabic* (Leiden: Brill, 1990), 1: 274.

Chapter 4

1. Halévy confirms that he did indeed stay with al-Qārah, whom he describes favorably. Joseph Halévy, "Voyage au Nedjran," *Bulletin de la Société de Géographie de Paris* 6 (1873), 19.

2. That is, "Adar 1, 5630 after creation, 2181 in the Seleucid calendar."

3. Halévy describes how, upon leaving Ṣan'ā', he rode on a donkey because his illness had left him too weak to walk long distances. Although Jews were not usually permitted to ride animals, special dispensation was given to sick Jews for whom this was necessary. Nonetheless, Halévy claimed that despite his guide's best efforts, this dispensation was frequently challenged. Halévy, "Voyage au Nedjran," 252–53.

4. The Qarāmiṭah were an Islamic sect that at one time enjoyed a considerable following in Yemen. According to Goitein, knowledge of the sect is no longer within Yemeni collective memory, so it is possible that the residents thought the cemetery was a Jewish one despite its Islamic name. See Ḥayyim Ḥabshūsh, *Ru'yā al-Yaman (Mas'ot Ḥabshūsh)*, ed. S. D. Goitein (Jerusalem: Ben-Zvi Institute, 1983), 35n9.

5. At this point, Ḥabshūsh ceases writing in Hebrew and starts writing in Arabic.

6. Ḥabshūsh is no doubt referring to Saadya's translation of the Bible into Arabic, known as the *Tafsīr* (the commentary). On the role that the work has played in Yemen, see Y. Qāfiḥ, *Perushe Rabbenu Saʿadya Gaon ʿal ha-Torah* (Jerusalem: Mossad ha-Rav Kook, 1976), 6–8; and J. Tobi, "Between *tafsīr* and *sharḥ*: Saʿadya Ga'on's Translation of the Bible Among the Jews of Yemen," *Studies in the History and Culture of Iraqi Jewry* 6 (1991), 127–38 (Hebrew).

7. I have been unable to identity this individual.

8. On Jacob Saphir, see Noah Gerber, *Ourselves or Our Holy Books? The Cultural Study of Yemenite Jewry* (Jerusalem: Ben-Zvi Institute, 2013), 28–51 (Hebrew).

9. For Saphir's account of these events, see Jacob Saphir, *Even Sapir* (Lyck: Mekitse Nirdamim, 1866), 106. Saphir is referred to by Ḥabshūsh as Ghādir al-Mās, a translation of his name into Arabic based on its Hebrew meaning.

10. The substance bears the scientific name *Withania somnifera (L.) dun.* M. Piamenta, *Dictionary of Post-Classical Yemeni Arabic* (Leiden: Brill, 1997), 2: 314.

11. On Halévy's travels in Abyssinia, see the Introduction section "Ḥayyim Ḥabshūsh and the European Explorers."

12. Song of Songs 1:5.

13. Ḥabshūsh substitutes this phrase for the Song of Song's "my mother's sons."

14. Song of Songs 1:6.

15. *Dāʿī* was the title given to important religious leaders of the Ismāʿīlī movement. Ḥabshūsh is referring to al-Ḥasan ibn Ismāʿīl Āl Shibām al-Makramī (r. AH 1262–89/1846–72), the forty-first of the Makramī Sulaymānī *dāʿī*s, who was eventually killed by the Ottomans. On him, see Farhad Daftary, *The Ismāʿīlīs: Their History and Doctrines*, 2nd ed. (Cambridge, UK: Cambridge University Press, 2007), 297.

16. On this figure, see the Introduction section "The People and Politics of Yemen."

17. Halévy also mentions having been imprisoned by Murshid al-Zubayrī on the charge of being a false messiah. Halévy, "Voyage au Nedjran," 257–59; and Joseph Halévy, "Rapport sur une mission archéologique dans le Yemen," *Journal Asiatique* 6 (1872), 15.

18. Cf. Joseph Halévy, "Inscriptions Sabéennes," *Journal Asiatique* 19 (1872), 142 (inscription 77). Referred to in Ḥabshūsh, *Ru'yā al-Yaman*, 45n31.

Chapter 5

1. The volume of these measurements varies greatly in Yemen. An *uqqah* is equal to approximately 1¼ kilograms. A Ṣanʿānī *qadaḥ* is equal to approximately 41 kilograms.

2. Halévy notes that the tribesmen were afraid to climb this mountain because they believed it to be inhabited by *jinn* who danced by the light of fires. Joseph Halévy, "Voyage au Nedjran," *Bulletin de la Société de Géographie de Paris* 6 (1873), 256.

3. This is a reference to the Pact of ʿUmar, which stipulates that Jewish houses must be lower than Muslim ones. On the pact, see the Introduction section "The People and Politics of Yemen."

4. Like Ḥabshūsh, Halévy remarks that the tribes of Nihm treat Jews more favorably than the tribes of Arḥab. Halévy, "Voyage au Nedjran," 261.

5. On the Ṭāghūt, see the Introduction section "The People and Politics of Yemen." On such sacrifices, see Paul Dresch, *Tribes, Government, and History in Yemen* (Oxford: Oxford University Press, 1989), 50–51.

6. See [58], later in this chapter.

7. Halévy also mentions the occurrence of a wedding. Halévy, "Voyage au Nedjran," 261.

8. A thick porridge made of crushed groats of wheat or durra.

9. The Day of the Morning (*yawm al-sabāḥ*) is the customary wedding banquet served on the morning after the wedding ceremony. Y. Qāfiḥ, *Halikhot Teman* (Jerusalem: Makhon Ben-Zvi, 1987), 142–43.

10. Ḥabshūsh does not end up telling this story, but he does reference Sālim Mask al-Aqḍaʿ elsewhere. See Schocken Library, no. 16944, 543, referred to in Ḥayyim Ḥabshūsh, *Ruʾyā al-Yaman (Masʿot Ḥabshūsh)*, ed. S. D. Goitein (Jerusalem: Ben-Zvi Institute, 1983), 52n16.

11. That is, "Rabīʿ al-Thānī 1311/Ḥeshvan 5654."

12. Although the Ottomans abolished the *jizyah* in most parts of the empire in 1856, they continued to impose it in Yemen. See Yehuda Nini, *The Jews of Yemen, 1800–1914* (New York: Harwood Academic, 1991), 62–66.

13. That is, Imām al-Manṣūr Muḥammad ibn Yaḥyā Ḥamīd al-Dīn (r. AH 1307–22/1890–1904). For his biography, see ʿAlī b. ʿAbdallāh al-Iryānī, *Al-Durr al-manthūr fī sīrat Mawlānā Amīr al-Muʾminīn al-Imām al-Manṣūr* (Damascus: Dār al-fikr, 2008).

14. Halévy also mentioned speaking to this man, who he said was 100 years old. Halévy, "Voyage au Nedjran," 262–63.

15. On the slaughtering of animals for the expiation of transgressions, see Dresch, *Tribes*, 50–51; and Shelagh Weir, *A Tribal Order: Politics and Law in the Mountains of Yemen* (Austin: University of Texas Press, 2007), 174–78.

16. Halévy does not mention Darb al-Ḥanshāt. Goitein, however, suggests that Halévy's description of al-Sūdah bears much in common with Ḥabshūsh's description of Darb al-Ḥanshāt (see [63] earlier in this chapter) and that Ḥabshūsh may have mistaken the one place for the other. See Ḥabshūsh, *Ruʾyā al-Yaman*, 61n34; and Halévy, "Voyage au Nedjran," 262–63.

17. Elsewhere, Ḥabshūsh wrote his own brief history of the seventeenth-century exile of the Jews to Mawzaʿ; see Ḥayyim Ḥabshūsh, "History of the Jews in Yemen," ed. Y. Qāfiḥ, *Sefunot* 2 (1958), 255–57 (Hebrew).

18. Halévy mentions having visited a fourteenth-century Jewish cemetery in this location with Hebrew inscriptions. Halévy, "Voyage au Nedjran," 262.

19. According to Hugh Scott, *ḍafar* seeds are from "a low-growing leguminose bush of the genus *Tephrosia*." See Hugh Scott, "Travels in the Yemen Seventy Years Ago," *Geographical Journal* 99 (1942), 275.

20. Glaser makes similar remarks; see Walter Dostal, *Ethnographica Jemenica: Auszüge aus den Tagebüchern Eduard Glasers mit einem Kommentar versehen* (Vienna: Österreichischen Akademie der Wissenschaften, 1993), 50.

21. Literally, "the principles and branches of the law" (*qawāʿid al-sharīʿah* and *furūʿ*). The terminology is drawn from Islamic jurisprudence.

22. *Baʿalei ha-peshaṭ* in Hebrew.

23. Jewish year 5608.

24. That is, Imām al-Nāṣir ʿAbdallāh b. al-Ḥasan (d. AH 1256/1840). On this imām's asceticism, see Bernard Haykel, *Revival and Reform in Islam: The Legacy of Muḥammad al-Shawkānī* (Cambridge, UK: Cambridge University Press, 2003), 184–87.

25. Halévy mentions only that they found "graffiti" on the rocks of Shayḥān. Joseph Halévy, "Rapport sur une mission archéologique dans le Yemen," *Journal Asiatique* 6 (1872), 17.

26. Halévy does not mention "Qalt al-Yahūd."

27. Ḥabshūsh writes what follows in mournful, if somewhat ungrammatical, rhymed prose.

28. Irfan Shahid, *Byzantium and the Arabs in the Fifth Century* (Washington, DC: Dumbarton Oaks Research Library and Collection, 1989), 339–40.

29. Abraha, a Christian Aksumite, was a Himyarite ruler (r. circa 535–565 CE). Christian Robin, "Arabia and Ethiopia," in Scott Fitzgerald Johnson, ed., *The Oxford Handbook of Late Antiquity* (Oxford: Oxford University Press, 2015), 284–88.

30. Qur'ān 3:146.

31. Cf. Halévy, "Voyage au Nedjran," 266–67; and Halévy, "Rapport sur une mission archéologique," 19–20.

32. Yemenis commonly referred to the script of ancient inscriptions as "Persian." See chapter 1, [6].

33. Halévy confirms this, adding that he did so to hide his transcriptions from prying eyes. Halévy, "Voyage au Nedjran," 5.

34. Gabriella Moscati Steindler suggests that Ḥabshūsh is linking the word to the Aramaic term *genāy*, meaning "disgrace" or "obscenity." Moscati Steindler, *Imagine dello Yemen* (Napoli: L'Istituto Orientale di Napoli, 1976), 63n141.

35. The Qarār (sing. Qarawī or Qarārī) were Arab Muslims whose status was inferior to that of the tribesmen; see Joseph Tobi, *The Jews of Yemen* (Leiden: Brill, 1999), 151–52. For a bibliography of this pariah caste, see Joseph Henninger, *Arabica Varia: Aufsätze zur Kulturgeschichte Arabiens und seiner Randgebiete* (Freiburg: Vandenhoeck und Ruprecht, 1989), 281–86. Halévy also describes the Qarār. See Halévy, "Voyage au Nedjran," 592–94.

36. On this sacrosanct caste, see Dresch, *Tribes*, 141–45; and Ettore Rossi, "Il diritto consuetudinario delle tribù arabe del Yemen," *Revista degli Studi Orientali* 23 (1948), 8. Rossi was one of the first scholars to appreciate the importance of Ḥabshūsh's descriptions of tribal relations.

37. According to Piamenta, the payment of tribal indemnities (*ṣāʿibah*) is "the yearly payment of six riyals and one ram which is due as long as the blood-money has not been handed over." M. Piamenta, *Dictionary of Post-Classical Yemeni Arabic* (Leiden: Brill, 1997), 2: 289.

38. On formulas for seeking protection, see R. Serjeant, "Customary Law of South-West Arabia," in *Recueils de la Société Jean Bodin*, tome 1, *La Coutume/Custom* (Brussels: De Boeck Université, 1992), 273.

39. The following addendum to the story occurs in one manuscript (Schocken Library, no. 16944, f. 472): "The elders of Nihm wrote to al-Mushīr [an Ottoman official] regarding their enemies, the people of Ḥaḍūr, describing what they had done. Immediately, al-Mushīr sent for Ibn ʿIyāsh, the sheikh of Ḥaḍūr, imprisoned him, and held him responsible for the slain man. When the leaders of Nihm learned that al-Mushīr had imprisoned the sheikh of Ḥaḍūr, they wrote to him a second time requesting that he free their enemy from prison, because they gained no advantage from his imprisonment. Nevertheless, the sheikh of Ḥaḍūr and the Nihmīs still attack each other and, to this day, they have taken from the sheikh twice the bloodwite—and the claim of the slain man still remains!"

40. By contrast, in Islamic law, the bloodwite of a non-Muslim is less than that of a Muslim. Y. Friedmann, *Tolerance and Coercion in Islam* (Cambridge, UK: Cambridge University Press, 2003), 47–50.

41. As Goitein notes, Ḥabshūsh offers an alternative explanation in the Schocken manuscript. The quadruple bloodwite of the Jews is awarded to them because "they are thought to be weak." Schocken Library, no. 16944, f. 472.

42. That is, the chiefs of the largest tribes of central Yemen.

43. *Qiṣāṣ* in Arabic.

44. That is, Imām al-Mutawakkil Muḥammad ibn Yaḥyā (r. AH 1261–65/1845–49). This imām is not to be confused with the other Muḥammad ibn Yaḥyā mentioned by Ḥabshūsh, that is, Imām al-Manṣūr Muḥammad ibn Yaḥyā Ḥamīd al-Dīn (r. AH 1307–1322/1890–1904).

45. On these events, see Nini, *Jews of Yemen*, 39.

46. AH 1251.

47. On al-Manṣūr ʿAlī ibn al-Mahdī ʿAbdallāh (r. AH 1251–52/1835–36, AH 1259–61/1843–45, AH 1265–66/1849–50, and AH 1267–68/1851) and the first revolt against him, see Haykel, *Revival and Reform*, 184–85.

48. AH 1261. On these events, see R. Serjeant, "The Post-Medieval and Modern History of Ṣanʿāʾ and the Yemenis," in R. Serjeant and Ronald Lewcock, eds., *Ṣanʿāʾ: An Arabian Islamic City* (London: World of Islam Festival Trust, 1983), 87–89.

49. The omitted portion, a description of how coins are struck, reads: "This is a description of how coins were made. About ten men melt a quantity of copper-silver alloy and pour it into sand that has been especially prepared for it. When they remove it from the sand, it has formed into thin strips, each of which is worth 20 dirhams. An official who has been appointed for this purpose gives it to workers who cut it into pieces—there are about fifty people who are thus employed and the place in which this is done is called the *mufrāṣah.* They then return the pieces of metal to the official. He in turn gives them to other workers—there are about one hundred of them—who press, beat, and flatten the pieces. The room in which all this is done is called the *midrābah.* When they bring the flattened pieces to the official, each piece is equal in measure, one not exceeding another in size by so much as a grain. The official then brings them to another place known as [94] the polishing house. After that, the official sends them to the mint, which is a place more guarded than all others. A judge representing the imām sits in the room. As for the forty people who work there, they cannot come and go like their fellows who work in the same house. These individuals have an iron engraving tool which has an obverse die upon which the name of the imām is inscribed and a reverse die upon which the name of the city is inscribed. The two impressions are made at the same time. One part of the tool holds the obverse side; inserting the coin between the dies, the second part strikes the coin with a hammer until the work is complete and the official removes the coin. After the judge's approval has been obtained, the pieces are designated current coins and are given to the moneychangers, who distribute them among the people."

50. This incident is described by Ḥabshūsh in another work; see Ḥabshūsh, "History of the Jews in Yemen," 273-274. Cf. Nini, *Jews of Yemen*, 38–40.

51. AH 1231. Goitein suggests that Ḥabshūsh's date is incorrect. The great famine of Ṣanʿāʾ was in 1808, and the Bakīl tribe's siege occurred in 1817. See Ḥabshūsh, *Ruʾyā al-Yaman*, 88n92.

52. See Y. Nini, "The Revolt of the Bakīl and Ḥāshid Confederation," *Sefunot* 3 (1984), 83–95 (Hebrew).

53. AH 1241.

54. AH 1251.

55. AH 1275.

56. AH 1303.

57. For a description of these events, see Dresch, *Tribes*, 217; and Caesar Farah, *The Sultan's Yemen: Nineteenth-Century Challenges to Ottoman Rule* (London: Tauris, 2002), 61.

58. Farah, *Sultan's Yemen*, 59.

59. The Torah portion Deuteronomy 32:1–32:52.

Chapter 6

1. See chapter 5, [78].

2. Halévy says that, before hiring a Muslim guide, he first tried to hire a Jewish one but could not because Jews did not wish to travel so close to Passover. Joseph Halévy, "Voyage au Nedjran," *Bulletin de la Société de Géographie de Paris* 6 (1873), 265; and Joseph Halévy, "Rapport sur une mission archéologique dans le Yemen," *Journal Asiatique* 6 (1872), 17.

3. A narrow-sleeved waistcoat. M. Piamenta, *A Dictionary of Post-Classical Arabic* (Leiden: Brill, 1997), 2: 205.

4. When Halévy received this *shamlah* as a gift, he declared it not suitable for human use, but later he would not part with it. See Ḥayyim Ḥabshūsh, *Ru'yā al-Yaman (Mas'ot Ḥabshūsh)*, ed. S. D. Goitein (Jerusalem: Ben-Zvi Institute, 1983), 32.

5. Halévy also mentions that his guide warned him of the hostility of the local tribes. Halévy, "Voyage au Nedjran," 270.

6. To the best of my knowledge, this word is not attested elsewhere.

7. Although Ḥabshūsh references *durūm* later in the manuscript, he does not discuss them in detail. Ḥabshūsh, *Ru'yā al-Yaman*, 190.

8. Halévy mentions an argument among the Jews of al-Ghayl over who would get the honor of hosting him. Halévy, "Voyage au Nedjran," 273.

9. On this garment, see Erich Brauer, *Ethnologie der jemenitischen Juden* (Heidelberg: Carl Winter, 1934), 85.

10. The rabbis instituted special blessings for bread made of one of five specified kinds of grains (*Mishnah Ḥallah* 1:1). Millet was not one of these grains, but it was often the only one available to Yemeni Jews living in these remote regions. As early as the time of Abraham, son of Maimonides (d. 1237), Yemeni Jews asked whether they could recite the blessings for bread over bread made from millet. Abraham Maimonides, *Teshuvot*, ed. A. Freimann (Jerusalem: Meḳitse Nirdamim, 1937), 126–28. Referred to in Ḥabshūsh, *Ru'yā al-Yaman*, 99n25.

11. This list of activities is somewhat surprising given that washing and cleaning are activities that most Jewish communities prohibit on the Sabbath.

12. Muslims regard the commandment to keep the Sabbath as having been abrogated, but, as this passage illustrates, many Muslims still considered its observance to be obligatory for Jews. See Ignaz Goldziher, "The Sabbath Institution in Islam," in Gerald Hawting, ed., *The Development of Islamic Ritual* (Aldershot, UK: Ashgate, 2006), 33–48; and Mark Wagner, *Jewish and Islamic Law in Early 20th-Century Yemen* (Bloomington: Indiana University Press, 2014), 79.

13. For an interesting parallel, see Reuben Shar'abi, *Yeḥi Re'uben* (Tel Aviv: Afikim, 2014), 43–44. Cited in Bat-Zion Eraqi Klorman, "Yemen: Muslim and Jewish Interactions in the Tribal Sphere," in Michael M. Laskier and Yaacov Lev, eds., *The Divergence of Judaism and Islam* (Gainesville: University Press of Florida, 2011), 132–33.

14. Halévy mentions only one Jew. Halévy, "Voyage au Nedjran," 581.

15. Banāt ʿĀd is the local Arabic name for an imposing temple located in the ancient city of Haram. The name *Banāt ʿĀd* means "the daughters of ʿĀd," a tribe mentioned in the Qurʾān. Ḥabshūsh calls the place Haram, and I have preserved this name, although it is sometimes referred to by other writers as Ḥaram.

16. Ḥabshūsh adds: "A furnace is something in which a hot fire blazes until it melts an object and changes its form such that one can no longer discern its nature."

17. In contrast, Halévy says that he discovered seventy-one fragmentary inscriptions there. Halévy, "Rapport sur une mission archéologique," 84.

18. Joseph Arūjas was an antiquities dealer in Ṣanʿāʾ; see J. Mordtmann and E. Mittwoch, *Sabäische Inschriften* (Hamburg: Friederichsen, 1931), 243; and Ḥabshūsh, *Ruʾyā al-Yaman*, 105n42.

19. Halévy recorded seventy-four inscriptions in this location, but most of them are quite short. Halévy, "Rapport sur une mission archéologique," 80–82.

20. Ḥabshūsh calls this place Barāqīsh, but it is usually referred to as Barāqish.

21. As Goitein notes, Halévy's transcriptions from Barāqīsh are divided into more lines than those from other places. See Ḥabshūsh, *Ruʾyā al-Yaman*, 112n52a; and Halévy, "Rapport sur une mission archéologique," 85–90.

22. Ḥabshūsh later explains that the idea that Muslims should shun Jews, to the extent of not even speaking their name, is a component of an unusually extreme anti-Jewish ideology. Ḥabshūsh, *Ruʾyā al-Yaman*, [184–85].

23. Halévy also refers to this mountain. Halévy, "Voyage au Nedjran," 604; and Halévy, "Rapport sur une mission archéologique," 30, 90–92.

24. Ḥabshūsh adds, "I saw the abandoned house of a Jew, and the gate and threshold were not made of a single stone." His meaning is not clear. It is possible that he is indicating that the gate itself was, atypically, also made of stone.

25. In contrast, Halévy mentions that, with the help of some Bedouin women, he himself caught fish in the river. Halévy, "Voyage au Nedjran," 583.

26. On Shapira, see P. Fenton, "Moses Shapira's Journey to the Yemen," in Eilat Ettinger and Danny Bar-Maoz, eds., *Mittuv Yosef: Yosef Tobi Jubilee Volume* (Haifa: University of Haifa, 2011), lxviii–lxxxi.

27. Shaddād ibn ʿĀd is a legendary pre-Islamic hero who is credited with building several great cities and monuments (now ruins). H. T. Norris, "Qiṣaṣ Elements in the Qurʾān," in A. F. L. Beeston, T. M. Johnstone, R. B. Serjeant, and G. R. Smith, eds., *Arabic Literature to the End of the Umayyad Period* (Cambridge, UK: Cambridge University Press, 1983), 248–49. King Og was an Amorite king, mentioned in the Bible. The two are associated with one another because of their reportedly great height.

28. Halévy also mentions seeing a monogram. Halévy, "Rapport sur une mission archéologique," 87.

29. On the Shawwāf tribe, see Paul Dresch, *Tribes, Government, and History in Yemen* (Oxford: Oxford University Press, 1989), 209–10.

30. That is, al-Manṣūr ʿAlī b. ʿAbbās al-Ḥusayn (r. AH 1189–1224/1775–1809).

31. See chapter 10, [188–89].

32. It is unlikely that this family emanates from the Ḥijāz. Goitein suggests that they received the name on account of their trade with the region. Ḥabshūsh, *Ruʾyā al-Yaman*, 122n71.

33. *Ḥubb al-waṭan* in Arabic.

34. See chapter 5, [83]. Ḥabshūsh uses the terms Qarawī and Qarārī interchangeably.

35. See [114] in this chapter.

36. Following Goitein, I omit a short tangent, present in the Schocken manuscript but not in Glaser's manuscript, that continues in this vein. Ḥabshūsh, *Ru'yā al-Yaman*, 127n77.

Chapter 7

1. According to the Pact of 'Umar, Jews were not allowed to carry weapons. In contrast, tribal law allowed Jews to carry weapons, although, in this case, their weapons were smaller than those of their patrons. On this, see the Introduction section "The People and Politics of Yemen." Halévy also comments on the courageous demeanor of the Jews of Khabb, but he does not mention that they carried weapons. Joseph Halévy, "Voyage au Nedjran II: De Sana à Nedjran," *Bulletin de la Société de Géographie de Paris* 13 (1877), 466–79.

2. See chapter 4, [47].

3. This tree has been identified as the *Ziziphus spina-christi*, or "Christ's Thorn Jujube." M. Piamenta, *A Dictionary of Post-Classical Arabic* (Leiden: Brill, 1997), 2: 392.

4. The reference is to Joseph Caro's (d. 1575) *Shulkhan 'Arukh*. On the reception of this Ottoman Jewish scholar's work in Yemen, see Aharon Gaymani, *Changes in the Heritage of Yemeni Jewry: On the Influence of the Shulkhan 'Arukh and Lurianic Kabbalah* (Ramat-Gan: Bar Ilan University Press, 2005) (Hebrew).

5. About 100 grams.

6. On Jewish migration to Ottoman Palestine, see Ari Ariel, *Jewish-Muslim Relations and Migration from Yemen to Palestine in the Late Nineteenth and Twentieth Centuries* (Leiden: Brill, 2014), 45–76.

Chapter 8

1. According to Halévy, the Jews of Khabb advised him against traveling to Najrān on the grounds that its inhabitants were hostile. They informed him that, some twenty years earlier, a rabbi from Jerusalem had attempted the journey but had died en route. Joseph Halévy, "Voyage au Nedjran II: De Sana à Nedjran," *Bulletin de la Société de Géographie de Paris* 13 (1877), 469.

2. Halévy does not mention this incident, remarking only that the guide delayed them with his long conversations with local shepherds. Halévy, "Voyage au Nedjran II," 471.

3. That is, the guide had fallen in love with her.

4. Halévy also mentions the guide's refusal to continue the journey. According to him, the guide refused because of his fear of the Banū Sulaymān tribe. Halévy, "Voyage au Nedjran II," 471.

5. Halévy refers to this guide as Ḥunbukh. The Ḥunbukh to whom Ḥabshūsh later refers is the guide who accompanies them on the return journey from Najrān. See chapter 10, [183]; and Halévy, "Voyage au Nedjran II," 471.

6. Here, the accounts of Halévy and Ḥabshūsh markedly differ. Halévy describes how he was forced to travel for three days with a caravan of merchants from Ḥaḍramawt whose religious fanaticism led them to maltreat him. Halévy, "Voyage au Nedjran II," 474.

7. Jewish dietary law in Yemen allowed Jews to eat even quite elaborate meals prepared by Muslims, but the presence of camel milk was frequently raised as an issue of concern. See Mark Wagner, *Jewish and Islamic Law in Early 20th-Century Yemen* (Bloomington: Indiana University Press, 2014), 71–72.

8. Halévy also tells a story about his guide and a lizard but with a different moral. According to Halévy, when he complained to his guide of his abuse at the hands of some Ḥaḍramī merchants, his guide caught a lizard, tore it in half, and swallowed it, to illustrate to Halévy what would become of him if he continued to complain. Halévy, "Voyage au Nedjran II," 475.

9. Halévy also recounts meeting a lost Bedouin woman. Halévy, "Voyage au Nedjran II," 478.

10. On the use of Hebrew as a secret language among Yemeni Jews, see Ori Shachmon, "Secret Languages, Hebrew in: Yemenite Judeo-Arabic," in Geoffrey Khan, ed., *Encyclopedia of Hebrew Language and Linguistics* (Leiden: Brill, 2013), 518–20.

11. Halévy mentions spending the night, tormented by mosquitoes, at the house of two Jewish brothers. Halévy, "Voyage au Nedjran II," 479.

12. *Kubānah* is a Yemeni slow-cooked bread *cholent*, that is, a food developed to balance the need for hot food with the Sabbath's cooking prohibitions. On its preparation, see Erich Brauer, *Ethnologie der jemenitischen Juden* (Heidelberg: Carl Winter, 1934), 103. On the *madhalah*, see S. D. Goitein, *Jemenica: Sprichwörter und Redensarten aus zentral-Jemen* (Leipzig: Harrassowitz, 1934), 273.

13. That is, Isaac Aboab's *Menorat ha-Ma'or*, a fourteenth-century Iberian collection of Talmudic narratives (*aggadot*).

14. The name Maṭrūd is derived from a verb meaning "to drive out."

15. Halévy also remarks that Najrānī Jews were treated better than Jews in other parts of Arabia. Joseph Halévy, "Rapport sur une mission archéologique dans le Yemen," *Journal Asiatique* 6 (1872), 38.

16. A mash, usually cooked for the Sabbath, consisting of wheat groats, meat, oil, and spices. Brauer, *Ethnologie der jemenitischen Juden*, 102–3.

17. Literally, "This is just animal grease (*wadak*), which they call *hāl*. It is not ghee and it is not *shaḥm*." *Shaḥm* is the Arabic translation of the Hebrew word *ḥelev*. *Ḥelev* refers to certain varieties of fat, equivalent to some kinds of tallow, that Jews are forbidden from eating, even if they are derived from a kosher animal. In making this statement, the woman's daughters are assuring Ḥabshūsh that the food that they are preparing contains neither the forbidden mixture of milk and meat nor forbidden tallow. On the prohibition of *shaḥm/ḥelev* in an early Judeo-Islamic context, see Ze'ev Maghen, *After Hardship Cometh Ease: The Jews as Backdrop for Muslim Moderation* (Berlin: de Gruyter, 2006), 151–53.

Chapter 9

1. Ḥabshūsh's term, "the East" (*al-mashāriq*), refers to northeastern Yemen, that is, Yemen both north and east of Ṣanʿāʾ. M. Piamenta, *Dictionary of Post-Classical Yemeni Arabic* (Leiden: Brill, 1997), 1: 254.

2. I have found no other examples of honor killings for expunging the loss of virginity in Jewish communities. However, other minority communities living in the Muslim world did engage in such practices. See, for example, Géraldine Chatelard, "Honneur chrétien et féminité, ou le marriage à la Jordanienne," in B. Heyberger, ed., *Chrétiens du monde arabe* (Paris: Autrement, 2003), 212–25. On sexual honor in Yemen, see Paul Dresch, *Tribes, Government, and History in Yemen* (Oxford: Oxford University Press, 1989), 44–57.

3. Halévy's belief that terminating a pregnancy constituted murder is not one that Jews have traditionally held and is likely the product of European Christian influence. It is therefore not surprising that Ḥabshūsh, who was familiar with the more permissive

Islamic attitude toward early-term abortion, was astonished by his position. On the European Jewish view, see Menachem Elon, "Abortion," in *Encyclopedia Judaica*, 1: 98–102. On the Islamic view, see Marion Holmes Katz, "The Problem of Abortion in Classical Sunni *fiqh*," in J. Brockopp, ed., *Islamic Ethics of Life* (Columbia: University of South Carolina Press, 2003), 25–50. On the influence of the Islamic view on Jews living in Muslim lands, see Abraham Stahl, *Family and Childrearing Among Oriental Jewry* (Jerusalem: Akademon, 1993), 301 (Hebrew).

4. Jewish law defines a bastard (*mamzer*) as the product of a sexual liaison that could never have resulted in a valid marriage, even ex post facto, for example, a liaison between a married adulterous woman and her extramarital partner, or an incestuous liaison. A child who is merely conceived out of wedlock is not assigned this status. Because Saʿīdah was unmarried, if she conceived a child from rape, the child would not be defined as a *mamzer*. B. Schereschewsky, "Mamzer," in *Encyclopedia Judaica*, 11: 839–42.

5. Polygamy among Yemeni Jews in the nineteenth century was relatively common and socially acceptable. S. D. Goitein, *The Yemenites* (Jerusalem: Ben-Zvi Institute, 1983), 313 (Hebrew); Stahl, *Family and Childrearing*, 133; and Erich Brauer, *Ethnologie der jemenitischen Juden* (Heidelberg: Carl Winter, 1934), 174–76.

Chapter 10

1. Halévy mentions having visited "Ṭaḥḍā." Joseph Halévy, "Rapport sur une mission archéologique dans le Yemen," *Journal Asiatique* 6 (1872), 91.

2. These scholars belong to the Makārimah (Sulaymānī) Ismāʿīlī sect that governed Najrān. On this sect, see Tahera Qutbuddin, "A Brief Note on Other Tayyibi Communities: Sulaymanis and ʿAlavis," in F. Daftary, ed., *A Modern History of the Ismailis* (London: Tauris, 2011), 355–58.

3. On the sacrosanct and protected (*hijrah* or *muhajjar*) status of markets, see Paul Dresch, "Guaranty of the Market at Ḥūth," in R. Serjeant, ed., *Arabian Studies* (Cambridge, UK: Cambridge University Press, 1990), 63–91.

4. Thamūd and ʿĀd are names of tribes mentioned in the Qurʾān. Here, each name refers not to the tribe but to its original forefather.

5. Qurʾān 4:85. Ḥabshūsh writes "Khudūd" rather than "Ukhdūd," and Halévy confirms that "Khudūd" is the local pronunciation. For reasons of clarity, however, I have altered the name to reflect the form in which the word appears in the Qurʾān. Halévy, "Rapport sur une mission archéologique," 39.

6. On the Najrānī Christians, see A. Beeston, "Judaism and Christianity in Pre-Islamic Yemen," in J. Chelhod, ed., *Le peuple yéménite et ses raciness* (Paris: Maisonneuve et Larose, 1984), 259–78.

7. Toward the end of the tenth century AH (seventeenth century), a succession dispute split the Ṭayyibī Ismāʿīlīs into the Dāʾūdī and Sulaymānī sects. In Yemen the Sulaymānī sect came to be known as the Makārimah. Farhad Daftary, *Mediaeval Ismāʿīlī History and Thought* (Cambridge, UK: Cambridge University Press, 1996), 5.

8. Halévy calls this place Bedr and also associates it with Karrāmī scholars. Halévy, "Rapport sur une mission archéologique," 39.

9. Many Christian Bibles were distributed to Yemeni Jews. Jacob Saphir reports that some Jews, reluctant to dispose of them, cut out the New Testament and kept the rest. Other Jews used the text to manufacture amulets for sale to Muslims. See Adam Mendelsohn, "Trading in Torah: Bootleg Bibles and Secondhand Scripture in the Age of European Imperialism," in G. Reuveni, ed., *The Economy in Jewish History* (New York:

Berghahn, 2001), 191; and Joseph Saphir, *Sefer Masa' Teman* (Jerusalem: Levin-Epstein Brothers, 1944), 119–20.

10. Because Ḥabshūsh does not introduce this individual, Goitein suggests that part of the manuscript may have been lost. Ḥayyim Ḥabshūsh, *Ru'yā al-Yaman (Mas'ot Ḥabshūsh)*, ed. S. D. Goitein (Jerusalem: Ben-Zvi Institute, 1983), 162n18.

11. Hugh Scott suggests that the word designates a puff adder. Hugh Scott, "Travels in the Yemen Seventy Years Ago," *Geographical Journal* 99.5/6 (1942), 275.

12. See chapter 6, [124].

13. Qur'ān 29:46.

14. Halévy notes that, despite dying his skin to make it appear darker, local women found it to be too light, and this prompted them to question him about his gender. Joseph Halévy, "Voyage au Nedjran," *Bulletin de la Société de Géographie de Paris* 6 (1873), 253.

15. That is, al-Manṣūr 'Alī b. 'Abbās al-Ḥusayn (r. AH 1189–1224/1775–1809).

16. The flesh of the Nile lizard (*saqanqūr*) was thought to be an aphrodisiac. M. Piamenta, *Dictionary of Post-Classical Yemeni Arabic* (Leiden: Brill, 1997), 1: 226.

17. Many of Ḥabshūsh's remarks about this imām are confirmed by a local chronicler. 'Abd al-Wāsi' b. Yaḥyā al-Wāsi'ī, *Ta'rīkh al-Yaman* (Cairo: al-Maṭba'a al-Salafiya, 1927), 59–60. Cf. Paul Dresch, *Tribes, Government, and History in Yemen* (Oxford: Oxford University Press, 1989), 214.

18. On the Orphans' Decree, see J. Tobi, "Conversion to Islam Among Yemeni Jews Under Zaydi Rule," *Pe'amim* 42 (1990), 118–21 (Hebrew).

19. Halévy also remarks on the lack of inscriptions in this region. Halévy, "Rapport sur une mission archéologique," 41.

20. See chapter 6, [105].

21. A *duqqah* is a "necklace consisting of 12 threaded . . . hollow silver ball beads of various sizes and patterns." A *labbah* is an "interworked filigree necklace covering the chest"; and a *lāzim* is a "necklace consisting of several strings of silver-gilt pellets and small plates of various shapes hanging on the chest." M. Piamenta, *Dictionary of Post-Classical Yemeni Arabic* (Leiden: Brill, 1997), 1: 153, 2: 443, 2: 448.

22. On this custom, see W. Leslau, "Linguistic Observations on a Native Yemenite Document," *Jewish Quarterly Review* 36 (1946), 277.

23. AH 1265.

24. The following account of political events is not reliable. Readers interested in the complex and volatile politics of the era should consult Dresch, *Tribes*, 212–18; and Caesar Farah, *The Sultan's Yemen: Nineteenth-Century Challenges to Ottoman Rule* (London: Tauris, 2002). In the following notes, I highlight some of the difficulties with Ḥabshūsh's account. To begin with, al-Mahdī 'Abdallāh ruled Ṣan'ā' from AH 1231 (1816) until his death in AH 1251 (1835), and the rebellion of the Bakīl occurred toward the beginning of his reign in 1818. Ḥabshūsh's death date for this imām is therefore incorrect. See Yehuda Nini, *The Jews of the Yemen, 1800–1914* (New York: Harwood Academic, 1991), 10; and al-Wāsi'ī, *Ta'rīkh al-Yaman*, 62–64.

25. Cf. Farah, *Sultan's Yemen*, 23–25. Also, Ibrāhīm Pāshā was Muḥammad 'Alī's son, not his nephew.

26. That is, Imām al-Nāṣir 'Abdallāh b. al-Ḥasan (r. AH 1252–1256/1836–1840).

27. Halévy reports a similar version of the story. Halévy, "Voyage au Nedjran," 27–28.

28. Cf. al-Wāsi'ī, *Ta'rīkh al-Yaman*, 66.

29. That is, al-Manṣūr ʿAlī b. al-Mahdī ʿAbdallāh (r. AH 1251–1252/1835–1836, AH 1259–1261/1843–1845, AH 1265–1266/1849–1850, and AH 1267–12681851).

30. Ḥabshūsh's claim that al-Manṣūr ʿAlī succeeded al-Nāṣir is incorrect. Imām al-Hādī Muḥammad (r. AH 1256–1259/1840–1843) succeeded him, followed by al-Manṣūr ʿAlī. The civil and political disorder of the period may well have been the source of Ḥabshūsh's confusion. See Bernard Haykel, *Revival and Reform in Islam* (Cambridge, UK: Cambridge University Press, 2003), xv; and Ḥabshūsh, *Ruʾyā al-Yaman*, 90.

31. In fact, al-Hādī Muḥammad (r. AH 1256–1259/1840–1843) ruled after al-Nāṣir, not before.

32. The governor was Faqīh Saʿīd ibn Ṣāliḥ al-ʿAnsī. He claimed to be the *mahdī al-muntaẓar* (the anticipated deliverer) and orchestrated an insurrection in AH 1255–1256 (1840). Bat-Zion Eraqi Klorman, *The Jews of Yemen in the Nineteenth Century: A Portrait of a Messianic Community* (Leiden: Brill, 1993), 55–59.

33. That is, Imām al-Mutawakkil Muḥammad ibn Yaḥyā (r. AH 1261–1265/1845–1849). Cf. chapter 5, [90–99].

34. See Farah, *Sultan's Yemen*, 30–38.

35. The Egyptians left in AH 1256 (1840). Farah, *Sultan's Yemen*, 29–30.

36. This occurred in 1872 as a result of the second Ottoman conquest of Yemen. Dresch, *Tribes*, 219–24.

37. Thomas Kuehn, *Empire, Islam, and Politics of Difference: Ottoman Rule in Yemen, 1849–1919* (Leiden: Brill, 2011), 33–34.

38. See chapter 6, [121].

39. The name of a female demon. Eduard Glaser and Walter Dostal, *Ethnographica Jemenica: Auszüge aus den Tagebüchern Eduard Glasers* (Vienna: Österreichische Akademie der Wissenschaften, 1993), 77.

Chapter 11

1. Halévy says that he was unable to find a guide willing to lead him all the way to Mārib but managed to find someone who was traveling to a Bedouin village nearby. Joseph Halévy, "Rapport sur une mission archéologique dans le Yemen," *Journal Asiatique* 6 (1872), 44.

2. Halévy confirms that the route he took to Mārib was circuitous, but he does not offer this explanation. Halévy, "Rapport sur une mission archéologique," 44–46.

3. Cf. Halévy, "Rapport sur une mission archéologique," 44–45, 93.

4. Ḥabshūsh discusses this matter in Ḥayyim Ḥabshūsh, "History of the Jews in Yemen," ed. Y. Qāfiḥ, *Sefunot* 2 (1958), 247–49 (Hebrew).

5. Halévy refers to the ruin as Kharībat Saʿūd. Halévy, "Rapport sur une mission archéologique," 46.

6. Halévy mentions this place and its salt but refers to it as al-Faṭiyyah. Halévy, "Rapport sur une mission archéologique," 46.

7. Halévy tells a similar story. According to him, a man posted to a tower on a hill to spy on tribal enemies robbed him but then sent his son to be his guide. Halévy, "Rapport sur une mission archéologique," 48.

8. Following Goitein, I translate the word *zīgh* as "gypsies." Although it is clear from context that the term refers to non-Arabs, its precise meaning is uncertain. Ḥayyim Ḥabshūsh, *Ruʾyā al-Yaman (Masʿot Ḥabshūsh)*, ed. S. D. Goitein (Jerusalem: Ben-Zvi Institute, 1983), 187n15.

Chapter 12

1. Halévy also mentions taking this route, offering the following explanation: Because of the trade between the two cities, the people of Mārib were accustomed to seeing strangers entering the city from the direction of Ṣanʿāʾ. However, they would have been suspicious of strangers entering through the eastern gate, because it faced the territory of a tribe with whom they were at war. Joseph Halévy, "Rapport sur une mission archéologique dans le Yemen," *Journal Asiatique* 6 (1872), 49.

2. Halévy also mentions receiving the hospitality of a local man. Halévy, "Rapport sur une mission archéologique," 49–50.

3. See Chapter 6, [111].

4. AH 1285.

5. On these traditions, see Aviva Klein-Franke, "The Jews of Yemen," in W. Daum, ed., *Yemen: 3000 Years of Art and Civilisation in Arabia Felix* (Innsbruck: Pinguin, 1987), 265–66.

6. On the Mārib dam, see Michael Schaloske, *Untersuchungen der Sabäischen Bewässerungsanlagen in Mārib* (Mainz: Philipp von Zabern, 1995).

7. Halévy recounts a similar story in greater detail. Halévy, "Rapport sur une mission archéologique," 53.

8. No doubt, Halévy had gleaned this information from Arnaud, who had previously visited the area. Thomas-Joseph Arnaud, "Relation d'un voyage à Mareb (Saba) dans l'Arabie méridionale, entrepris en 1843," *Journal Asiatique* 5 (1845), 320.

9. Halévy's version of the events is remarkably similar to that of Ḥabshūsh, with the exception that Halévy claims to act alone. Halévy, like Ḥabshūsh, even notes how, anticipating a hostile encounter, he was able to hide his inscriptions and later retrieve them. Halévy, "Rapport sur une mission archéologique," 53–58.

10. AH 1305.

11. The page numbering here follows Goitein's estimate. Ḥayyim Ḥabshūsh, *Ruʾyā al-Yaman (Masʿot Ḥabshūsh)*, ed. S. D. Goitein (Jerusalem: Ben-Zvi Institute, 1983), 344.

12. In Halévy's version, he was harassed on this mountain by an agent of an Indian antiquities dealer, whose interference had previously compelled him to prematurely leave Mārib. Although Halévy refers to this individual as Moussellil and Ḥabshūsh refers to him as Ḥājj Ḥusayn, it seems likely that they are referring either to the same person or to someone closely associated with him. Halévy, "Rapport sur une mission archéologique," 58, 50–51.

13. Halévy mentions that some Muslims in Ṣanʿāʾ suspected him of being a British spy. Joseph Halévy, "Voyage au Nedjran," *Bulletin de la Société de Géographie de Paris* 6 (1873), 18.

14. Here, Ḥabshūsh engages in wordplay. The word for courage (*shajāʿah*) is from the same root as the name of the mountain (Ashjaʿ).

15. Elsewhere, Ḥabshūsh describes the customary evening meal to which Yemeni Jews invite guests following the end of a *shivʿah*, that is, the week-long period of mourning following the death of first-degree relatives. As in our text, the meal is referred to as *al-ʿashā*. Ḥayyim Ḥabshūsh, "History of the Jews in Yemen," ed. Y. Qāfiḥ, *Sefunot* 2 (1958), 282.

16. See Chapter 4, [41].

17. On the false messiahs Shukr Kuḥayl I and II, see the Introduction section "The People and Politics of Yemen."

18. Ḥabshūsh colorfully describes the date as "the year 2170 of the era of the formidable and destructive, 'two-horned' king [Alexander of Macedon], that is to say, 5619 of the Seleucid era."

19. On Aḥmad al-Ḥaymī's control of Ṣan'ā', see Caesar Farah, *The Sultan's Yemen: Nineteenth-Century Challenges to Ottoman Rule* (London: Tauris, 2002), 58–64; and Yehuda Nini, *The Jews of Yemen, 1800–1914* (New York: Harwood Academic, 1991), 12.

20. Al-Manṣūr Muḥammad b. 'Abdallāh al-Wazīr declared himself imām in AH 1270 (1854) and died in AH 1308 (1891). Bernard Haykel, *Revival and Reform in Islam* (Cambridge, UK: Cambridge University Press, 2003), 195.

INDEX

abortion, 6–7, 169, 173–75
Abyssinia, Jews of, 16–19, 37, 92–93
Académie des Inscriptions et Belles-Lettres, 4, 20–21
Aden, 23, 40–41, 66
alchemy, 73, 90
Alliance Israélite Universelle, 15–21, 37
Arabic. *See* linguistic style and composition of *A Vision of Yemen*; Yemeni-Arabic words defined by Ḥabshūsh
architecture, pre-Islamic, 115, 130, 135–37, 145–46, 191, 199–200
Arḥab (region), 93–95, 110, 115, 120, 150

Arnaud, Thomas, 43, 196
Austria and Austrian officials, 27–28, 36, 57, 63

banditry, 20, 84, 94, 100, 152–53, 196–98, 201, 206–7
Barāqīsh (town), 142, 144–47
Bibles, 11, 44, 128, 180, 244n9. *See also* missionaries (Christian)
biblical figures: Ham, 117, 152; Ishmael's sons (Dumah, Massa. and Mishma), 66, 83; Joseph, 67–68, 93; Queen of Sheba, 8, 54; Samson, 75; Saul, 104; Solomon, 8, 54, 78, 199–200
biblical references: Genesis, 66–68, 83, 93; Exodus, 76; Leviticus, 81, 231n11; Deuteronomy, 128, 231n11; Judges, 75; Samuel, 69, 104; Isaiah, 73–74; Jeremiah, 78; Ezekiel, 231n11; Psalms, 69, 73–74, 76, 79–80, 128; Proverbs, 76; Song of Songs, 92–93; Lamentations, 83
bloodwite penalties for manslaughter (*diyah*), 50–51, 102, 117–21, 148–49
books: trade and exchange of, 27, 44, 67–68, 89, 128, 144, 180; magical, 73, 91, 203
Britain. *See* Aden; missionaries (Christian); Montefiore, Moses

cats, 82–84, 183
charity. *See* hospitality; rabbis collecting alms
children and youths: arranged marriage of, 156; concealing gender of, 171; education of, 14–16, 19, 71–72, 104, 132; forced to work, 109; at home, 98, 125, 133, 184, 189; ; in polygamous families, 7, 176–77 in public 76, 81–82, 86, 148, 165; treatment in law and warfare, 51, 149. *See also* Orphans' Decree; clothing,

hairstyles, and jewelry: children's attire
Christians and Christianity, 15–18, 44–45, 179–80, 208. *See also* missionaries (Christian)
clothing and fashions: children's attire, 129, 171; female attire, 75–76, 106–7, 132, 165; male attire, 45, 47, 84–85, 128–29, 132, 139, 153, 184, 192; hairstyles 45, 111–12, 155, 171, 184; jewelry, 107, 141, 186, 194; occasions for wearing finery, 49, 104; dress restrictions placed on Jews, 45, 47; Jews dressed similarly to non-Jews, 70, 155, 165, 184; distinctive Ṣanʿānī clothes, 99
coffee: as charitable donation, 199; distinctive preparation of, 106, 132, 193; sabbath restrictions, 164; served to guests, 73, 74–76, 79, 94, 115, 131, 166, 172, 183–84, 192–93, 198, 202, 205; trade, 52, 109

Darb al-Ḥanshāt (village), 108–9
death: positive attitude toward death in battle, 70, 149; suicide, 121–25. *See also* bloodwite penalties for manslaughter; graves, cemeteries, and burial practices
demons. *See* magic and supernatural powers
dhimmīs / *dhimmah*. *See* interreligious relations
dialect. *See* linguistic style and composition of *A Vision of Yemen*; Yemeni-Arabic words defined by Ḥabshūsh
dietary restrictions (Jewish), 134, 157, 160–62, 168
disease and medicine: abortifacients, 173; aphrodisiacs, 183; apothecaries, 86–87; epilepsy, 189; eyesight, 93; Halévy's illness and treatment, 70–71, 86–87; precious stones and occult remedies, 91–92; scorpion bite treatment, 154; snakebite treatment, 91–92; plagues, 46, 66; unhealthy living conditions, 47, 179
disguise and deception: Ḥabshūsh's, 9, 35, 71–72, 76–78, 80, 152, 168–89, 209, 211; Halévy's, 3, 15, 18, 85; Glaser's, 3, 27–30; girls dressed as boys, 171
diyah. *See* bloodwite penalties for manslaughter (*diyah*)
Dor Deʿah (Generation of Knowledge, Yemeni Jewish movement), 53–54

Egyptian involvement in Yemeni politics, 43, 122–23, 187–88
Ethiopia. *See* Abyssinia, Jews of

Faitlovich, Jacques, 19
Falashas. *See* Abyssinia, Jews of
famine, 12, 42, 46, 52, 55, 66, 105, 113, 126–27, 200, 206
fishing, 110, 143–44
food, 74–75, 99, 105, 106–7, 110, 115, 126–27, 131–35, 140, 154–55, 157, 160–61, 165, 186, 189, 192. *See also* coffee; dietary restrictions; famine; hookahs; sabbath
forgery of antiquities, 33–34

al-Ghayl (village), 130–35, 140, 142–43, 149–50, 189
Ghaymān (town), 52, 70–79
Glaser, Eduard, 3, 25, 26, 27–31, 35–36, 63
Goitein, Shlomo Dov, 34–35, 57–58
graves, cemeteries, and burial practices, 30, 54–55, 88–90, 101, 108–9, 115, 125, 130, 136, 144–45, 151–52, 154, 179, 200, 206
gunpowder, 71, 123, 160

Ḥabshūsh, Ḥayyim, 8–13, 37–38; as an antiquities forger, 33–34; attachment to Yemen, 4, 54–55, 114, 144–45, 150–57; attitudes toward magic and rationalism, 9, 51–52, 77–79, 168–70; friendships with Muslims, 11, 55, 86, 151; *Halikhot Tema* (The Ways of Yemen) book, 11; immediate relatives, 7, 12, 68, 79, 88, 176; relationship with hired Muslim guides, 158–62, 180–82, 191–92. *See also* Ḥabshūsh / Halévy relationship

Ḥabshūsh / Halévy relationship, 3–8, 32–34, 63, 67, 70, 80, 88, 92–92, 130, 134, 139–41, 133, 144, 146, 154, 156–57; payment for services rendered; 68–69, 78–79, 109, 134–35, 139–40, 202
Hadhlūl (Muslim guide to Ḥabshūsh and Halévy), 159–64
Halacha. *See* Jewish law
Halévy, Joseph, 13–25, 36–37; in Abyssinia, 16–17, 21, 92–93; in Adrianople, 14–16; arrival in Yemen, 63, 66–69; attitudes toward honor killing, abortion, and polygamy, 6–8, 173–77; in Bucharest, 16; descriptions of his guide, 34; disdain for superstition, 5, 32; imprisonment 95–96; interest in contemporary Yemenis, 80, 116–17, 134, 165; involvement in internal Yemeni-Jewish religious disputes, 53–54, 112, 156–57; family, 13, 189, 217n43; linguistic knowledge, 14, 17–18; in Morocco, 16; scholarship on Semitics, 22–23; writings about Yemen, 3–4, 21, 23, 35; Zionism, 224n137. *See also* Ḥabshūsh / Halévy relationship; orientalism
Ḥanokh ha-Levi, Moshe 44, 66
Ḥarāz (region), 66–67, 70, 94
Herzl, Theodor, 221n94
Hibshoosh, Yehiel, 12–13
Himyarites. *See* architecture, pre-Islamic; inscriptions, pre-Islamic
holidays: festival of ʿArafāt, 85; Passover, 134; Shavuʿot (Pentecost), 159
homes, descriptions of, 76, 99, 114, 131, 164, 188–89
honor and shame. *See* bloodwite penalties for manslaughter; hospitality; inter-religious relations; marriage and wedding customs; rape; Ṭāghūt (tribal law); tribal identity and politics
hookahs, 73, 79, 94, 106–7, 115, 194–95
hospitality: begrudged and refusal of, 142, 163, 205; comparison of Jewish and Muslim forms of, 94; extended to members of other religious groups, 73–76, 79–80, 108, 142, 162, 192–93, 199; interactions between men and women, 74–75, 95–96, 131, 138–39, 142, 154, 162; within the Jewish community, 20, 25, 66–67, 90, 94, 110, 114–15, 129, 131–34, 141, 155, 164, 186, 205, 210–11; targeting of strangers and dangers to hosts, 72, 80–84, 95–98; at weddings, 106–8
Hujar (caste), 40, 117–18, 121
Ḥunbukh (Muslim guide to Ḥabshūsh and Halévy), 180–82

Ibn Qamlā (local ruler), 148, 151–2
Ibrāhīm Pasha (Egyptian general), 187
illegitimate children, 7–8, 124, 169, 175, 244n4
imāms (Zaydī rulers), by reign: al-Mutawakkil (r. AH 1054–87/1654–76), 46–47; al-Manṣūr ʿAlī b. ʿAbbās al-Ḥusayn (r. AH 1189–1224/1775–1809), 150; al-Mahdī ʿAbdallāh (r. AH 1231—51/1816–35), 52, 126, 186–87; ʿAlī ibn al-Mahdī ʿAbdallāh (r. AH 1251–52/1835–36, AH 1259–61/1843–45, AH 1265–66/1849–50), and AH 1267–68/1851), 122–25, 127, 187; al-Nāṣir ʿAbdallāh b. al-Ḥasan (r. AH 1252–56/1836–40), 111, 187; al-Mutawakkil Muḥsin ibn Aḥmad al-Shahārī (d. 1295/1878), 65, 87, 95; Muḥammad ibn Yaḥyā Ḥamīd al-Dīn (r. AH 1307–22/1890–1904), 65–66, 102, 121–24, 127, 187; Yaḥyā Ḥamīd al-Dīn (d. 1948), 13
imperialism, 4, 30–31, 35–36, 41–42, 52, 55. *See also* Ottoman Empire, officials, and reforms
Indians in Yemen, 24, 40, 87
inscriptions, pre-Islamic, and transcription efforts, 3, 20, 24, 33–34, 43; accusations of forgery and misrepresentation, 33, 78–79, 140–42; in Arḥab region, 93–94, 96; 110, at Banāt ʿĀd, 134–35, 151; at Barāqīsh, 142, 145–47; in Barrān (with red ink), at al-Bayḍāʾ, 140–41; in Darb

al-Ḥanshāt, 109; in Ghaymān, 71, 74, 78–79; at Haram (al-Farʿ), 148; in al-Madīd, 87–88; in Najrān, 178; in and around Mārib, 30, 199, 201–3; in and around Milḥ, 104, 115–16; orientalist versus native guide effort in collection process, 31, 33–34, 69, 97, 109, 116, 13–35, 142–43, 146, 199; protecting and concealing transcriptions, 190, 195, 203–5, 209–10; in Raghwān, 191; in Ṣanʿāʾ, 68–69; in Shirāʿ, 97; Yemeni destruction of, 146; Yemeni interest in, 3, 8–9, 67–69, 87, 151, 203

interreligious relations: anti-Jewish edicts and legal restrictions, 10–11, 45–48, 124; enslavement, 47; expulsions, 46–47, 108; forced conversion, 46, 48–49, 150; friendships, tolerance, and working relations, 11, 29, 55, 86, 98, 108–9, 120, 130, 133, 142–43, 151, 154, 162, 181–82, 203; imprisonment and extortion, 65, 90, 95, 121–25, 187; individual violence, 90–91, 120–21, 131, 153, 158, 172, 182; Jews in possession of supernatural powers, 51, 71–72, 82, 120, 187, 203–4; *jizyah* (poll-tax), 45–46, 49, 102, 109; mob violence, 12, 72, 81–86, 90–91; Muslim attitudes toward and enforcement of Jewish religious observances, 133–34, 159–60; Muslim-Jewish relations under Islamic law, 44–46, 48; negative attitudes toward friendly interactions, 142, 181, 198, 205; under Ottoman influence, 42, 48, 102–4, 109–10, 127; treatment of foreign visitors to Yemen, 41, 44, 80–84, 90; tribal patronage and protection of Jewish clients, 40–41, 49–51, 90–91, 94–95, 97–98, 100–101, 103–5, 109, 120–21, 148–49, 155, 167, 172, 184, 207. *See also* bloodwite penalties for manslaughter; Ḥabshūsh, Ḥayyim: relationship with hired Muslim guides; Ṭāghūt (tribal law)

Jawf (region), 23, 33, 128–54, 188–91

Jewish law (halacha), 7, 111–12, 155–57, 164, 165, 174–75. *See also* dietary restrictions (Jewish); Sabbath

jinn (demons). *See* magic and supernatural powers

jizyah (poll tax). *See* interreligious relations

Judeo-Arabic language, 5–6, 8, 31, 58–59, 89

Kabbalah. See *The Zohar* and Jewish mysticism

Khabb (region), 155–59

kohl, 93, 104, 106, 107, 131

kosher food. *See* dietary restrictions (Jewish)

linguistic style and composition of *A Vision of Yemen*, 5–6, 31, 58–59, 89–90

Latrines Decree, 48

liturgy (Jewish), 11, 54

lost Israelite tribes, 3, 44, 70, 137, 180

al-Madīd (village in the region of Nihm), 87–88, 96, 98–104, 109–12

magic and supernatural powers: amulets and protective objects, 67, 92, 186; belief that Jews possess supernatural powers, 51–52; 71–74, 97, 204; connected with inscriptions, 3, 8, 67, 71, 73–74; demons, 13, 67, 77–79, 116, 189–90; exorcism, 15; Ḥabshūsh mistaken for a demon, 137–38, 147; Ḥabshūsh pretending to have occult powers, 72–74, 76–79, 168–69; occult healing, 91–92; rejection of superstition, 5, 9, 13, 15, 32, 78, 168–69. *See also* alchemy

Maimonides, Moses, 54, 128

Maʿīn (region in the Jawf), 137–40

Mārib (town), 23–24, 30, 43, 69, 77, 88, 190, 194, 199–201

markets, 85–87, 90, 117, 177–78, 184

marriage and wedding customs, 99, 105–7, 156–57, 182

Mawzaʿ (town), 47, 108

al-Mazāʿiqah (neighborhood in the environs of Ṣanʿāʾ), 90–91, 93

medicine. *See* disease and medicine

merchants, 8, 40–41, 66, 109, 123, 137, 158

messianism, 11, 13, 52–53, 95, 211–12
Milḥ (village), 104, 110, 112, 115–16, 120–21, 128–29, 152
missionaries (Christian), 11, 16–17, 44, 180
Montefiore, Moses (philanthropist), 11–12
Moshe of Baghdad (traveler to Yemen), 90
mosques: 47, 71–72, 79, 94, 136, 143, 148, 179; Great Mosque of Ṣanʿāʾ, 11, 85; Mosque of Solomon (in Mārib), 199–200
Muḥammad, Prophet, 46, 55, 181–82
Muḥammad ʿAlī (ruler of Egypt), 43
Muḥṣunah, and her brothers, 74–76, 79
Muslim denominations in Yemen, 39–40, 42, 179
Muslim-Jewish relations. *See* interreligious relations
mysticism. See *The Zohar* and Jewish mysticism
mythical rulers, 73, 113–14, 145, 200, 203. *See also* Sheba, Queen of; Solomon (king)
mythological Jewish kingdoms in Yemen, 39, 44
Najrān (region), 6–8, 24, 44, 158–80
natural disasters, 52, 133–34. *See also* disease and medicine; famine
newspapers, Hebrew, 8, 17, 63
Nihm (region), 87–88, 95, 98, 100, 104, 120–21. *See also* al-Madīd

occupations, 9, 11, 40, 48, 71–72, 86–87, 93, 108–10, 157, 194, 200
oil (applied to the skin), 104, 106, 131
Orientalism, 3–4, 8, 27–33, 35–36, 42–43. *See also* imperialism
Orphans' Decree, 48–49, 150, 184
Ottoman Empire, officials, and reforms, 29–31, 36, 39, 41–43, 48, 52, 66, 102–3, 125–27, 188

polygamy, 6–7, 149, 176–77, 186
poverty, 71, 74–76, 93, 109, 124, 129, 131, 140–41, 189. *See also* natural disasters; prices, valuation, taxation, and economic history
prayer services and prayer rituals: Jewish, 13, 75, 80, 85, 111, 125, 129, 131–34, 164–67, 189, 194, 198, 201; Islamic, 29, 73, 76, 82, 148, 204. *See also* liturgy (Jewish); mosques; synagogues
prices, valuation, taxation, and economic history: cost of goods, 103, 107, 110, 120, 126, 141, 180, 191; currency equivalents, 65, 69; economic crises, 47, 52, 122; fines imposed on the Jewish community, 124–25, 187; inflation and standard of living, 42, 125, 183; wages, 69, 79, 135, 161, 183

Qāfiḥ, Yaḥyā (Jewish leader and scholar), 27, 53–54
al-Qārah family: Meʾir, 67, 69; Sulaymān, 66, 80; Yaḥyā, 66–67, 70, 80, 84, 87–88, 128, 190
Qarār / Qarārī, / Qarawī (caste), 40, 50–51, 116–17, 148–49, 151–52
Qoraḥ, ʿAmram (scribe to Ḥabshūsh), 57
Qurʾān, Quranic references, and Quranic figures, 45, 53, 114, 134, 179, 182. *See also* Sheba, Queen of; Solomon (king)

rabbis collecting alms, 3, 20, 25, 43, 84, 96, 110, 129, 141, 189. *See also* hospitality
race and color, 18–19, 21–23, 92–93, 117
rape, 6, 169–77
al-Rawḍah (town), 88–93
Renan, Ernest, 20–22, 24
Revue sémitique d'épigraphie et d'histoire ancienne, 37–38
Rhodokanakis, Nikolaus 57
Sabaeans, 8–9, 11–12, 25, 30, 43, 88; 234–35n18. *See also* architecture, pre-Islamic; inscriptions, pre-Islamic; Semitic linguistics
Sabbath, 80, 131–34, 159–60, 164–66, 188–89, 201
Sālim ibn Saʿīd (guide to Ḥabshūsh and Halévy) and his brothers Harūn and Yaḥyā, 128–31, 134–36, 140–43, 151–52, 154, 189–90, 195
Ṣanʿāʾ (city), 6, 11, 39–40, 47, 65–66, 81–86, 88–90, 94–95, 99, 101, 121–25, 184, 187
Saphir, Jacob, 20, 43, 90, 93

Sar Shalom ben Aharon ha-Cohen al-ʿIrāqī, 81–83
Sar Shalom ha-Levi, 65
al-Sawdāʾ, ruins of, 135–36, 140
sayyids (descendants of the Prophet Muḥammad), 40, 65–66, 90–91, 102, 122, 148, 159, 167, 171–72, 181, 200. *See also* Zaydī rulers
Semites. *See* race and color
Semitic linguistics, 21–22, 37–38
Shapira, Moses (Moshe ben Netanel), 44, 144
sharīʿah (Islamic law). *See* bloodwite penalties for manslaughter; interreligious relations
sharīfs. See *sayyids*
al-Shawkānī, Muḥammad (Muslim religious leader), 48
Sheba, Queen of, 8, 54, 179, 200. *See also* Biblical references and figures; mythical rulers
Shebans. *See* Sabaeans; Sheba, Queen of
Shiʿism. *See* Muslim denominations
Shirāʿ (village in the region of Arḥab), 93–97, 109
Shukr Kuḥayl (first and second, messianic figures), 53, 95, 211–12. *See also* messianism
silversmiths and coin minting, 87, 109, 123–25, 194, 200, 239n49. *See also* occupations
Ṣirwāḥ, 24, 115, 201–5
slaves and slavery, 45–47, 50–51, 148–49, 152
smoking. *See* hookahs
snakes and snakebites, 77–78, 91–92, 129, 180–81
Solomon (king), 8, 54, 78, 199–200
Sunnīs. *See* Muslim denominations
superstition. *See* magic and supernatural powers
synagogues, 13, 42, 45–47, 54, 80, 94–96, 98–99, 131–33

Ṭāghūt (tribal law), 40–41, 49–51, 98–101, 117–20, 148–49, 178, 206, 225n10
Tanẓīmāt. *See* Ottoman Empire, officials, and reforms
taxes. *See* interreligious relations; prices, valuation, taxation, and economic history
treasure hunting and treatment of antiquities, 13, 28, 33–34, 52, 73–74, 116, 136–38, 146, 151, 199–200, 203
tribal identity and politics, 7, 20, 39–40, 49–50, 70–72, 91, 94–95, 99–101, 104, 117–23, 127, 148–49, 167, 186, 225n10

Vision of Yemen, A: publication and reception history, 8, 31–35, 38, 57

wailing, public, 100, 125, 148–49, 172, 206–7
weaving, 202
women, 6–8, 71–78, 117–19, 125, 131–33, 162, 167–78, 186; betrothal and weddings of, 99–100, 106–7, 156; experiencing poverty, 74–76, 129; hair care and covering, 75, 111–12, 131, 133, 194; interactions with unrelated men, 74–75, 95–96, 131, 138–39, 142, 154, 159, 162, 165, 182, 195; occupations of, 71, 96, 109–10, 138, 202; scandalous behavior of, 99–100; social status within tribes, 50–51, 117–120, 148–49; tombstones of, 144. *See also* abortion; clothing and fashions; hospitality; marriage and wedding customs; polygamy; rape

Yemeni-Arabic words defined by Ḥabshūsh: *awshāj*, 110; *ḍafar*, 110; *dharār*, 73; *durūm*, 130; *ḥayyah*, 181; *ḥazzah*, 132; *himūṣ*, 133; *ḥindīd*, 110; *kubānah*, 166; *lizaq*, 160; *madhalah*, 166; *madhāq*, 75; *maqrawī*, 117; *qarāqish*, 75; *ruṭab*, 170; *ṣamgh*, 84; *shamlah*, 85; *shayāṭīn* 87; *ṭarūsh*, 133; *waḥar*, 160; *zuqāq*, 69
Yūsuf ibn Yaḥyā al-ʿArūsī, 90–93

Zaydīs. *See* imāms (Zaydī rulers); Muslim denominations
Zionism and land of Israel, 12, 27, 37–38, 54, 56, 157, 221n94
Zohar, The, and Jewish mysticism, 16, 27, 54, 111–12

The authorized representative in the EU for product safety and compliance is:
Mare Nostrum Group
B.V Doelen 72
4831 GR Breda
The Netherlands

www.ingramcontent.com/pod-product-compliance
Lightning Source LLC
Chambersburg PA
CBHW022004220426
43663CB00007B/947

* 9 7 8 1 5 0 3 6 0 7 7 3 6 *